ODDS-ON INVESTING

ODDS-ON INVESTING

Survival and Success in
The New Stock Market

EUGENE D. BRODY

BETSY L. BLISS

JOHN WILEY & SONS
New York • Chichester • Brisbane • Toronto

Library of Congress Cataloging in Publication Data:

Brody, Eugene D., 1931-
   Odds-on investing.

   "A Wiley-Interscience publication."
   Includes index.
   1. Put and call transactions. 2. Hedging (Finance).
I. Bliss, Betsy, 1942-   joint author. II. Title.
HG6041.B73   332.6'45   78-18222
ISBN 0-471-04478-4

This book is dedicated to
all those who have loved and lost—money

Foreword

This book is must reading for anyone who truly wants to understand conservative trading. The concept of selling more calls than one is long in stocks is usually brushed off as "too speculative." I am firmly in agreement with Mr. Brody that not only is this concept not "too speculative," but it is actually more conservative.

This book should be read and re-read. It is clear that Mr. Brody is not out for the big "kill," but neither does he want to "be killed." He ably weaves in and out of the intricacies of this type of trading and skillfully shows its conservative nature.

He goes a step further than most commentators in recognizing that establishing the initial position is one thing. Then, how should one react as the market moves up or down? This is the key to the value of this book.

Mr. Brody, in his clear, lucid writing, has taken a giant step forward for the American investor.

LEON POMERANCE
Former Chairman of the Board
Chicago Board Options Exchange

Preface

Webster defines *odds-on* as "that (which) is more likely to win . . .
having a better than even chance to win; that (which) does not involve
much risk. . . ."

This book shows you how to invest with advantage—how to lift the
burden of disadvantage that plagues nearly every investor today. It will
tell you how to *survive* and, indeed, how to *succeed* in a market environment vastly different from past market conditions.

This is not a get-rich-quick book. It is about *not losing* in the stock
market. Few investors stop to consider the pernicious *arithmetic of
losing*—the costly numbers game that painfully points out that once you are
behind, you must earn more than compensatory returns just to get even, let
alone get ahead. Fewer still recognize that much conventional market
wisdom puts you in an *odds-against* rather than an *odds-on* stance. There
have been radical changes in investment techniques, concepts, percep-
tions, and even the markets themselves in the past fifteen years. To make
money in today's markets, you must understand the implications of these
changes. Then you must do a mental makeover.

This book is also about a new mental attitude that will enable you to
survive and succeed in today's new stock market. You will learn how to *run
your money as you would run a business*—with discipline, risk-avoidance
procedures, and the flexibility to make adjustments that will allow your
total portfolio to be profitable, whether the stock market advances or
declines.

You have probably picked up this book because you have accumulated some capital (a difficult enough achievement in the current tax
climate) and you want to earn a better-than-average return on it. We hope
we can help you to clarify some of your investment choices and decisions, and to reorient your thinking so that your capital can grow in the
future.

EUGENE D. BRODY
BETSY BLISS

New York, New York
April 1978

Acknowledgements

We could not have written this book without the special help and advice of

ROGER W. ACH, II
SOL ERDMAN
ADDY MANIPELLA

Many thanks,

EUGENE D. BRODY
BETSY BLISS

Contents

List of Tables

ODDS-ON INVESTING

CHAPTER ONE

Starting Over
for Investment Success

The new stock market that has evolved over the past 20 years is a pretty formidable contender for you, the individual investor.

To survive in the new market environment, you must adapt. In investment terms, "to survive" does not mean merely continuing to exist. Rather, it means earning a return on capital that compares favorably with the amount of risk taken. In other words, "survival" is synonymous with "success."

This book is a survival manual. It introduces an approach that shifts the odds back in your favor, allowing you not only to protect yourself against losing in today's treacherous market but to earn an attractive return as well.

This new approach involves, first, a mental makeover—a radical reworking of your long-harbored attitudes toward investing, toward stocks themselves, and toward the market—and, second, a technique, called variable hedging, that allows you to capitalize on, rather than be victimized by, modern market volatility.

Volatility is the hallmark of the new stock market. It is what makes stock market profits so elusive. It is why everything you learned from 1946 to 1966 about market money-making no longer applies, or only partially applies, and why the risks and penalties for being wrong today are so much greater.

The new stock market makes investors painfully aware of an old trap, which we call "the arithmetic of losing." The "arithmetic" quantifies how costly losing can be—for, once you are behind, you must earn more than compensatory returns just to get even, let alone ahead. A 10% loss in any one year on a 15% compounded rate of return requires a 47% gain the following year just to get back on track!

For example, if you have $100 earning a 15% return, you will have $115 at the end of the first year and $132.25 at the end of the second. But, if your investment of $100 declines 10% to $90 at the end of the first year instead of earning a 15% return, you must gain 47% to be back on track at $138 by the end of the second year. Similarly, a 5% loss on a 10% rate goal requires a 27.4% gain to get back to your hoped-for return.

Just to stay even, an investment that is down 20% must appreciate 25%. For example, a $100 investment that has declined 20% to $80 must earn 25% or $20 merely to get back to the original starting point. An investment down 30% has to appreciate 43%; one down 40% must appreciate 66 ⅔% to get even.

These are the grim mathematical realities you must face if your goal is to preserve capital and to earn a fair return on it.

If losing is excruciatingly easy, making money in today's markets is more difficult than ever before. By almost any measure, the last decade has proved unrewarding for most stock investors—even the professionals. Table 1-1 shows the 1965–1974 performance of the 10 major banks' commingled equity accounts. These sorry returns, moreoever, include the reinvestment of income. By our definition, this is not "surviving."

Even so, that period of professionals' sorry returns yielded some extraordinary money-making opportunities. The Dow Jones Industrial Average was at the same level in 1976 as it was in 1966. Yet in the interim, considering only 20-point changes in direction, the Dow traveled a total distance of almost 8000 points!

When asked what he thought the market would do, one of the wisest investors of all times, J. P. Morgan, replied, "It will fluctuate." Yet over the years investors have ignored his sage observation and have never

TABLE 1-1   Ten Major Banks' 10-Year Performance of Commingled Accounts 1965-1974

	10-Year Performance (%)	Size of Fund (millions of $)
Crocker Bank	+2.1	22.0
Citibank	+2.07	126.0
Colorado National	+2.0	12.0
U.S. Trust	+1.6	45.5
Girard Bank	+1.4	58.0
Chemical Bank	+1.3	60.0
Wilmington Trust	+1.3	16.2
N.C. Natl. Trust	+1.28	40.0
First of Boston	+1.14	122.0
Irving Trust	+0.035	14.0

Source: *New York Times* March 6, 1975.

learned to systematically take advantage of fluctuating stock prices. This "survival manual" shows you how.

Why is survival/success such a challenge in today's stock market? That is a query often heard from old-timers who remember (and younger investors who have heard about) yesterday's salad days (although it was never as easy to make money then as some would have you believe). The market itself has changed in terms of participants, rules, and stock leadership. But, more than any other factor, the predominance of "megabuck" institutions in today's market has spawned volatility—and has created an environment too risky for the investor who employs traditional investing techniques and who falls prey to common psychological snares.

One of the most popular games investors play with themselves reflects the irrational conviction—backed by their own capital—that they can predict the market's future moves. This is a no-win strategy in itself. Used on an unpredictable marketplace, it puts investors in the poor-odds position of having constantly to guess correctly to "win." And it *is* guessing, since any effective "beat the market" system would have to self-destruct if it were adopted by everyone. If anyone were ever to develop such a system, he would be wise to keep it for himself.

Add to this the equally popular tender trap of falling in love with one's stocks. Such passion, in practice, seems particularly to bloom when a stock declines below the price paid for it. The notion that one can nudge stocks upward through affection always fails, for stocks cannot appreciate the sentiment!

Finally, investors often delude themselves into believing that by buying well-known stocks of high quality they are being conservative. This is what the banks (see Table 1-1) thought, too.

Does this mean that you should not be in stocks? No. It means that you have to approach the job of preserving and enhancing capital in a new way. We will make a case for the statement that the investor cannot make money anymore by simply buying the big, recognizable stocks—because these institutionally held securities are now more dependent than ever on external variables rather than on fundamental improvements in their underlying companies' businesses. What's more, these variables are unpredictable and unanalyzable for purposes of translation into stock price movement.

We will show you that to survive/succeed in the new stock market, you must take one of two approaches, or both. One is to unearth the companies that will someday become the big stocks—and be willing to wait for that judgment to have proven wise. (This approach has been subjectively analyzed by many others and is not covered in this book.)

The other approach is to use the big stocks in a new and different way. This involves revolutionizing your whole concept of investment—

abandoning the idea that you "win" by "putting your eggs in the right basket" and embracing instead the concept of making money by *capitalizing on the most likely occurrences.* Even more important, this new way means learning to be in stocks as a business—a business that produces "working capital" in the form of immediate cash earnings, while the "long-term capital" (the stocks themselves) are the "bricks and mortar," or fixed assets, whose residual value may in fact increase over time rather than depreciate.

The evolution of the stock market has brought about the means for you to be in stocks as a business. A survival tool has finally been provided for the individual investor. It is a way to shift the odds in your favor, and it is a method as yet unrecognized by most investors. As long as it remains unrecognized, it will produce returns in a favorable proportion to risk. It is a way to use the new options markets to decrease your vulnerability to volatility and potential large losses while simultaneously producing an annualized return well in excess of the low-risk rates available elsewhere.

This technique, moreover, is a radical departure from the no-win strategy that attempts to outsmart all other investors—and, indeed, the market itself—by buying at the bottom and selling at the top—a strategy that has proved to be difficult if not impossible. There is little evidence to support the notion that any system, technique, or group of investors has been able to consistently outperform the market averages or correctly time market moves.

Instead, this procedure is constructed to allow you to take advantage of, rather than be victimized by, wide swings in stock prices—to put J. P. Morgan's prediction into profitable practice. It allows you to gain from other investors' attempts to outsmart the market. Moreoever, you can use it to make money regardless of whether the market goes up or down.

This technique is called variable hedging. In brief, it involves transferring your stocks' volatility—through options—to traders who are willing to speculate on near term price movements. You will be "renting out" volatility (price changes) while you keep the stocks' dividends, residual values, and holding periods for tax purposes. If this appears complicated, it is actually easy to understand once you have a basic understanding of the options market. And, contrary to options' widely held (but not necessarily accurate) reputation for being speculative, it is a very conservative approach.

We will show you how to construct, and adjust, your own variable hedging program. But first we must analyze the modern market environment, the foibles of standard investment techniques, and the fundamentals of options.

CHAPTER TWO

The New Stock Market

The individual investor currently faces a stock market that is vastly different from what it was a few years ago. The market has evolved in four major areas:

- The participants have changed. There are fewer individual and more institutional investors, each of the latter commanding tremendous buying and selling power.

- The rules have changed. Many structural changes in the brokerage industry now aggravate stock price swings.

- Institutional managers' "performance standards" have created curious aberrations.

- Stock leadership has narrowed as a result of the "two-tier" market—consisting of "institutional favorites" and noninstitutional stocks—that has evolved along with increased institutional participation.

The combination of these factors has produced a much more volatile marketplace—one which, by definition, poses more risks than ever before for the individual.

We will examine each of these changes in more detail in order to assess their impact. First, however, we should take a look—for perspective's sake—at how our securities markets have evolved to their present state.

In the early years of the United States there was no stock market per se. Securities markets were mainly composed of the debt securities of the new nation. Sales were conducted by auction, but in a one-sided manner; buyers competed to buy, while sellers took turns conducting the auction In either case it was the actual buyer and the actual seller who stood in the auction arena; there were no middlemen.

As volume picked up, some traders made it their business to remain in the marketplace, thus becoming the first stockbrokers. Conflicts began to develop between the auctioneers and the brokers, since the brokers felt the auctioneers were trying to monopolize the business. The result of this conflict was the famous Buttonwood Agreement, under which the brokers agreed to give each other preference in their dealings and to charge a fixed minimum commission. And this was the genesis of the New York Stock Exchange.

Though there were brokers and commissions from the earliest days, the whole arena of stock trading remained shrouded in secrecy and populated by insiders for nearly a century. In the beginning, communications were such that the trader whose broker owned a swift horse enjoyed a considerable advantage. Later, the telegraph brought traders from around the country and around the world into our markets—and, at the beginning of this century, the telephone enhanced the public's access to information affecting individual securities and securities markets. Nevertheless, most of the participants were still wealthy speculators, brokers, merchants, entrepreneurial types and empire builders seeking greater personal power through corporate control. Market participants continued to fit this stratified sociological profile into the twentieth century, and it was not until the 1920s that the public, as we think of it, entered the market in a big way.

Thus, 50 years ago, the concept of investing as we know it today did not exist. The individual was the dominant force, and what institutions existed bought mostly high-grade bonds. Investment trusts were being formed in the 1920s, and some fledgling institutions began to nibble at common stocks after the publication of Edgar Lawrence Smith's classic *Common Stocks As Long Term Investments*.

However, it was not until after World War II that mutual funds, pension funds, and large insurance companies and banks showed an accelerating interest in common stocks. (Interestingly enough, the postwar period started out with these institutions favoring bonds with 2% yields and ignoring stocks with 8% yields. By the time we got to the "buy-and-hold" investment philosophy of just a few years ago we had seen a 180-degree turn—bonds with 8% yields were ignored for growth stocks with 2% yields!) This coincided with increased public interest in the market, greater press coverage, brokerage firm expansion, and the New York Stock Exchange's public relations campaign urging citizens to "own a share of America." This statement neglected to mention that what people were really buying was the price changes in their "share of America," since they received neither the assets nor the earnings (except partially, through dividends).

These two kinds of shareholdings, individual and institutional, grew together through the 1960s, culminating in the "paper crunch" and the market crash late in that decade. Table 2-1 vividly portrays the decline of the individual as shareholder and the increasing dominance of the institutional investor in the past two decades:

TABLE 2-1   Historical Summary—Public Volume Shares Bought and Sold
on the NYSE

Period	Total	Millions of Shares Per Day		Percentage Distribution	
		Individuals	Institutions	Individuals	Institutions
First Quarter 1976	44.1	18.8	25.3	42.7	57.3
First Quarter 1974	23.2	9.5	13.7	41.1	58.9
First Half 1971	26.6	10.7	15.9	40.3	59.7
Second Quarter 1971	25.0	9.4	15.6	37.6	62.4
First Quarter 1971	28.3	12.1	16.2	42.6	57.4
Full Year 1969	18.0	7.9	10.1	44.1	55.9
Second Half 1969	18.0	7.8	10.2	43.5	56.5
First Half 1969	18.1	8.1	10.0	44.6	55.4
October 1966	10.7	6.1	4.6	57.0	43.0
March 1965	8.9	5.4	3.5	60.7	39.3
October 1963	9.4	6.5	2.9	69.1	30.9
September 1961	5.7	3.8	1.9	66.7	33.3
September 1960	5.1	3.5	1.6	68.6	31.4
June 1959	5.1	3.6	1.5	70.6	29.4
September 1958	7.0	5.0	2.0	71.4	28.6
October 1957	3.8	2.7	1.1	71.1	28.9
March 1956	5.6	4.2	1.4	75.0	25.0
June 1955	5.3	4.0	1.3	75.5	24.5
December 1954	6.1	4.8	1.3	78.7	21.3
March 1954	3.3	2.3	1.0	69.7	30.3
March 1953˙	4.0	3.0	1.0	75.0	25.0
September 1952	2.6	1.8	0.8	69.2	30.8
		Millions of Dollars Per Day			
First Quarter 1976	1,270	337	893	29.7	70.3
First Quarter 1974	708	219	489	31.0	69.0
First Half 1971	940	299	641	31.8	68.2
Full Year 1969	742	283	459	38.1	61.9
October 1966	444	233	211	52.5	47.5
March 1965	343	182	161	53.1	46.9
October 1963	386	250	136	64.8	35.2
September 1961	240	147	93	61.2	38.8
September 1960	186	112	74	60.2	39.8

Source: New York Stock Exchange *Public Transactions Study: 1976*

In past decades the individual investor accounted for substantial stock market trading volume. But as greater amounts of investment money were concentrated in the hands of professional portfolio managers who invested for pension funds, bank trust departments, insurance companies, and mutual funds, their share of trading volume also increased dramatically.

This trend has been aggravated by the exit from the market of individual investors, particularly the shorter term stock traders, many of whom simply gave up after "getting burned" in the market's sharp swings of the last few years.

Fewer participants make for a "thinner" (that is, more volatile) marketplace. Fewer and larger buyers and sellers tend to cause bigger swings in stock prices. Suppose, for instance, that an institutional portfolio manager decides to sell his whole position in one stock. Since that position may often be at least 100,000 shares, his selling may knock the price of the stock down 5% or 10% or more—particularly when he sells it all at once. The price of a large block of stock under such circumstances often decreases so quickly that other holders of the same stock have no chance to react until after the fact. There is a significant variation in the impact when this occurs: that stock may be one of an individual investor's four or five holdings and a substantial percentage of his net worth. In contrast, it is probably one of hundreds of securities owned by an institution and a minuscule part of its assets.

The likelihood that large buyers or sellers will produce wide price swings in stocks has increased in recent years because of other developments. In the early 1960s, when an institutional seller would go to the floor of the New York Stock Exchange to sell, for example, a 50,000 share block, he was aided in his efforts by both the specialist and floor traders. Under Exchange rules the specialist is charged with the duty of maintaining an orderly market; in so doing, he is sometimes required to "position" stock (i.e., buy it for his own account). In those days floor traders would also pool their assets to position the seller's stock, thus insuring that the block could be accommodated without too sharp a decline in the stock's price. They were anticipating that the public traders would be attracted by the discount print and that they could feed their stock out on the snap-back.

In 1964 new Exchange rules largely discouraged floor traders. With their exit, a great deal of the large block business moved "upstairs" to the trading rooms of block trading firms, another phenomenon of the 1960s. A block trading firm tries to match major buyers and sellers and persuade them to agree on a price before taking their trades to the floor of the exchanges where such transactions are "printed." Thus the specialist

TABLE 2-2 Market Value of Stockholdings of Institutional Investors and Others
(Billions of Dollars, End of Year)

	1968	1969	1970	1971	1972	1973	1974	1975
1. Private Noninsured Pension Funds	61.5	61.4	67.1	88.7	115.2	90.5	63.3	88.6
2. Open-End Investment Companies	50.9	45.0	43.9	52.6	58.0	43.3	30.3	38.7
3. Other Investment Companies	8.3	6.3	6.2	6.9	7.4	6.6	4.7	6.0
4. Life Insurance Companies	13.2	13.7	15.4	20.6	26.8	25.9	21.9	28.3
5. Property-Liability Insurance Companies [a]	14.6	13.3	13.2	16.6	21.8	19.7	12.8	14.3
6. Common Trust Funds	4.8	4.6	4.6	5.8	7.4	6.6	4.3	5.7
7. Personal Trust Funds	83.6	79.6	78.6	94.1	110.2	94.7	67.7	92.8
8. Mutual Savings Banks	2.4	2.5	2.8	3.5	4.5	4.2	3.7	4.4
9. State and Local Retirement Funds	5.8	7.3	10.1	15.4	22.2	20.6	17.4	25.8
10. Foundations	22.0	20.0	22.0	25.0	28.5	24.5	18.4	22.7
11. Educational Endowments	8.5	7.6	7.8	9.0	10.7	9.6	6.7	8.7
12. Subtotal	275.6	261.3	271.6	338.2	412.7	346.1	251.3	336.0
13. Less: Institutional Holdings of Investment Company Shares	3.4	4.0	4.9	5.8	6.5	6.3	5.8	7.8
14. Total Institutional Investors	272.2	257.3	266.8	332.4	406.2	339.8	245.4	328.2
15. Foreign Investors [b]	28.8	26.9	28.7	32.9	41.3	37.0	28.2	48.2
16. Other Domestic Investors [c]	680.3	582.1	563.9	638.4	694.7	487.8	335.3	439.9
17. Total Stock Outstanding [d]	981.4	866.3	859.4	1003.7	1142.3	864.6	608.9	816.3
Institutional Investors Percentage of Stock Outstanding	27.7	29.6	31.1	33.1	35.6	39.3	40.3	40.2

Source: Securities and Exchange Commission, *Statistical Bulletin*, May 1976, P. 14.

[a] Excludes holdings of insurance company stock.
[b] Includes estimate of stock held as direct investment.
[c] Computed as residual (line 16-17-14-15). Includes both individuals and institutional groups not listed above.
[d] Includes both common and preferred stock. Excludes investment company shares but includes foreign issues outstanding in the U.S.

lost his predominance as the controlling element of his stocks' price movement. He was therefore no longer so willing to position sellers' stock, for he never knew what was going on ''upstairs'' in dozens of firms around the country. He did not want to take the chance of buying a block for his own account, only to have an upstairs trade appear a few minutes later that could knock the stock down well below his cost. What is more, an upstairs trade by a block trading firm often involves positioning. This means that the firm itself buys or sells short the excess on either side of the trade and will be working out of this risk position at a later time on the floor of the exchange.

Another stabilizing factor disappeared in 1968, when the New York Stock Exchange banned a practice known as the ''give-up.'' When give-ups were permissible, an institutional buyer or seller could do all of his large block business with one firm and still ''pay'' his other brokers commissions for services he had received from them, such as research and economic analysis. This was accomplished by the institutional customer instructing the broker who executed his trades to give up a percentage of the commissions generated to other houses. Customarily, then, the trade would be done by one of the large block trading houses that specialized in absorbing large blocks of stock without disturbing the market; after the trade, the executing broker would mail checks for give-up commissions to the customer's other brokers, who had been designated to receive such credit.

When give-ups disappeared, institutional customers were forced to spread their buy and sell orders around to all the firms with which they wished to do business. Thus after the abolition of give-ups, the institutional customer would have to pay the small research-oriented firm directly through commissions from executions of trades, even though that firm lacked expertise in block trading. The net effect was that more and more block trades were given to smaller and less well capitalized firms that were hesitant to take on the capital risks of positioning large blocks of stock. Hence they executed these trades on an agency basis; that is, they bought or sold stock on the exchanges at whatever prices the supply and demand on the specialists' books could accommodate or tried to find a buyer by ''shopping'' the block, which in itself caused the stock to drop. Obviously, then, the end of give-ups introduced another element which added to the market's volatility.

Still other structural changes of more recent vintage exacerbated this volatility. On May 1, 1975, the S.E.C. declared all commissions negotiable. The real impact of this decision has been to benefit the institutional stock market participants while the individual investor continues to pay top dollar. Their very size as brokerage firm accounts has enabled institutions to demand and receive substantial commission cuts. Individuals have difficulty gaining such leverage. As a consequence, block trading firms that deal with these large institutions have become more chary about positioning blocks of stock themselves, since under the negotiated rate structure they are now less able to offset their capital risk.

Thus without the willingness of floor traders, specialists, and now block trading firms to accommodate larger sellers and buyers by positioning for their own accounts, these institutional participants are forced to fill their orders by finding offsetting institutional orders or by means of existing bids and offers on the specialists' books at the various exchanges. This makes for a much more volatile market, since a "buy" or "sell" order involving, say, 50,000 to 100,000 shares to be filled on the floors of the exchanges is likely to push that stock up or down several points before it is completed.

But these structural changes are not the only contributors to the market's new volatility. Another factor is the behavior and mind set of institutional money managers. These are a new breed, as historical perspective shows. In the early days of Wall Street, the investment world was not regarded as a place of great career opportunity—quite the reverse. To the public mind, Wall Street was a place for scions of wealthy families and other well-connected people where breeding was a very important consideration. This environment did not attract the most talented young people, or the hungriest, and a management gap, particularly in the 1930s and 1940s, was created in the securities industry.

New blood did not flow into the business for many years. Even after World War II there was fear of a postwar depression—a fear that proved ill-founded but was nevertheless not conducive to encouraging aggressive careerists to tackle the Street. Fortunately, by the early 1950s, one of the great benefits of World War II, the GI Bill, began to produce mature graduates whose sense of egalitarianism had been nurtured by the nationalistic mood of the 1940s. These men felt that many doors were open to them that had not been open years before. Sons and grandsons of immigrants and the disadvantaged in general, they now had college educations and military experience as part of their makeup. The post-war depression had not occurred, and the post-war bull market was beginning. By the early 1960s it was apparent that Wall Street had ceased to emphasize blood line and had become an industry where ability and performance counted. Previously anonymous money managers were being written up in the major media as folk-hero alchemists. Performance became the name of the game, and money for management came primarily to those who performed. This unfortunately led to high risk taking and eventually to investment disaster.

Today's money manager is a product of two conflicting strains. He is subject to cutthroat competition—challenged, for the sake of his job, to have his portfolio "perform" better than those of his competitors. At the same time, he is bridled by caution, since under the Employees' Retirement Income Security Act of 1974 (ERISA) he or his superiors may be held personally liable for losses in a pension fund portfolio. He is therefore very careful to act with prudence.

The so-called "prudent man rule" is one in which the courts have held that fiduciaries must employ investment practices that a man "acting in a like capacity and familiar with like matters would use in the conduct of an enterprise of like character with like aims." Stated more simply, the test of prudence is whether men in similar situations would do similar things. The inevitable investment result is to be concentrated in the "big" stocks. Trustees also tend to award management contracts to the big investment advisors to avoid criticism.

These strains affect the securities marketplace, since institutional investors often judge their professional investment performance very frequently—many of them quarterly.

The resulting pressure on professional money managers to show quarter-by-quarter gains in their portfolios has produced a number of aberrations in the marketplace—and has contributed to our modern market's volatility (and sometimes seeming irrationality).

One aberration is the tendency to be "trigger-happy." For the sake of his job, a money manager cannot afford to keep in his portfolio stocks which do not "perform"—that is, go up. Consequently, he is extremely sensitive to political and economic news developments that affect the market in general and specific stocks in particular. To be "safe" rather than "sorry," he may allow a potentially adverse news items to trigger a sell decision. The market's volatility is increased when many managers choose this path simultaneously.

Another aberration is a curious confusion between short and long-term investment objectives. A pension fund portfolio manager, for instance, should logically look for stocks offering a combination of income and long-term capital appreciation potential, since he is investing money that will be needed to provide benefits to pensioners in the distant future. The manager would probably consult his own internal stock analysts or brokerage firm analysts for long-term stock recommendations and buy those stocks with that objective in mind. However, because he is judged on a quarterly basis, that manager is likely—for practical considerations—to have to sell his "long-term" investment in the near term if the stock does not "perform" Thus today's market is often characterized by little equation between long-term security analysis and near-term market action.

Still another curiosity is the professionals' mania for "relative performance"—that is, they feel that their portfolios must do better than the market averages or other managers' performance. There is a subtle difference between such standards and the standards individual investors set for themselves. If you are investing your own money, you are concerned with absolute gains or losses in your portfolio. But if you are managing other peoples' money and your salary is based on your portfolios' "relative performance," your stock market perspective may be quite different. For example, if the Standard & Poors 500 Index has declined 20% over the past year and your managed money has declined only 10%, chances are that you, your bosses, and your client are delighted with your "excellent relative performance." An individual investor cannot afford to be so cavalier about his own money. He knows how difficult it was to accumulate that capital after taxes and how hard it will be to get even again.

The chess game money managers play in trying to outperform the averages often creates stock price swings that are completely unrelated to the merits of the stocks themselves. While the individual investor sees the stocks in his portfolio going up or down on big volume, he may think the big fellows know something he does not. Perhaps they may. But often they are simply shuffling around their portfolios in an attempt to beat the averages, without any apparent regard for their judgments on the stocks involved.

Here is how it works: Each of the 500 stocks in the S&P 500 has a particular weighting in that average, determined by the number of shares outstanding multiplied by the stock's current market price. If stock X begins to decline more than the S&P 500, it automatically becomes underweighted in the average relative to the immediately preceding period, as a result of the above formula. A portfolio manager trying to outperform that average will instantly conclude that if his portfolio is to do better than the averages, he certainly must weight that particular stock even less than the weighting it carries in the average. So he reduces his position by selling the stock. Because he probably owns a substantial position in that stock, his selling depresses the price even more, touching off sell decisions on the part of other managers, which further weakens that stock. In short, a situation develops where all the big "players" are trying to sell at once, while potential buyers, not unaware of what is happening, are holding back. The relative performance mentality thus creates a kind of vicious cycle that causes greatly increased volatility.

The cycle works similarly when the market begins to go up: a professional manager may be 90% invested (that is, 90% of his portfolio is in stocks, 10% in cash equivalents) when the market starts to climb. Since he is competing with a fully (100%) invested S&P 500 Index, he suddenly finds himself already behind the averages. He typically reacts by buying over-weighted amounts of the volatile or "high Beta" stocks, which he feels are sure to move up more than the averages. When his competitors do likewise, these stocks suddenly jump up. Result: buying panic. The increase in volatility in recent years becomes clearer upon study of Table 2-3. The number of months of high volatility is steadily increasing, while the number of months of low volatility is decreasing.

Currently the institutional investment world is caught up in a vogue called "indexing." This consists of buying stocks in the S&P indexes in the exact proportion that they are carried in these indexes. This fad has emerged as many money managers have become frustrated trying to outperform the broad market. They have concluded, in effect, that market success is random, so, "if you can't beat it, join it." They are trying to *become* the market.

This tendency to concentrate megabuck institutional portfolios in the big, recognizable stocks—called "institutional favorites" or, in Street parlance, "the nifty fifty" (since those favorites include about 50 names)—is exacerbated by the concentration of research information produced by Wall Street brokerage firms.

Today, stock research information is being produced by fewer and fewer brokerage firms, following the consolidation of many Wall Street houses in recent years. Moreover, there is a "star system" among stock analysts; therefore, most institutional money managers receive their information and recommendations from the same small cadre of "top" analysts. Since buy and sell decisions are made by a concentrated group of managers who are the recipients of the same buy and sell rec-

TABLE 2-3   Number of Months of Percentage Changes in the Dow Jones Industrial Average Ranges in 5-Year Segments—1947–1976

| 5 Year Period | Percentage Monthly Range | | | | | |
	0–1.99	2–3.99	4–5.9	6–7.9	8–9.99	10+
1972–1976	—	11	23	14	4	8
1967–1971	—	18	24	9	6	3
1962–1966	9	29	14	3	3	2
1957–1961	5	24	25	4	—	2
1952–1956	3	26	23	6	1	1
1947–1951	1	23	24	10	—	2

ommendations at approximately the same time, the market reacts violently to the star analysts' changes of opinion. We see "air pockets" on the downside and "buying panics" on the upside.

This was not always the case. Instant announcement and quickly-communicated analysis of corporate and economic developments is a phenomenon of the last quarter century. Prior to the 1930s information was a rare commodity in the stock market.

We have seen that the invention of the telegraph and telephone has greatly improved communications about stock prices and news events; even after the advent of these devices, however, corporate developments in the earlier days of the stock market largely remained secret—except when it was advantageous to insiders to make some facts generally known. As a matter of fact, technical analysis, or "charting," was an attempt on the part of traders to figure out the activities of the insiders by analyzing stock price changes.

From a time perspective, security analysis is still in its infancy. It is an art that depends mainly on published information, interviews with corporate officials, and the proper weighting of countless external variables. None of these was accessible a century ago, so that security analysis is a relatively new thing. This letter from the New York Stock Exchange to the Delaware, Lackawanna & Western Railroad Co.* and the response shows the prevailing attitude in 1866:

New York
19 Broad Street, Room 17
22nd March, 1866

To the Secretary of the
   Delaware, Lackawanna & WesternRail-Road Co.

Sir;

The Stock Exchange of New York desires to collect Reports and Documents connected with Finance and Rail-Roads, and to this end have appointed a committee.

I therefore beg to request you will direct, that from time to time, as they may be issued, the Reports of your Company be sent to the Secretary of the New York Stock Exchange, George H. Brodhead, Esq. and if not occa-

---

*Source: Birl E. Shultz, *The Securities Market; And How It Works.* N.Y. and London. Harper and Bros, 1942. p. 8.

sioning you too much trouble, you will greatly oblige by furnishing also, the Reports and statements from a period as far back as they have been preserved.

I am, respectfully,
G. L. Gerrard
Chairman of the Committee

P.S. Answer will oblige.

The answer to this communication written in longhand on the inside page of the request follows:

The Delaware, Lackawanna & Western Rail-Road Co. makes no Reports and publishes no statements—and have not done anything of the kind for the last five years.

A.C. Odell
Treasurer

How can the individual investor hope to survive the big risks he is now taking by playing in an investment arena dominated by big players and big stocks? How can he overcome the built-in volatility that characterizes a high-risk marketplace where relative performance standards and concentrated holdings of relatively few buyers and sellers predominate? To survive/succeed, one must adapt, with new techniques and new attitudes. And since a whole new attitude toward stocks is the foundation of this book, we will start there . . .

CHAPTER THREE

The Games Investors Play (with Themselves)

Here is your strategy for surviving/succeeding in the new stock market:

- First, remove yourself from the position of having to make the right guesses within a high stakes, volatile environment.

- Second, change your whole purview of investing—from the idea that you "win" by "putting your eggs in the right basket" to the concept that you will make money by capitalizing on the most likely occurrences.

- Third, learn to manage your stock inventory the way a businessman manages his product inventory—with discipline, flexibility, and an ability and willingness to play the probabilities.

That is a lot to digest all at once. Now that we've said it, let's look at the various parts of our game plan.

The previous chapter gave us some insights into why today's stock market has become a high-risk, highly volatile arena for the individual investor. In succeeding chapters we will describe techniques for implementing this three-part strategy. But first, we all need a dose of self-help psychology in order to change some of our self-defeating, ingrained attitudes about stocks and investing.

Many investors make the mistake of taking a speculator's stance: trying to outguess the market on a near-term basis through a combination of tips, hunches, guesses, whims, and responses to news with the hope that one day they will be lucky enough to be one of those bragging about the great success story—for instance, finding the new Xerox and holding it through its period of spectacular price increase. Not likely. This is how losses are accumulated in stocks people "like."

Others, more cautious, do not aim for pie-in-the-sky. Their objective is to win good returns on their investments by putting their blue chips away and forgetting them. This was correct for the 1949–1968 period, but it has been unrewarding since then. Not a policy for all seasons.

But common to both the swinger and the sedate stock market investor is a mistake nearly every investor makes: he puts himself in the position of having to decide (and be right) that "the market is going up" or "the market is going down." Based on that decision, he buys or sells, further commits funds to the marketplace, or withdraws them.

This psychology is shared by nearly every market participant, from the biggest to the smallest. It is the driving force that creates the supply and demand that is reflected in each day's market averages. And yet this is a no-win strategy.

The investor who makes the mistake of having to second-guess the direction in the risky, irrational, unpredictable environment that is to-day's stock market has little chance of success. If he must constantly guess whether or not the market is going up—and must be correct to "win"—the odds are against him. Here's why:

Nobody knows what the stock market will do day by day, despite the advice of all our "experts"—not only those on Wall Street, but in government, business, labor, and private economists' circles. The "experts" themselves don't agree on the short and long-term outlook for either the economy or stocks. Moreover, most of the time most of them are wrong—though not so consistently off-base that we might make money merely by relying on the converse of their predictions. Notice how frequently the statement, "Experts were surprised by the stock market's action yesterday," or words to that effect appear in the financial columns of your newspaper.

The market has a mind and life of its own. It always has; and it probably will continue to behave in seemingly capricious cycles. Were it otherwise, the most rational investors would be the most successful; the smartest would be the richest! For further evidence, keep in mind the record in Table 1-1, of the big banks' stock market performance over 10 years. With access to the best brainpower in the country, the professionals' top performance was a 2.1% portfolio gain—including the reinvestment of income. Surely, with the swings the market experienced in that period, the performance could have been outstanding, if anyone had had an inkling or educated guess as to which way the market was headed.

If you study the history of 100 years of market tops and bottoms—with accompanying newspaper analyses, columns, and even advertisements—the repetition of these inaccurate projections is readily discernible.

In the post-war period alone we have seen dozens of investment vogues that were the subject of serious treatises in their day, and that now, with hindsight, seem pure folly. During World War II and through the 1940s, investment professionals developed "formula plans." They would examine recent trading ranges for stocks, and then structure their portfolios so that they held their largest positions in particular stocks when they were at the bottom of their ranges. The classic example was the Vassar College endowment—a plan initiated by that noble institution's economics department! As a stock traded up toward the top of its range, the formula required a portfolio manager to sell off his holdings, so that at the top he had his smallest position in that stock. This plan was quite effective until the early 1950s, when the market broke out over its 1929 highs—and caught the formula practitioner with virtually no positions in any stocks.

Perhaps as a reaction to this embarrassment and also as a consequence of the post-World War II bull market, the next vogue was "buy and hold"—a sure way not to get caught without stocks in position in a strong uptrend. According to this philosophy, a portfolio manager could rest easy if he bought a group of stocks of "outstanding" companies and simply held them for appreciation. These stocks were known as "one-decision" stocks—that is, all you had to do was decide to buy them. This worked fine for a while, too, until the stock leadership of the market changed entirely and once-stars became each day's "new lows."

The late 1960s' "one-decision" mentality (as if continuing to hold a stock were not a decision) helped create the "two-tier" market, which still survives to some extent. With institutional portfolio managers singling out a few dozen stocks as their "one-decision" candidates, the market itself became divided into two tiers—a "top tier" of "institutional-grade" stocks selling for high multiples, and a "bottom tier" consisting of the rest of the stocks in the marketplace, many of them selling at bargain prices.

Both the "one-decision" vogue and the "two-tier" market have taken their lumps in recent years. The result: several new philosophies, all in reaction to past failures. The folly of "buy-and-hold"—which became "hold" all the way up and then all the way down in the rise and fall of the "growth" stocks—is reflected today in portfolio managers' extreme skittishness about holding declining stocks. Once burned and twice cautious, this group of professionals is now so collectively nervous that, as we mentioned in the last chapter, they tend to sell on the slightest hint of bad news. This willingness to sell early creates near-panic selling way out of proportion to the reality of whatever is considered the bad news—thus often creating self-generating, one-way stock market declines and adding to the market's overall volatility.

Many former "buy-and-hold" adherents have taken two other routes.

One is trying to beat the market through "market timing," or scrupulous attention to technical market analysis, creating quick turnover (and thus heightening volatility). The other, as mentioned in the previous chapter, is no longer trying to beat the market, but just keeping up with it, by "indexing." In a decade investors may view market timing and indexing as we view "formula plans" and "one-decision" investing.

One of the reasons that the stock market is a showplace for recurring folly is that each generation of investors tends to project into the future its immediate past experience. Reminiscent of a teenager in love, each generation thinks that what is happening now is unlike anything that has ever happened before: each cycle is a whole new experience. Aggravating this entirely natural phenomenon is another phenomenon. Most of the institutional money managers today are the products of graduate-level business schools, having been attracted tc the business field by the disproportionately large profits of an abnormal period that was not then recognized as an aberrance.

By their nature, business schools stress the study of companies and corporate finance but do not emphasize (and often fail even to consider) the history of financial markets. Thus when their graduates become portfolio managers, they do not respect the differences between stocks and companies, or between stock market cycles and business cycles. Without making such distinctions, the M.B.A. money manager may not appreciate that markets have lives of their own, or that companies can do well without their stocks doing well, and vice versa.

Many investors of both professional and amateur rank make the additional mistake of falling in love with their stock portfolios. They will refuse to buy a particular stock "because I've always hated Polaroid," or to sell another "because Kodak has always done well by me in the past." On closer examination, one usually finds that a particular investor "loves" the stocks that are still in his portfolio and that "love" began to blossom when the stock declined below the price he paid for it.

The problem with emotional involvement with your stocks is that they are hardly appreciative of your passion for them. Hence there is rarely a correlation between a stock's love quotient and its price movement. So many people loved IBM in the high 270s that few would tender it to the company at 280 in March 1977. Yet, some 6 weeks later, IBM was under 260, and, a year later, it was under 240. In fact, for the previous ten years, lovers of IBM had had their passion unrequited. Such is the heartbreak of love.

But enough of market modes and moves. By now it should be obvious why few win at the game of correctly anticipating the market's future direction. Forcing investors to guess whether "the market's going up" or "the market's going down" creates too gamey an environment for risking capital.

What's more, the psychological burden of second-guessing the stock market is too emotionally taxing. If you allow yourself to employ this no-win strategy with your money on the line, you are faced with daily decisions, that is, you buy or sell. This is a black or white situation, with no gray, no temporizing. What do we mean? Suppose you own U.S. Steel, and today it went down. Should you sell it now? Will it bounce up again? Will it go down further? Suppose instead that today it went up. Should you take your profits? Should you hope for more? The old saw says, "Cut your losses and let your profits run." But where do you begin to cut your losses? At 5%? 10%? 15%? Taking a 10% loss four times in a row is a big loss! No matter what you decide, your decision comes back to haunt you every day—that is, the stock market pages of your newspaper tell you what would have happened had you done otherwise. In contrast, you never know the results of alternative decisions in most other areas of life. If you consult a doctor for an ailment and follow his advice, you can not know what would have happened if you had not. You can only guess.

As you will learn from this book, your strategy for surviving/succeeding in the new stock market requires a whole new set of attitudes towards investing. *Instead of trying to outguess the market, you will learn to make money on other investors' expectations.* You will be concerned, not with making money by enjoying a lucky "big hit," but with making money by *identifying low-risk situations in which you will be paid money to assume that stocks will not behave uncharacteristically.* Your goal will not be to find a stock that has a possibility of a spectacular rise, but rather to find a whole series of stocks for which you will receive money if they conform to historical probabilities—that is, if they do not rise or fall outside price boundaries determined by their historical volatility in any specific time period.

In other words, you will be kicking your self-defeating habits and avoiding the mistakes most investors make. *You will be learning to invest not by having to guess whether the market will go up or down, but by playing the odds that it will merely fluctuate within certain ranges*—and if it does not, you can adjust those ranges successfully and profitably.

And what stocks will you pick for constructing an investment program where the odds are on your side? You will be using the options market to "rent out" the volatility of the self-same "institutional grade" stocks in which the big institutions concentrate their buying and selling.

We will leave the mechanics to later chapters following an explanation of options in general. But the theory is easily understood here. It is simply put: once a stock becomes "widely held" and of "institutional grade" and, as the academics say, "efficiently priced," it is impossible to consistently make any significant profits trading in it. Therefore, you can profitably finance someone else's attempts to do so. Own the substance—sell the froth!

CHAPTER FOUR

The Efficient Market

- Question: When is a "good" investment not a good investment?
- Answer: When everyone *thinks* of it as a "good" investment.

The contradictions inherent in the above question and answer illustrate another dimension of the mental makeover you will need to survive/succeed in the new stock market.

The radical but necessary reworking of your conventional attitudes towards investing includes disposing of the delusion that buying well-known stocks of high quality is "wise" and "conservative."

You may impress your banker with a portfolio filled with the big, recognizable stocks—but you will not make any money simply by owning them. This does not mean that these stocks will not go up. You just can not tell which ones will, or when they will.

That is because these institutionally-held securities are already "efficiently priced." They constitute the "efficient market." But efficiently priced does not mean "fairly" priced.

Market "efficiency" means that all known information is immediately discounted by all investors and reflected in the market price of stocks. In other words, no one has an information edge. In the ideal efficient market, everyone knows all possible-to-know information simultaneously, interprets it similarly, and behaves rationally. But, human beings being what they are, this of course rarely happens.

In the real world it is very difficult to know whether what you know is fully known, and, if it is, whether the implications to be drawn are correct. The investor's question is always, "Has this fact been fully reflected in the price?" This question brings up other unknowns: Are there other factors also affecting the price of this stock that some investors have not yet taken into consideration? How can I be sure that I am the only one who is correctly interpreting the facts and therefore will benefit when others realize what I realize? When do I give up on that idea? Is it knowable at all?

There are many levels of insight into a major economic or technological development. Take the jet engine, for instance. In the early 1960s it was clear that airlines would convert their fleets to jet power. Everyone knew this. It was not a speculative thought. But the courses of investment action immediately following the information input were quite disparate. Investor A, for instance, reacted by buying the shares of a jet engine manufacturer, while Investor B selected the shares of an airplane manufacturer. Investor C invested in the airlines whose cost structure and profitability would be dramatically affected by the jet engine introduction. Investor D considered the subtler implications of the information and reasoned that, since the size of the world in travel hours would be diminished, previously far-off spots, such as the Caribbean, would have enhanced appeal for vacationers. In his view, a land investment in a tropical island made the most sense. For some period of time, each would be correct. Each investment required a different amount of time for the market to recognize it and to fully discount its economic implications—although everyone knew about the jet engine at the same time.

The academics' generalization that today's stock market is efficient fails to make the following distinction: today's "efficient" market is composed of stocks which *are* efficiently priced and also those that are inefficiently priced, but it is dominated by those that are efficiently priced. To make money, it is crucial that you learn to separate the two categories.

Efficiently priced stocks are widely held and most favored by institutions. Institutions are in the business of gathering and evaluating information on stocks. Moreover, they have become the major participants in valuing certain stocks. Because of these two realities—and also because portfolio managers tend to think alike—it can be inferred that their largest holdings are efficiently priced; that is, all there is to know is known and reflected in the prices of these stocks. Therefore, these stocks are no longer attractive investments. They are priced "right."

How can these "good investment stocks" not be good investments? The confusion is in the vernacular and investment implications of the word "good." Most investors identify a "good investment" as stock in a company that is well recognized and respected, has "good" management, "stable" or "predictably rising" earnings, "safe" dividends, and a "good" balance sheet—a stock which is highly unlikely to cause you to lose all your money. But a lot of these "good investment" stocks have gone down a lot over the last few years. The fact is that a "good investment stock" is not really a smart investment, because it has no real appreciation potential. Everyone recognizes its premium quality, and the premium for this quality is already built into the price of the stock. *A truly good investment is an inefficiently priced stock that someday will be recognized for its quality—and then priced up accordingly.*

There is a way to test our thesis that the institutionally held (and therefore efficiently priced) stocks are no longer good investments. Comparing the institutionally held stocks for their attractiveness as investments *before* they were institutionally favored with *after* would be a primitive but easy method to confirm this contention. For this comparison, we will use "Vickers Favorite Fifty," a list of the most widely held institutional stocks that is published every quarter by Vickers Associates, Inc., Huntington, N.Y. This list happens to relate to mutual funds, but, if it were to relate to banks or pension funds, the names and dates would not differ significantly. The following pages include charts of every stock that made its way onto this list in the last 18 years, with an arrow denoting the quarter in which it became one of the Favorite Fifty.

As the charts show graphically, there is little potential left for a good return once a stock becomes an institutional favorite. The charts do not imply that the institutions are not intelligent investors. They do, however, imply that money is made while institutions are accumulating these stocks and while the stocks are becoming recognized as "good investments." Once they are widely held and recognized, the potential for profit sags. That does not mean they can not go up, but it does mean it is hard to pick which ones and when. The chances of being right are slim.

What does this mean for the clever investor? Two things:

■ If one were to buy stocks, one would not look to the largest institutional holdings to make shrewd investments. One would instead consider stocks that might *become* large institutional holdings.

■ Efficiently-priced stocks *do* fluctuate; in fact, they have a *more predictable volatility* than lesser-known stocks, since their investment characteristics have been established and recognized and they are under continuous analysis by institutions and brokerage analysts.

Thus these stocks are the perfect candidates for renting out volatility profiably to other investors.

To better understand this investment concept as it relates to your new attitudes, let us consider a real estate analogy. If the institutional stocks are existing property in an established neighborhood, and the lesser known stocks are undeveloped land on the outskirts of town, you, as an investor, have a choice:

If you want to make a spectacular investment, you do not buy the established property with little potential for a big gain. Instead, you try to make a judgmental prediction of the real estate market by taking the bigger risk on the undeveloped land, hoping it will eventually yield a handsome return by becoming part of the suburbs.

If you instead prefer to make a steady, good, efficient market return with much less risk and without relying as much on a market prediction, you buy existing property in the established stable neighborhoods and rent it out.

How can you conduct your stock business like the landlord of good property? It is possible, thanks to the new standardized options markets.

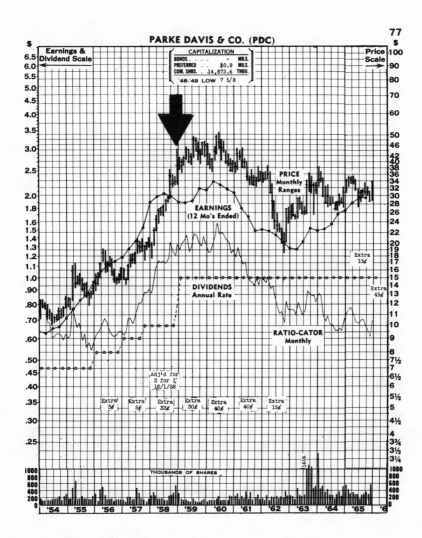

PARKE DAVIS & CO. (PDC)

*All charts from CYCLI-GRAPHS Courtesy of Securities Research Company, Boston, Mass.

27

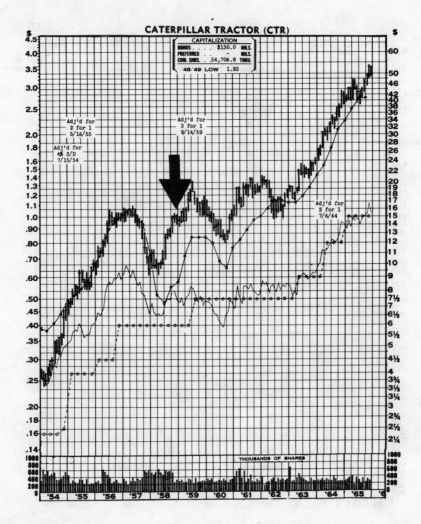

CATERPILLAR TRACTOR (CTR)

CAPITALIZATION		
BONDS	$130.0	MILS.
PREFERRED	-	MILS.
COM. SHRS. .	54,706.8	THOU.

'48-'49 LOW 1.93

Adj'd for
2 for 1
5/16/55

Adj'd for
4% S/D
7/15/54

Adj'd for
3 for 1
9/14/59

Adj'd for
2 for 1
7/6/64

THOUSANDS OF SHARES

'54 '55 '56 '57 '58 '59 '60 '61 '62 '63 '64 '65 '6

28

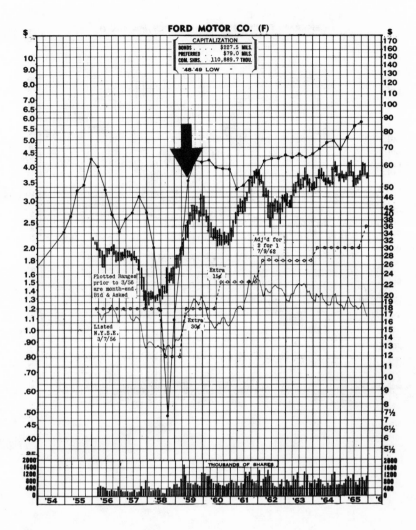

FORD MOTOR CO. (F)

CAPITALIZATION
BONDS . . . . $227.5 MILS.
PREFERRED . . $79.0 MILS.
COM. SHRS. . 110,889.7 THOU.

'48-'49 LOW -

Adj'd for
2 for 1
7/9/62

Extra
15¢

Plotted Ranges
prior to 3/56
are month-end
Bid & Asked

Extra
30¢

Listed
N.Y.S.E.
3/7/56

THOUSANDS OF SHARES

'54 '55 '56 '57 '58 '59 '60 '61 '62 '63 '64 '65 '6

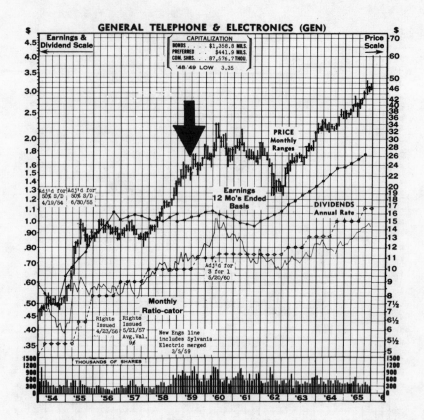

GENERAL TELEPHONE & ELECTRONICS (GEN)

Earnings & Dividend Scale

CAPITALIZATION
BONDS . . . . $1,358.8 MILS.
PREFERRED $441.9 MILS.
COM. SHRS. . . 87,576.7 THOU.
'48 '49 LOW 3.35

Price Scale

PRICE Monthly Ranges

Earnings 12 Mo's Ended Basis

DIVIDENDS Annual Rate

Adj'd for 50% S/D 4/19/54

Adj'd for 50% S/D 6/30/55

Adj'd for 3 for 1 5/20/60

Monthly Ratio-cator

Rights Issued 4/23/56

Rights Issued 5/21/57 Avg. Val. 9¢

New Engs line includes Sylvania Electric merged 3/5/59

THOUSANDS OF SHARES

'54 '55 '56 '57 '58 '59 '60 '61 '62 '63 '64 '65 '6

30

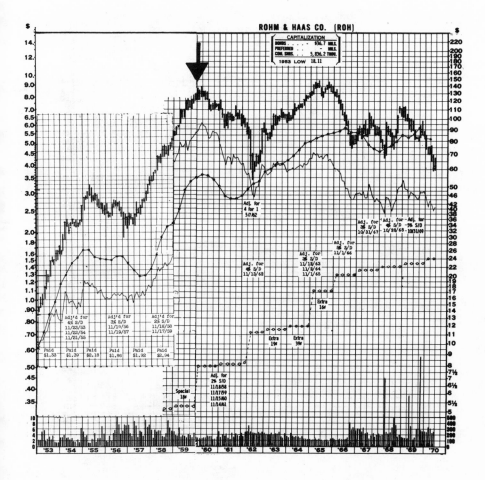

ROHM & HAAS CO. (ROH)

CAPITALIZATION
BONDS . . . . . $36.7 MIL.$
PREFERRED . . . . MIL.$
COM. SHRS. . . . 5,836.2 THOU.
1953 LOW 18.11

Adj. for
4 for 1
5/1/62

Adj. for
3% S/D
10/31/67   Adj. for
          4% S/D   Adj. for
          10/28/68 -5% S/D
                    10/31/69

Adj. for
5% S/D
11/1/66

Adj. for
3% S/D
11/12/63
11/1/65

Adj. for
4% S/D
11/13/68

Extra
16¢

Adj'd for
4% S/D
11/23/53
11/22/54
11/21/55

Adj'd for
3% S/D
11/19/56
11/19/57

Adj'd for
2% S/D
11/18/58
11/17/59

Extra
19¢   Extra
      39¢

Paid
$1.33   Paid
        $1.39   Paid
                $2.18   Paid
                        $1.86   Paid
                                $1.92   Paid
                                        $2.94

Adj. for
2% S/D
11/8/58
11/17/59
11/15/60
11/14/61

Special
19¢

'53 '54 '55 '56 '57 '58 '59 '60 '61 '62 '63 '64 '65 '66 '67 '68 '69 '70

31

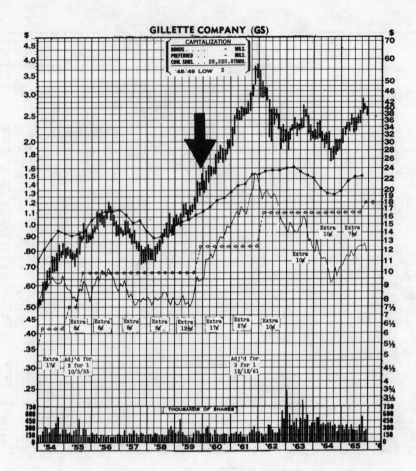

GILLETTE COMPANY (GS)

CAPITALIZATION
BONDS . . . . . - MILS.
PREFERRED . . . - MILS.
COM. SHRS. . . . 28,320.8THOU.

'48-'49 LOW 2

THOUSANDS OF SHARES

'54 '55 '56 '57 '58 '59 '60 '61 '62 '63 '64 '65 '

32

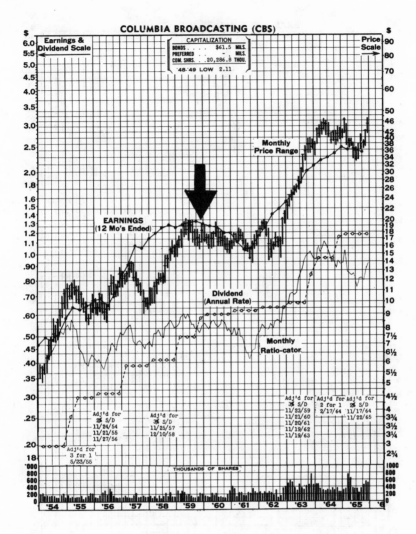

COLUMBIA BROADCASTING (CBS)

CAPITALIZATION
BONDS . . . . $61.5 MILS.
PREFERRED . . - MILS.
COM. SHRS. . . 20,286.8 THOU.

'48-'49 LOW 2.11

Earnings & Dividend Scale

Price Scale

Monthly Price Range

EARNINGS
(12 Mo's Ended)

Dividend
(Annual Rate)

Monthly
Ratio-cator

Adj'd for
2% S/D
11/24/54
11/21/55
11/27/56

Adj'd for
3 for 1
5/23/55

Adj'd for
3% S/D
11/25/57
12/10/58

Adj'd for
3% S/D
11/23/59
11/21/60
11/20/61
11/19/62
11/19/63

Adj'd for
2 for 1
2/17/64

Adj'd for
2% S/D
11/17/64
11/22/65

THOUSANDS OF SHARES

'54 '55 '56 '57 '58 '59 '60 '61 '62 '63 '64 '65 '6

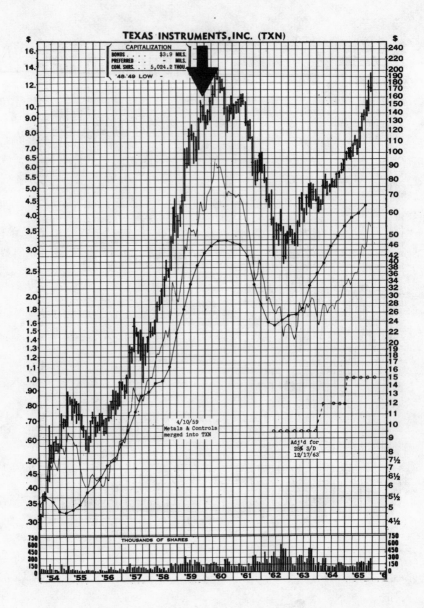

TEXAS INSTRUMENTS, INC. (TXN)

CAPITALIZATION
BONDS . . . . $3.9 MILS.
PREFERRED . . – MILS.
COM. SHRS. . . 5,024.2 THOU.
'48-'49 LOW –

4/10/59
Metals & Controls
merged into TXN

Adj'd for
25% S/D
12/17/63

THOUSANDS OF SHARES

'54 '55 '56 '57 '58 '59 '60 '61 '62 '63 '64 '65 '6

34

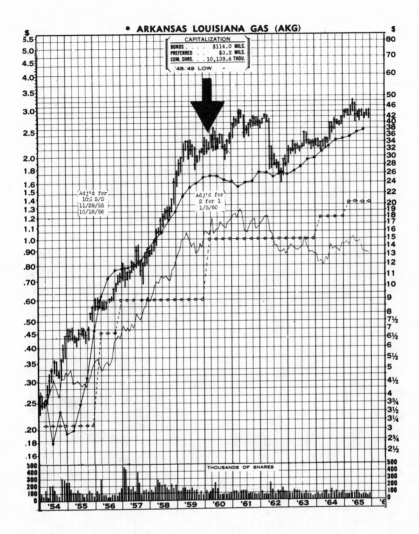

● ARKANSAS LOUISIANA GAS (AKG)

CAPITALIZATION
BONDS . . . . $114.0 MILS.
PREFERRED . . $3.2 MILS.
COM. SHRS. . . 10,139.6 THOU.
'48-'49 LOW -

THOUSANDS OF SHARES

Adj'd for
10;5 S/D
11/29/55
10/18/56

Adj'd for
2 for 1
1/5/60

'54   '55   '56   '57   '58   '59   '60   '61   '62   '63   '64   '65

35

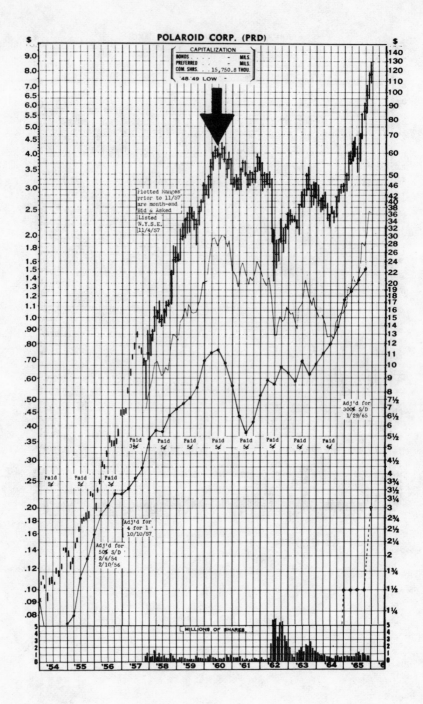

POLAROID CORP. (PRD)

CAPITALIZATION

BONDS	—	MILS.
PREFERRED	—	MILS.
COM. SHRS.	15,750.8	THOU.

'48 '49 LOW —

Plotted Ranges prior to 11/57 are month-end Bid & Asked
Listed N.Y.S.E. 11/4/57

Adj'd for 300% S/D 1/29/65

Paid 3½¢	Paid 5¢	Paid 5¢	Paid 5¢	Paid 5¢	Paid 5¢	Paid 5¢	Paid 4¢

Paid 2¢	Paid 2¢	Paid 3¢

Adj'd for 4 for 1 10/10/57

Adj'd for 50% S/D 2/6/54 2/10/56

MILLIONS OF SHARES

'54 '55 '56 '57 '58 '59 '60 '61 '62 '63 '64 '65 '6

36

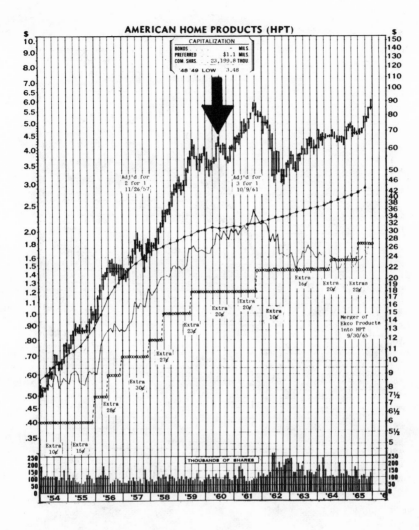

AMERICAN HOME PRODUCTS (HPT)

CAPITALIZATION

BONDS . . . . . — MILS.
PREFERRED . . . $1.1 MILS.
COM. SHRS. . . . 23,199.8 THOU.

'48 '49 LOW 3.48

Adj'd for
2 for 1
11/26/57

Adj'd for
3 for 1
10/9/61

Extra
16¢

Extra
20¢

Extras
22¢

Extra
20¢

Extra
20¢

Extra
10¢

Merger of
Ekco Products
into HPT
9/30/65

Extra
23¢

Extra
27¢

Extra
30¢

Extra
28¢

Extra
10¢

Extra
15¢

THOUSANDS OF SHARES

'54 '55 '56 '57 '58 '59 '60 '61 '62 '63 '64 '65 '6

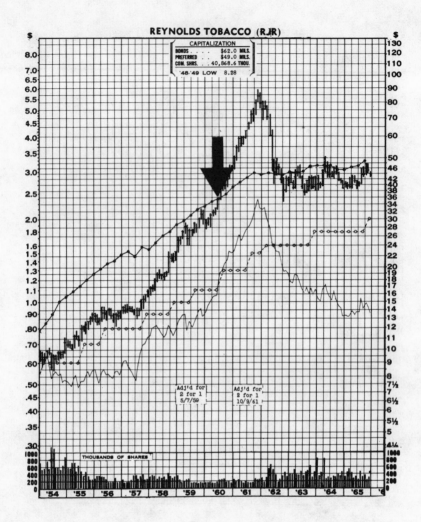

REYNOLDS TOBACCO (RJR)

CAPITALIZATION
BONDS . . . . $62.0 MRS.
PREFERRED . . $49.0 MRS.
COM. SHRS. . 40,868.6 THOU.

'48-'49 LOW 8.28

Adj'd for
2 for 1
5/7/59

Adj'd for
2 for 1
10/9/61

THOUSANDS OF SHARES

'54 '55 '56 '57 '58 '59 '60 '61 '62 '63 '64 '65

38

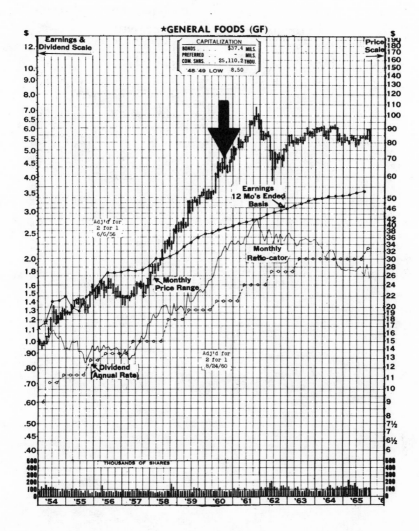

★GENERAL FOODS (GF)

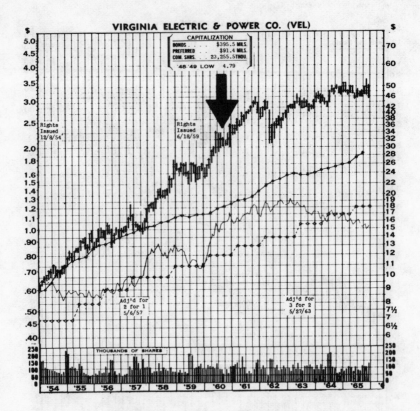

VIRGINIA ELECTRIC & POWER CO. (VEL)

CAPITALIZATION
BONDS . . . . $395.5 MILS.
PREFERRED . . . $91.4 MILS.
COM. SHRS. . . . 23,255.5THOU.
'48 '49 LOW 4.79

Rights
Issued
12/8/54

Rights
Issued
6/18/59

Adj'd for
2 for 1
5/6/57

Adj'd for
3 for 2
5/27/63

THOUSANDS OF SHARES

'54 '55 '56 '57 '58 '59 '60 '61 '62 '63 '64 '65

AMERICAN MACHINE & FOUNDRY (AMF)

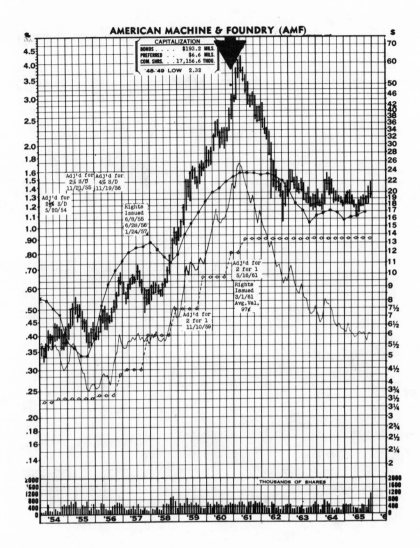

CAPITALIZATION

BONDS	$193.2 MILS.
PREFERRED . . .	$6.6 MILS.
COM. SHRS. . .	17,156.6 THOU.

'48-'49 LOW 2.32

Adj'd for
2½ S/D
5/20/54

Adj'd for
2% S/D
11/21/55

Adj'd for
4% S/D
11/19/56

Rights
Issued
6/8/55
6/28/56
1/24/57

Adj'd for
2 for 1
11/10/59

Adj'd for
2 for 1
5/16/61

Rights
Issued
3/1/61
Avg.Val.
97¢

THOUSANDS OF SHARES

'54 '55 '56 '57 '58 '59 '60 '61 '62 '63 '64 '65 '6

41

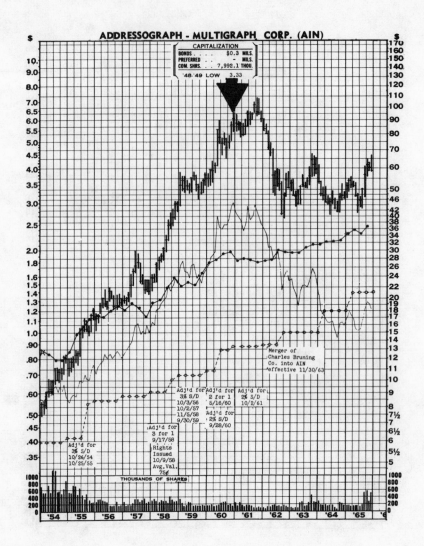

ADDRESSOGRAPH - MULTIGRAPH CORP. (AIN)

CAPITALIZATION
BONDS . . . . $0.3 MILS.
PREFERRED . . . - MILS.
COM. SHRS. . . . 7,992.1 THOU.

'48 '49 LOW 3.33

Merger of
Charles Bruning
Co. into AIN
effective 11/30/63

Adj'd for
3% S/D
10/3/56
10/2/57
11/5/58
9/30/59

Adj'd for
2 for 1
5/16/60

Adj'd for
2% S/D
10/2/61

Adj'd for
2% S/D
9/28/60

Adj'd for
3 for 1
9/17/58

Rights
Issued
10/9/58
Avg. Val.
75¢

Adj'd for
3% S/D
10/26/54
10/25/55

THOUSANDS OF SHARES

'54 '55 '56 '57 '58 '59 '60 '61 '62 '63 '64 '65

42

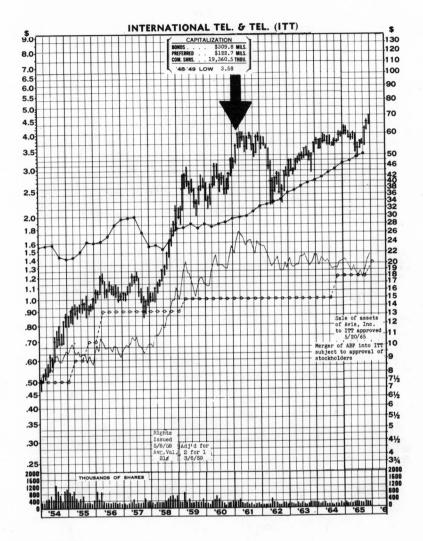

INTERNATIONAL TEL. & TEL. (ITT)

CAPITALIZATION
BONDS . . . . $309.8 MILS.
PREFERRED . . . $122.7 MILS.
COM. SHRS. . . 19,360.5 THOU.

'48-'49 LOW 3.58

Sale of assets
of Avis, Inc.
to ITT approved
5/20/65

Merger of ABP into ITT
subject to approval of
stockholders

Rights
Issued
5/8/58
Avg.Val. 21¢   Adj'd for
2 for 1
3/6/59

THOUSANDS OF SHARES

'54   '55   '56   '57   '58   '59   '60   '61   '62   '63   '64   '65   '6

43

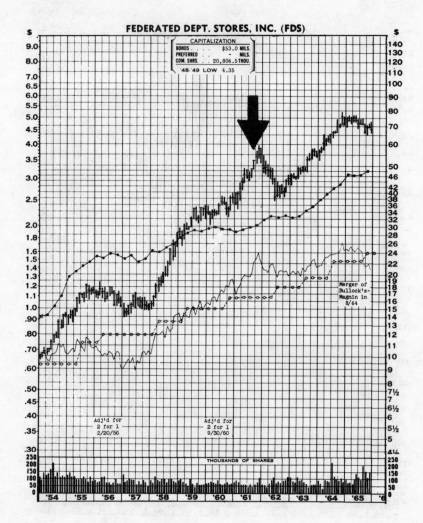

FEDERATED DEPT. STORES, INC. (FDS)

CAPITALIZATION
BONDS . . . . $53.0 MILS.
PREFERRED . . . - MILS.
COM. SHRS. . . . 20,806.5 THOU.
'48-'49 LOW 4.35

Merger of
Bullock's-
Magnin in
8/64

Adj'd for
2 for 1
2/20/56

Adj'd for
2 for 1
9/30/60

THOUSANDS OF SHARES

'54 '55 '56 '57 '58 '59 '60 '61 '62 '63 '64 '65 '6

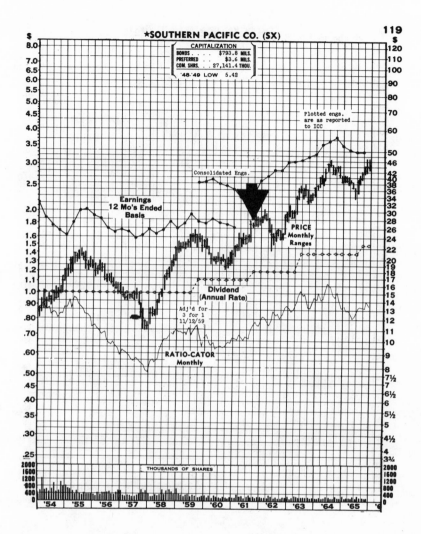

★SOUTHERN PACIFIC CO. (SX)

CAPITALIZATION
BONDS . . . . $793.8 MILS.
PREFERRED . . $3.6 MILS.
COM. SHRS. . . 27,141.4 THOU.

'48-'49 LOW 5.42

Plotted engs.
are as reported
to ICC

Consolidated Engs.

Earnings
12 Mo's Ended
Basis

PRICE
Monthly
Ranges

Dividend
(Annual Rate)

Adj'd for
3 for 1
11/12/59

RATIO-CATOR
Monthly

THOUSANDS OF SHARES

'54 '55 '56 '57 '58 '59 '60 '61 '62 '63 '64 '65

45

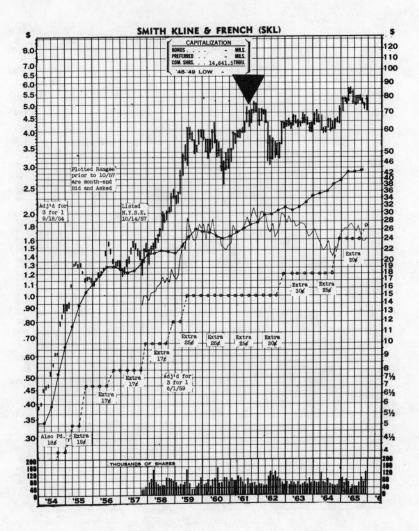

SMITH KLINE & FRENCH (SKL)

CAPITALIZATION
BONDS . . . . — MILS.
PREFERRED . . . — MILS.
COM. SHRS. . . 14,641.5 THOU.
'48-'49 LOW —

Plotted Ranges prior to 10/57 are month-end Bid and Asked

Adj'd for 3 for 1 9/18/54

Listed N.Y.S.E. 10/14/57

Extra 20¢

Extra 30¢ Extra 25¢

Extra 25¢ Extra 25¢ Extra 25¢ Extra 30¢

Extra 17¢

Extra 17¢

Adj'd for 3 for 1 6/1/59

Extra 17¢

Also Pd. 18¢ Extra 18¢

THOUSANDS OF SHARES

'54 '55 '56 '57 '58 '59 '60 '61 '62 '63 '64 '65

46

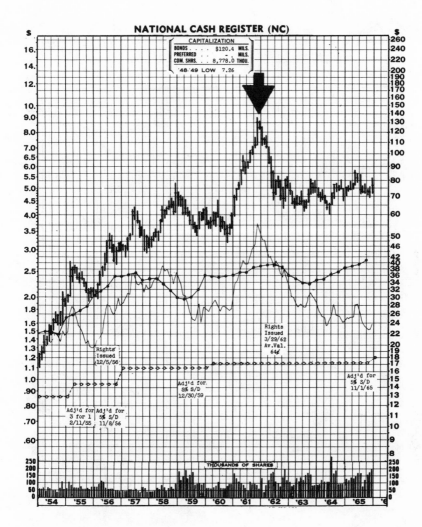

NATIONAL CASH REGISTER (NC)

Rights
Issued
12/5/56

Rights
Issued
3/29/62
Av.Val.
64¢

Adj'd for
5% S/D
11/1/65

Adj'd for
5% S/D
12/30/59

Adj'd for
3 for 1
2/11/55

Adj'd for
5% S/D
11/8/56

THOUSANDS OF SHARES

'54 '55 '56 '57 '58 '59 '60 '61 '62 '63 '64 '65 '6

47

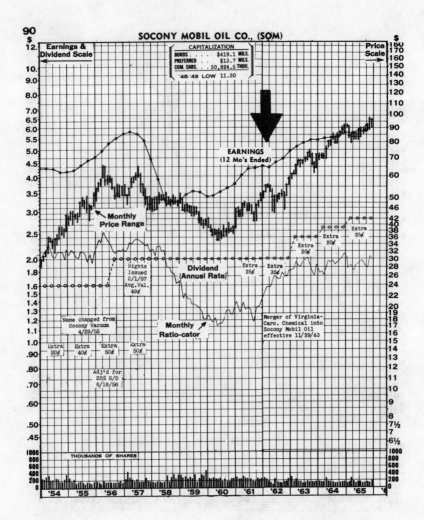

SOCONY MOBIL OIL CO., (SOM)

Earnings & Dividend Scale

Price Scale

CAPITALIZATION
BONDS . . . $419.1 MILS.
PREFERRED . . $13.7 MILS.
COM. SHRS. . . 50,824.5 THOU.
'48-'49 LOW 11.30

EARNINGS
(12 Mo's Ended)

Monthly Price Range

Rights Issued 2/1/57 Avg. Val. 49¢

Dividend (Annual Rate)

Extra 25¢

Extra 35¢

Extra 20¢

Extra 20¢

Extra 25¢

Name changed from Socony Vacuum 4/29/55

Monthly Ratio-cator

Merger of Virginia-Caro. Chemical into Socony Mobil Oil effective 11/29/63

Extra 20¢

Extra 40¢

Extra 50¢

Extra 50¢

Adj'd for 25% S/D 6/18/56

THOUSANDS OF SHARES

'54 '55 '56 '57 '58 '59 '60 '61 '62 '63 '64 '65

48

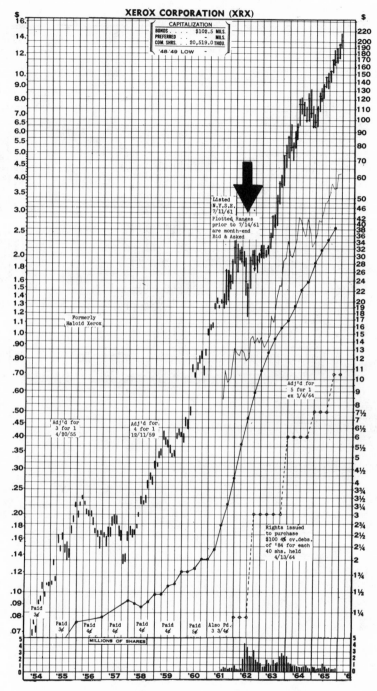

XEROX CORPORATION (XRX)

CAPITALIZATION

BONDS	$102.5 MILS.	
PREFERRED	–	MILS.
COM. SHRS.	20,519.0 THOU.	

'48-'49 LOW –

Listed
N.Y.S.E.
7/11/61
Plotted Ranges
prior to 7/14/61
are month-end
Bid & Asked

Formerly
Haloid Xerox

Adj'd for
3 for 1
4/20/55

Adj'd for
4 for 1
12/11/59

Adj'd for
5 for 1
ex 1/6/64

Rights issued
to purchase
$100 4% cv.debs.
of '84 for each
40 shs. held
4/13/64

Paid
3¢

Paid
3¢

Paid
4¢

Paid
4¢

Paid
4¢

Paid
4¢

Paid
5¢

Also Pd.
3 3/4¢

MILLIONS OF SHARES

'54 '55 '56 '57 '58 '59 '60 '61 '62 '63 '64 '65 '6

49

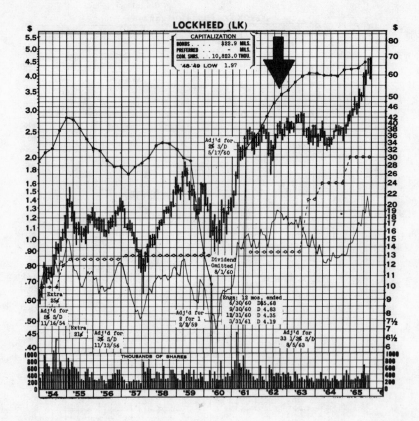

LOCKHEED (LK)

CAPITALIZATION
BONDS . . . . $22.9 MILS.
PREFERRED — MILS.
COM. SHRS. . . 10,823.0 THOU.
'48-'49 LOW 1.97

Adj'd for
2% S/D
5/17/60

Dividend
Omitted
8/1/60

Engs: 12 mos. ended
6/30/60 D$5.68
9/30/60 D 4.63
12/31/60 D 4.35
3/31/61 D 4.19

Extra
25¢

Adj'd for
5% S/D
11/16/54

Extra
21¢

Adj'd for
3% S/D
11/13/56

Adj'd for
2 for 1
2/2/59

Adj'd for
33 1/3% S/D
9/5/63

THOUSANDS OF SHARES

'54 '55 '56 '57 '58 '59 '60 '61 '62 '63 '64 '65

50

GRACE (W.R.) & COMPANY (GRA)

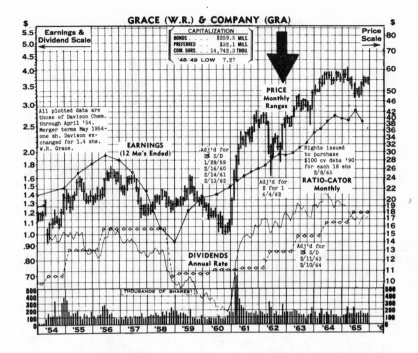

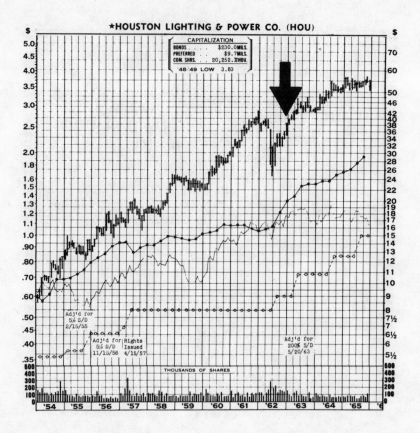

★HOUSTON LIGHTING & POWER CO. (HOU)

CAPITALIZATION
BONDS . . . . $230.0MILS.
PREFERRED . . . $9.7MILS.
COM. SHRS. . . 20,252. THOU.

'48-'49 LOW 3.83

Adj'd for
5% S/D
2/15/55

Adj'd for Rights
5% S/D Issued
11/15/56 4/15/57

Adj'd for
200% S/D
5/20/63

THOUSANDS OF SHARES

'54   '55   '56   '57   '58   '59   '60   '61   '62   '63   '64   '65

52

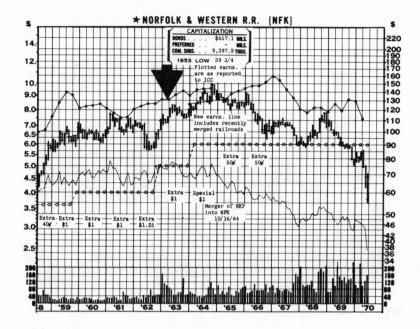

★ NORFOLK & WESTERN R.R. (NFK)

CAPITALIZATION

BONDS	$657.1	**MILS.**
PREFERRED . .	-	**MILS.**
COM. SHRS. . .	9,397.9	**THOU.**

1953 LOW 39 3/4

Plotted earns.
are as reported
to ICC

New earns. line
includes recently
merged railroads

Extra
50¢   Extra
50¢

Extra
$1   Special
$1

Merger of NKP
into NFK
10/16/64

Extra-Extra — Extra — Extra — Extra
40¢ · $1 $1 $1 $1.25

'58 '59 '60 '61 '62 '63 '64 '65 '66 '67 '68 '69 '70

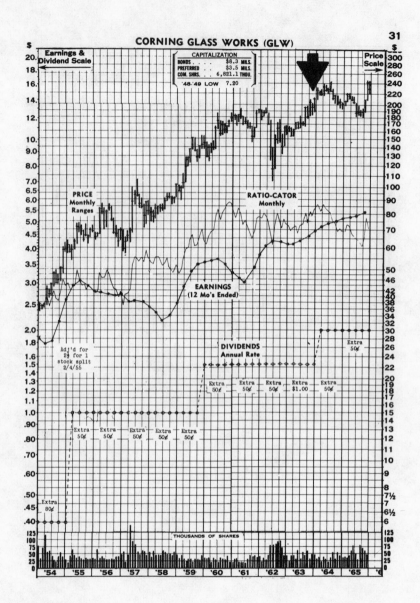

CORNING GLASS WORKS (GLW)

Earnings & Dividend Scale

Price Scale

CAPITALIZATION	
BONDS	$8.3 MILS.
PREFERRED . . .	$3.5 MILS.
COM. SHRS. . .	6,821.1 THOU.

'48-'49 LOW 7.20

PRICE
Monthly
Ranges

RATIO-CATOR
Monthly

EARNINGS
(12 Mo's Ended)

Adj'd for
2½ for 1
stock split
2/4/55

DIVIDENDS
Annual Rate

Extra
50¢

Extra
50¢

Extra
50¢

Extra
50¢

Extra
$1.00

Extra
50¢

Extra
50¢

Extra
50¢

Extra
50¢

Extra
50¢

Extra
50¢

Extra
80¢

THOUSANDS OF SHARES

'54 '55 '56 '57 '58 '59 '60 '61 '62 '63 '64 '65 '6

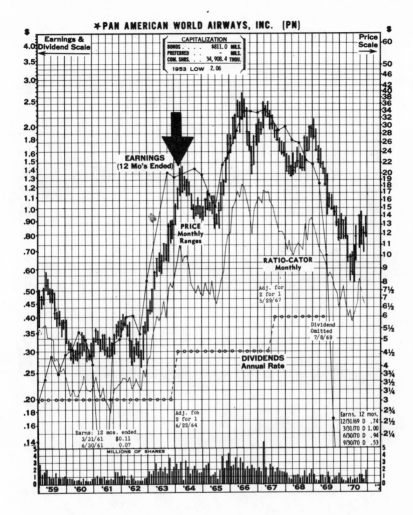

✳PAN AMERICAN WORLD AIRWAYS, INC. (PN)

Earnings & Dividend Scale

Price Scale

CAPITALIZATION		
BONDS	$811.0	MILS.
PREFERRED . .	-	MILS.
COM. SHRS. . .	34,908.4	THOU.
1953 LOW	2.06	

EARNINGS
(12 Mo's Ended)

PRICE
Monthly
Ranges

RATIO-CATOR
Monthly

Adj. for
2 for 1
5/29/67

Dividend
Omitted
7/8/69

DIVIDENDS
Annual Rate

Adj. for
2 for 1
6/22/64

Earns. 12 mos.		
12/31/69	D	.74
3/31/70	D	1.00
6/30/70	D	.94
9/30/70	D	.53

Earns: 12 mos. ended
3/31/61 $0.11
6/30/61   0.07

MILLIONS OF SHARES

'59 '60 '61 '62 '63 '64 '65 '66 '67 '68 '69 '70 '7

55

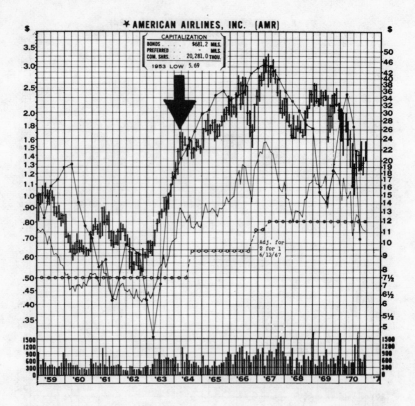

★ AMERICAN AIRLINES, INC. (AMR)

CAPITALIZATION
BONDS . . . . $681.2 MILS.
PREFERRED . . . — MILS.
COM. SHRS. . . . 20,281.0 THOU.

1953 LOW 5.69

Adj. for
2 for 1
6/13/67

'59 '60 '61 '62 '63 '64 '65 '66 '67 '68 '69 '70 '7

56

AVON PRODUCTS, INC. (AVP)

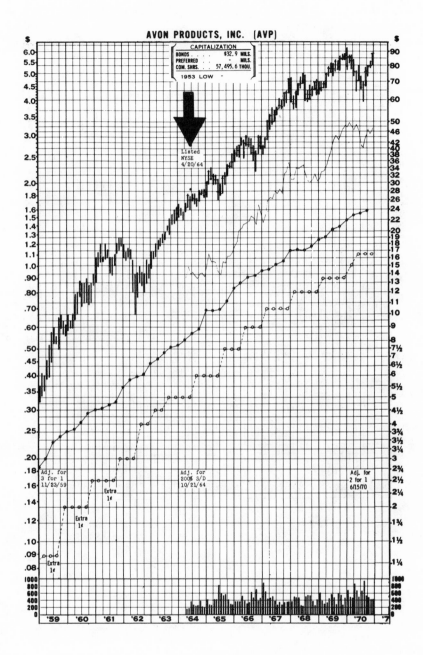

CAPITALIZATION
BONDS . . . . $32.9 MILS.
PREFERRED . . . - MILS.
COM. SHRS. . . 57,495.6 THOU.

1953 LOW -

Listed
NYSE
4/20/64

Adj. for
3 for 1
11/23/59

Extra
1¢

Extra
1¢

Extra
1¢

Adj. for
200% S/D
10/21/64

Adj. for
2 for 1
6/15/70

'59 '60 '61 '62 '63 '64 '65 '66 '67 '68 '69 '70 '7

57

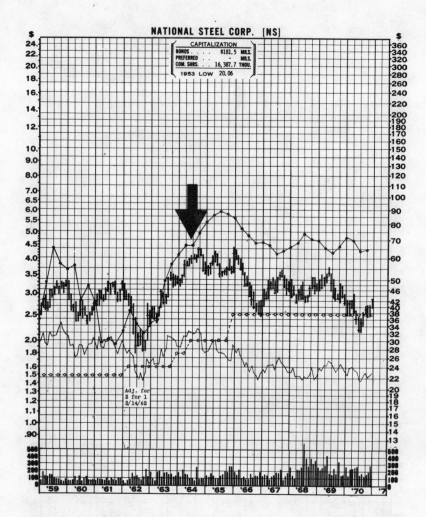

NATIONAL STEEL CORP. (NS)

CAPITALIZATION
BONDS . . . . $181.5 MILS.
PREFERRED . . — MILS.
COM. SHRS. . . 16,387.7 THOU.
1953 LOW 20.06

Adj. for
2 for 1
2/14/62

58

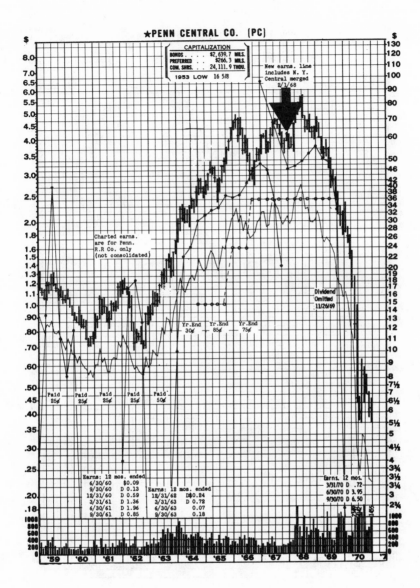

★PENN CENTRAL CO. (PC)

CAPITALIZATION
BONDS . . . . $2,639.7 MILS.
PREFERRED . . . $266.3 MILS.
COM. SHRS. . . 24,111.9 THOU.
1953 LOW 16 5/8

New earns. line
includes N. Y.
Central merged
2/1/68

Charted earns.
are for Penn.
R.R Co. only
(not consolidated)

Dividend
Omitted
11/26/69

Yr.End   Yr.End   Yr.End
30¢   85¢   75¢

Paid   Paid   Paid   Paid   Paid
25¢   25¢   25¢   25¢   50¢

Earns: 12 mos. ended
6/30/60 $0.09
9/30/60   D 0.13
12/31/60   D 0.59   Earns: 12 mos. ended
3/31/61   D 1.36   12/31/62   D$0.24
6/30/61   D 1.96   3/31/63   D 0.72
9/30/61   D 0.85   6/30/63   0.07
                       9/30/63   0.18

Earns. 12 mos.
3/31/70 D .72
6/30/70 D 3.95
9/30/70 D 6.50

'59   '60   '61   '62   '63   '64   '65   '66   '67   '68   '69   '70   '7

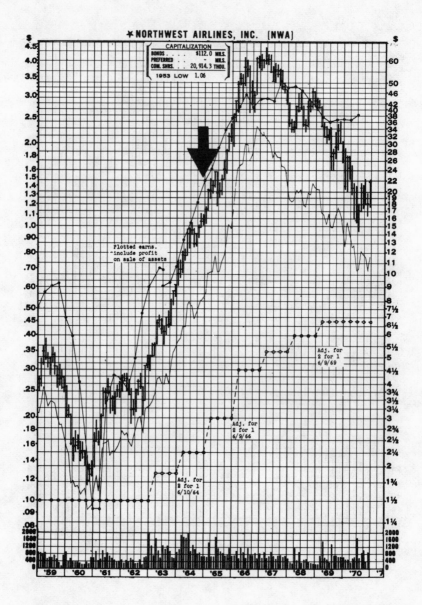

★NORTHWEST AIRLINES, INC. (NWA)

CAPITALIZATION
BONDS . . . . $112.0 MILS.
PREFERRED . . - MILS.
COM. SHRS. . . 20,914.3 THOU.
1953 LOW 1.06

Plotted earns.
include profit
on sale of assets

Adj. for
2 for 1
6/9/69

Adj. for
2 for 1
6/9/66

Adj. for
2 for 1
6/10/64

'59 '60 '61 '62 '63 '64 '65 '66 '67 '68 '69 '70 '7

60

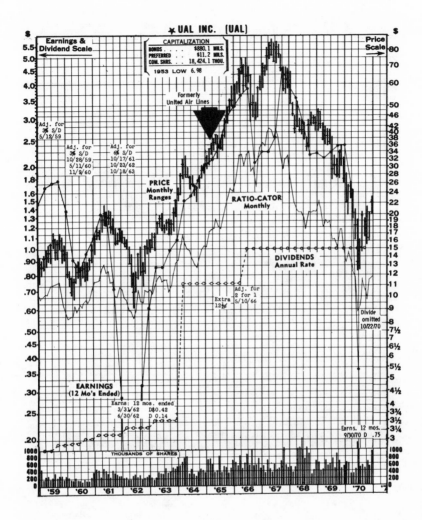

★ UAL INC. (UAL)

CAPITALIZATION
BONDS . . . . $880.1 MLS.
PREFERRED . . $11.2 MLS.
COM. SHRS. . . 18,424.1 THOU.
1953 LOW 6.98

Earnings & Dividend Scale

Price Scale

Formerly United Air Lines

PRICE Monthly Ranges

RATIO-CATOR Monthly

DIVIDENDS Annual Rate

EARNINGS (12 Mo's Ended)

Earns: 12 mos. ended
3/31/62   D$0.42
6/30/62   D 0.14

Adj. for 3% S/D 5/12/59

Adj. for 3% S/D 10/28/59 5/11/60 11/9/60

Adj. for 6% S/D 10/17/61 10/23/62 10/18/63

Extra 12½¢

Adj. for 2 for 1 5/10/66

Divide omitted 10/22/70

Earns. 12 mos. 9/30/70 D .75

THOUSANDS OF SHARES

'59 '60 '61 '62 '63 '64 '65 '66 '67 '68 '69 '70

61

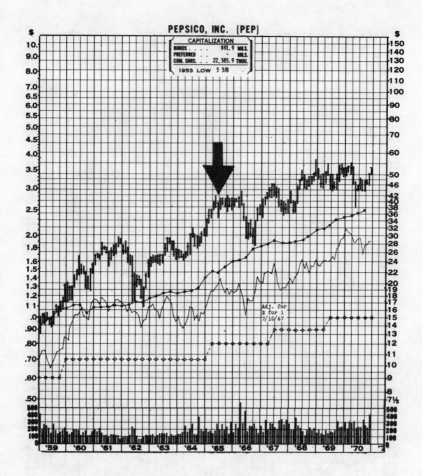

PEPSICO, INC. (PEP)

CAPITALIZATION
BONDS . . . . $91.9 MILS.
PREFERRED . . . – MILS.
COM. SHRS. . . 22,385.9 THOU.

1953 LOW 5 3/8

Adj. for
2 for 1
7/10/67

'59 '60 '61 '62 '63 '64 '65 '66 '67 '68 '69 '70

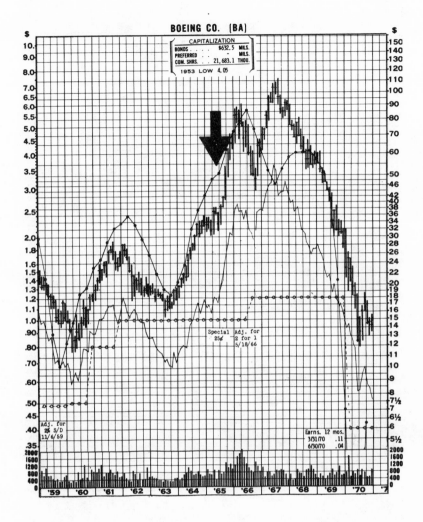

BOEING CO. (BA)

CAPITALIZATION
BONDS . . . . $632.5 MILS.
PREFERRED . . - MILS.
COM. SHRS. . . 21,683.1 THOU.
1953 LOW 4.05

Special Adj. for
25¢ 2 for 1
5/18/66

Adj. for
2% S/D
11/6/59

Earns. 12 mos.
3/31/70 .11
6/30/70 .04

'59 '60 '61 '62 '63 '64 '65 '66 '67 '68 '69 '70 '7

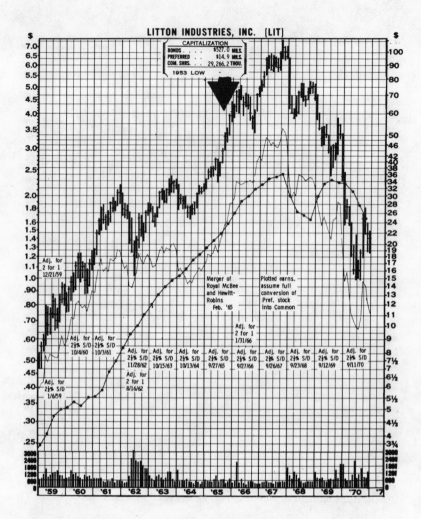

LITTON INDUSTRIES, INC. (LIT)

CAPITALIZATION
BONDS . . . . $527.0 MILS.
PREFERRED . . $14.9 MILS.
COM. SHRS. . . 29,266.2 THOU.

1953 LOW

Adj. for
2 for 1
12/21/59

Adj. for
2½% S/D
10/4/60

Adj. for
2½% S/D
10/3/61

Adj. for
2½% S/D
11/28/62

Adj. for
2½% S/D
10/15/63

Adj. for
2½% S/D
10/13/64

Adj. for
2½% S/D
9/27/65

Adj. for
2½% S/D
9/27/66

Adj. for
2½% S/D
9/26/67

Adj. for
2½% S/D
9/23/68

Adj. for
2½% S/D
9/12/69

Adj. for
2½% S/D
9/11/70

Adj. for
2½% S/D
1/6/59

Adj. for
2 for 1
8/16/62

Merger of
Royal McBee
and Hewitt-
Robins
Feb. '65

Adj. for
2 for 1
1/31/66

Plotted earns.
assume full
conversion of
Pref. stock
into Common

'59 '60 '61 '62 '63 '64 '65 '66 '67 '68 '69 '70 '7

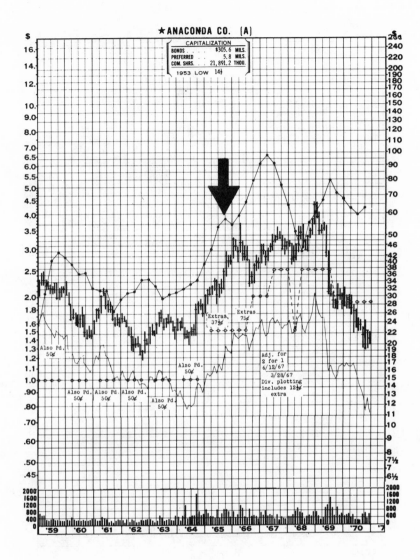

★ANACONDA CO. (A)

CAPITALIZATION
BONDS . . . . $305.6 MILS.
PREFERRED . . . 5.8 MILS.
COM. SHRS. . . . 21,891.2 THOU.

1953 LOW 14½

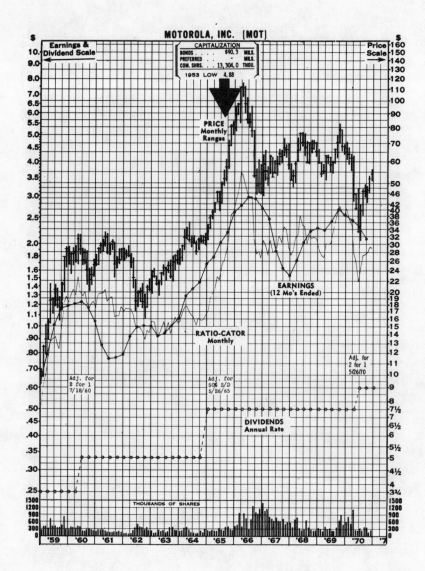

MOTOROLA, INC. [MOT]

Earnings & Dividend Scale

Price Scale

CAPITALIZATION
BONDS . . . . $90.3 MILS.
PREFERRED . . . . MILS.
COM. SHRS. . . . 13,304.0 THOU.

1953 LOW 4.88

PRICE
Monthly
Ranges

EARNINGS
(12 Mo's Ended)

RATIO-CATOR
Monthly

Adj. for
2 for 1
7/18/60

Adj. for
50% S/D
5/26/65

Adj. for
2 for 1
5/26/70

DIVIDENDS
Annual Rate

THOUSANDS OF SHARES

'59 '60 '61 '62 '63 '64 '65 '66 '67 '68 '69 '70 '7

66

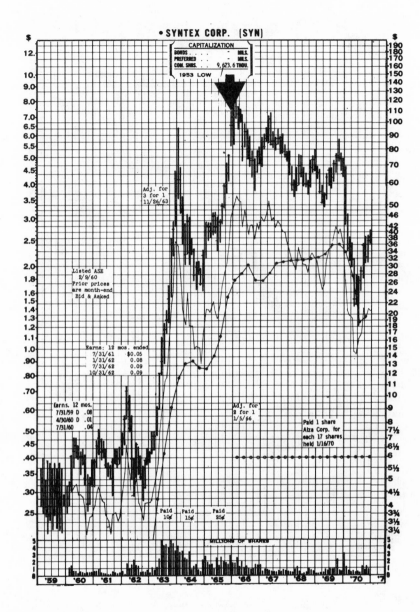

● SYNTEX CORP. (SYN)

CAPITALIZATION
BONDS . . . - MILS.
PREFERRED . . - MILS.
COM. SHRS. . . 9,623. 6 THOU.

1953 LOW

Adj. for
3 for 1
11/26/63

Listed ASE
2/9/60
Prior prices
are month-end
Bid & Asked

Earns: 12 mos. ended
7/31/61 $0.05
1/31/62   0.08
7/31/62   0.09
10/31/62   0.09

Earns. 12 mos.
7/31/59 D .08
4/30/60 D .01
7/31/60   .04

Adj. for
2 for 1
1/5/66

Paid 1 share
Alza Corp. for
each 17 shares
held 1/16/70

Paid   Paid   Paid
10¢   15¢   25¢

MILLIONS OF SHARES

'59 '60 '61 '62 '63 '64 '65 '66 '67 '68 '69 '70 '7

67

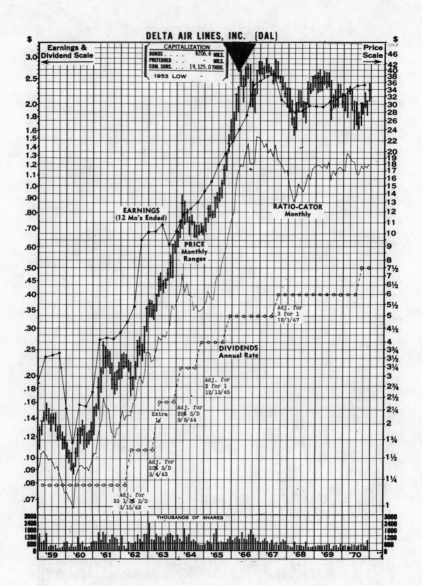

DELTA AIR LINES, INC. (DAL)

Earnings & Dividend Scale

Price Scale

CAPITALIZATION
BONDS . . . . $206.6 MILS.
PREFERRED . . . . - MILS.
CON. SHRS. . . . 19,125.0 THOU.

1953 LOW -

EARNINGS (12 Mo's Ended)

PRICE Monthly Ranges

RATIO-CATOR Monthly

DIVIDENDS Annual Rate

Adj. for 3 for 1 12/1/67

Adj. for 2 for 1 12/13/65

Adj. for 25% S/D 9/8/64

Extra 1¢

Adj. for 50% S/D 3/4/63

Adj. for 33 1/3% S/D 3/15/62

THOUSANDS OF SHARES

'59 '60 '61 '62 '63 '64 '65 '66 '67 '68 '69 '70

68

UNION OIL CO. OF CALIFORNIA (UCL)

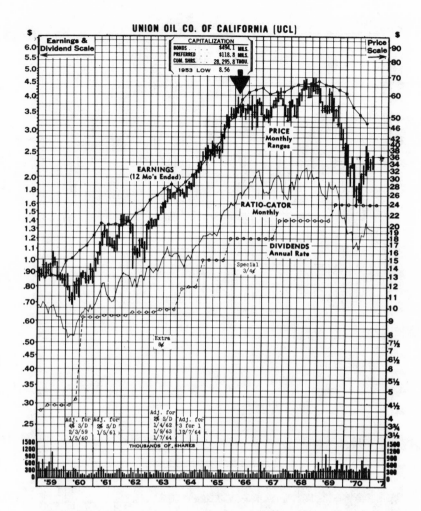

Earnings & Dividend Scale

Price Scale

CAPITALIZATION	
BONDS	$494.1 MIL.S.
PREFERRED	$118.8 MIL.S.
COM. SHRS.	28,295.8 THOU.
1953 LOW	8.56

EARNINGS (12 Mo's Ended)

PRICE Monthly Ranges

RATIO-CATOR Monthly

DIVIDENDS Annual Rate

Special 3/4¢

Extra 8¢

Adj. for 4% S/D 2/3/59 1/5/60

Adj. for 2% S/D 1/5/61

Adj. for 2% S/D 1/4/62 1/9/63 1/7/64

Adj. for 3 for 1 12/7/64

THOUSANDS OF SHARES

'59 '60 '61 '62 '63 '64 '65 '66 '67 '68 '69 '70 '7

69

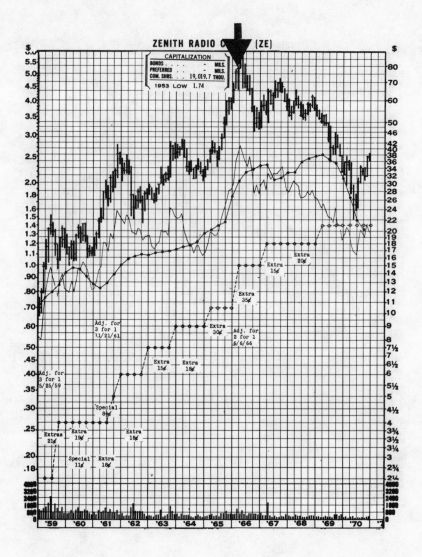

ZENITH RADIO C... (ZE)

CAPITALIZATION
BONDS . . . . - MILS.
PREFERRED . . . - MILS.
COM. SHRS. . . . 19,019.7 THOU.

1953 LOW 1.74

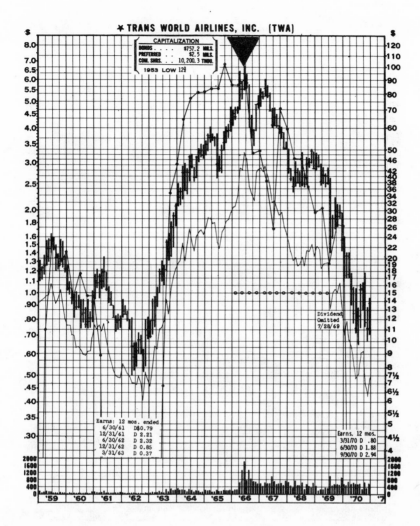

✶ TRANS WORLD AIRLINES, INC. (TWA)

CAPITALIZATION
BONDS . . . . $757.2 MILS.
PREFERRED . . $2.5 MILS.
COM. SHRS. . . 10,200.3 THOU.
1953 LOW 12½

Dividend
Omitted
7/28/69

Earns: 12 mos. ended
6/30/61   D 0.79
12/31/61   D 2.21
6/30/62   D 2.32
12/31/62   D 0.85
3/31/63   D 0.37

Earns. 12 mos.
3/31/70 D .80
6/30/70 D 1.88
9/30/70 D 2.94

'59 '60 '61 '62 '63 '64 '65 '66 '67 '68 '69 '70 '7

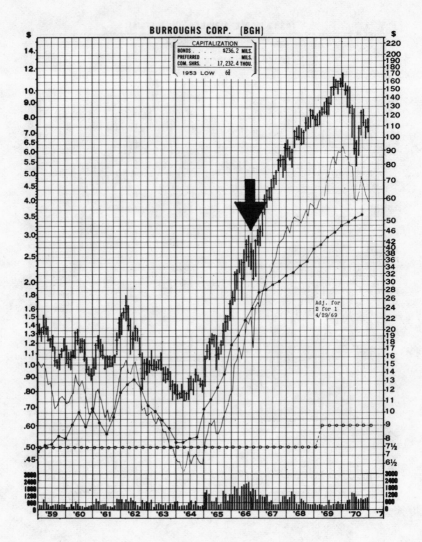

BURROUGHS CORP. [BGH]

CAPITALIZATION
BONDS . . . . $236.2 MILS.
PREFERRED . . - MILS.
COM. SHRS. . . 17,232.4 THOU.

1953 LOW 6⅛

Adj. for
2 for 1
4/29/69

ATLANTIC RICHFIELD CO. (ARC)

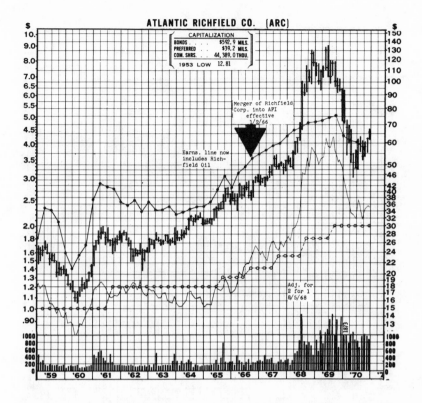

CAPITALIZATION
BONDS . . . . $592.9 MILS.
PREFERRED . . . $39.2 MILS.
COM. SHRS. . . . 44,389.0 THOU.

1953 LOW 12.81

Merger of Richfield Corp. into AFI effective 1/2/66

Earns. line now includes Richfield Oil

Adj. for 2 for 1 8/5/68

73

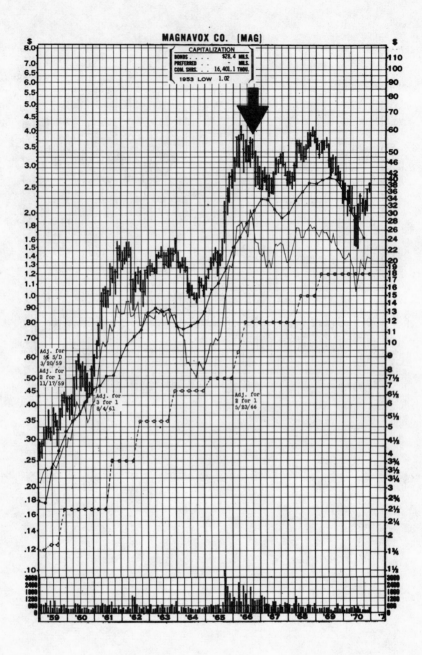

MAGNAVOX CO. (MAG)

CAPITALIZATION
BONDS . . . . $28.4 MILS.
PREFERRED . . - MILS.
COM. SHRS. . . 16,401.1 THOU.
1953 LOW 1.02

Adj. for
5% S/D
3/20/59
Adj. for
2 for 1
11/17/59

Adj. for
3 for 1
8/4/61

Adj. for
2 for 1
5/23/66

'59 '60 '61 '62 '63 '64 '65 '66 '67 '68 '69 '70 '7

74

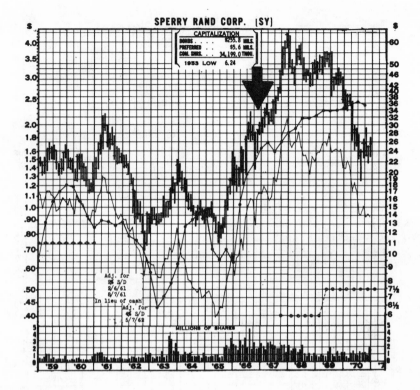

SPERRY RAND CORP. (SY)

CAPITALIZATION
BONDS . . . . $255.8 MILS.
PREFERRED . . 85.6 MILS.
COM. SHRS. . . 34,199.0 THOU.

1953 LOW 6.24

Adj. for
2% S/D
8/6/61
8/7/61
In lieu of cash
Adj. for
4% S/D
5/7/62

MILLIONS OF SHARES

'59 '60 '61 '62 '63 '64 '65 '66 '67 '68 '69 '70 '7

75

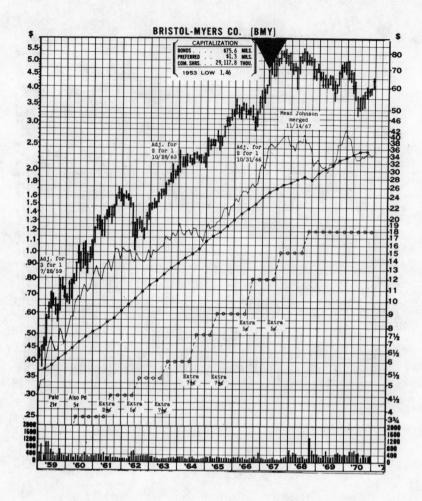

BRISTOL-MYERS CO. (BMY)

CAPITALIZATION

BONDS	. . . .	$75.6	MLS.
PREFERRED	. . .	$1.3	MLS.
COM. SHRS.	. . .	29,117.8	THOU.

1953 LOW 1.46

Mead Johnson merged 11/14/67

Adj. for 2 for 1 10/28/63

Adj. for 2 for 1 10/31/66

Adj. for 3 for 1 7/28/59

Extra 5¢   Extra 5¢

Extra 7½¢   Extra 7½¢

Paid 2½¢   Also Pd 5¢   Extra 2½¢   Extra 5¢   Extra 7½¢

'59 '60 '61 '62 '63 '64 '65 '66 '67 '68 '69 '70 '7

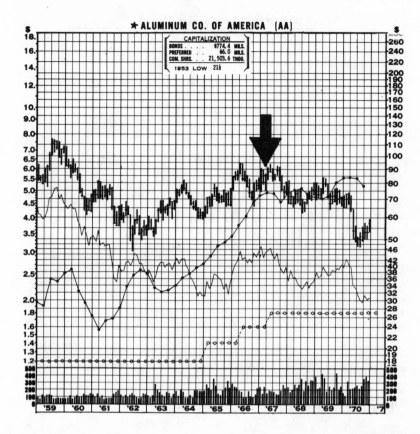

★ ALUMINUM CO. OF AMERICA (AA)

CAPITALIZATION
BONDS . . . . $774.4 MILS.
PREFERRED . . 66.0 MILS.
COM. SHRS. . . 21,503.6 THOU.
1953 LOW 21½

'59 '60 '61 '62 '63 '64 '65 '66 '67 '68 '69 '70 '7

77

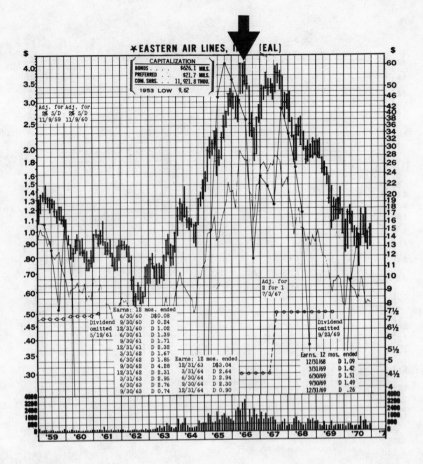

✶EASTERN AIR LINES, INC. (EAL)

CAPITALIZATION
BONDS . . . . . $626.1 MILS.
PREFERRED . . . $21.7 MILS.
COM. SHRS. . . 11,921.8 THOU.

1953 LOW 9.62

Adj. for   Adj. for
2% S/D   2% S/D
11/9/59   11/9/60

Adj. for
2 for 1
7/3/67

Earns: 12 mos. ended
6/30/60   D$0.08
Dividend   9/30/60   D 0.24
omitted   12/31/60 D 1.02
5/19/61   6/30/61   D 1.39
           9/30/61   D 1.71
           12/31/61 D 2.32
           3/31/62   D 1.67
           6/30/62   D 1.85
           9/30/62   D 4.28
           12/31/62 D 2.31
           3/31/63   D 2.95
           6/30/63   D 2.76
           9/30/63   D 0.74

Earns: 12 mos. ended
12/31/63 D$3.04
3/31/64   D 2.64
6/30/64   D 2.94
9/30/64   D 2.30
12/31/64 D 0.90

Dividend
omitted
9/23/69

Earns. 12 mos. ended
12/31/68 D 1.09
3/31/69   D 1.42
6/30/69   D 1.51
9/30/69   D 1.49
12/31/69 D .26

'59 '60 '61 '62 '63 '64 '65 '66 '67 '68 '69 '70

78

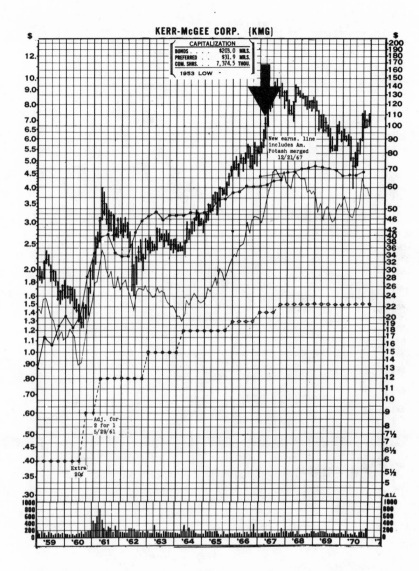

KERR-McGEE CORP. (KMG)

CAPITALIZATION
BONDS . . . . $203.0 MILS.
PREFERRED . . $31.9 MILS.
COM. SHRS. . . 7,374.5 THOU.

1953 LOW -

New earns. line
includes Am.
Potash merged
12/21/67

Adj. for
2 for 1
5/29/61

Extra
20¢

'59 '60 '61 '62 '63 '64 '65 '66 '67 '68 '69 '70 '7

79

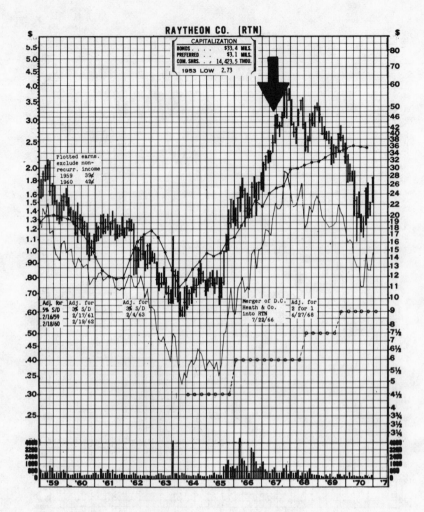

RAYTHEON CO. (RTN)

CAPITALIZATION
BONDS . . . . $33.4 MILS.
PREFERRED . . . $3.1 MILS.
COM. SHRS. . . 14,423.5 THOU.
1953 LOW 2.73

Plotted earns.
exclude non-
recurr. income
1959   39¢
1960   42¢

Adj. for   Adj. for   Adj. for   Merger of D.C.   Adj. for
5% S/D   3% S/D   3% S/D   Heath & Co.   2 for 1
2/16/59   2/17/61   2/4/63   into RTN   6/27/68
2/18/60   2/19/62   7/22/66

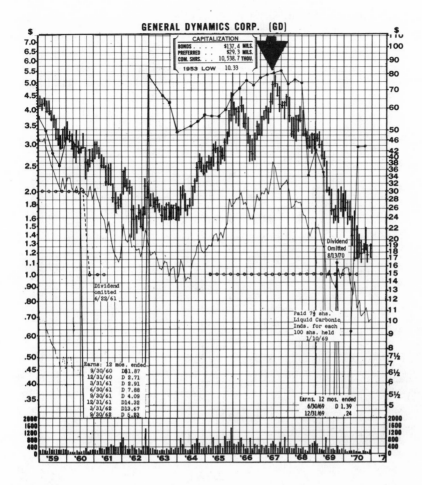

GENERAL DYNAMICS CORP. (GD)

CAPITALIZATION
BONDS . . . . $137.4 MILS.
PREFERRED . . $29.3 MILS.
COM. SHRS. 10,538.7 THOU.

1953 LOW 10.33

Dividend
Omitted
8/13/70

Dividend
omitted
6/22/61

Paid 7½ shs.
Liquid Carbonic
Inds. for each
100 shs. held
1/10/69

Earns: 12 mos. ended
9/30/60   D$1.87
12/31/60   D 2.71
3/31/61   D 2.91
6/30/61   D 7.88
9/30/61   D 4.09
12/31/61   D14.32
3/31/62   D13.67
9/30/62   D 5.83

Earns. 12 mos. ended
6/30/69   D 1.39
12/31/69   .24

'59 '60 '61 '62 '63 '64 '65 '66 '67 '68 '69 '70 '7

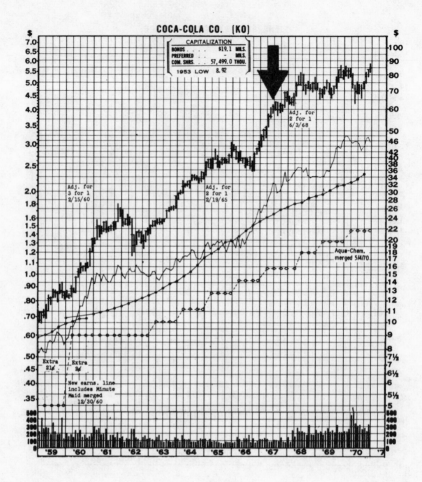

COCA-COLA CO. (KO)

CAPITALIZATION
BONDS . . . . $19.1 MILS.
PREFERRED . . . - MILS.
COM. SHRS. . 57,499.0 THOU.
1953 LOW 8.92

Adj. for
2 for 1
6/3/68

Adj. for
3 for 1
2/15/60

Adj. for
2 for 1
2/19/65

Aqua-Chem.
merged 5/4/70

Extra 21¢   Extra 3¢

New earns. line
includes Minute
Maid merged
12/30/60

'59 '60 '61 '62 '63 '64 '65 '66 '67 '68 '69 '70 '7

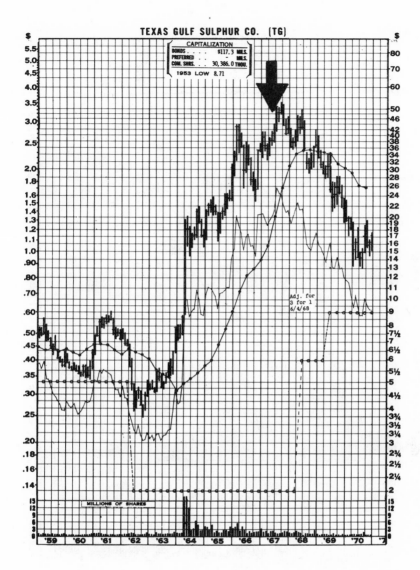

TEXAS GULF SULPHUR CO. (TG)

CAPITALIZATION
BONDS . . . . $117.3 MILS.
PREFERRED . . . - MILS.
COM. SHRS. . . . 30,386.0 THOU.
1953 LOW 8.71

Adj. for
3 for 1
6/4/68

MILLIONS OF SHARES

'59 '60 '61 '62 '63 '64 '65 '66 '67 '68 '69 '70 '7

83

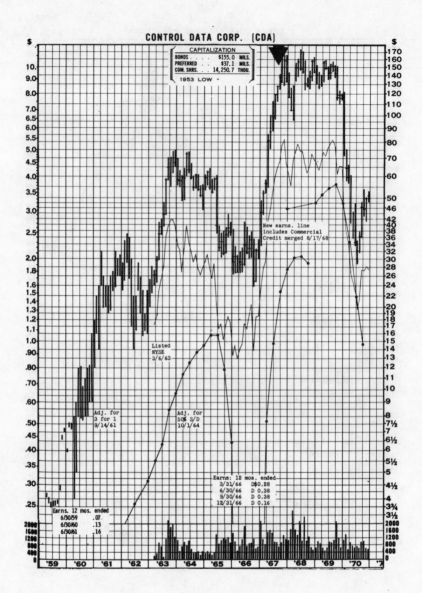

CONTROL DATA CORP. (CDA)

CAPITALIZATION
BONDS . . . . $155.0 MILS.
PREFERRED . . . $37.1 MILS.
COM. SHRS. . . . 14,250.7 THOU.

1953 LOW -

New earns. line
includes Commercial
Credit merged 8/17/68

Listed
NYSE
3/6/63

Adj. for
3 for 1
9/14/61

Adj. for
50% S/D
10/1/64

Earns. 12 mos. ended
3/31/66   D&0.28
6/30/66   D 0.38
9/30/66   D 0.38
12/31/66   D 0.16

Earns. 12 mos. ended
6/30/59   .07
6/30/60   .13
6/30/61   .16

84

★ SEABOARD COAST LINE INDUSTRIES, INC. (SCI)

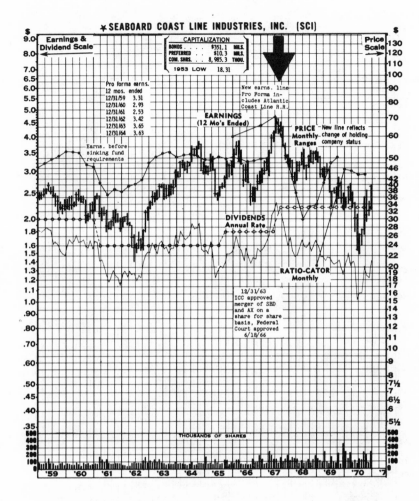

Earnings & Dividend Scale

Price Scale

CAPITALIZATION
- BONDS . . . . $351.1 MILS.
- PREFERRED . . $10.3 MILS.
- COM. SHRS. . . 8,985.3 THOU.

1953 LOW 18.31

Pro forma earns.
12 mos. ended
- 12/31/59   3.31
- 12/31/60   2.93
- 12/31/61   2.53
- 12/31/62   3.42
- 12/31/63   3.65
- 12/31/64   3.63

New earns. line
Pro Forma includes Atlantic
Coast Line R.R.

Earns. before
sinking fund
requirements

**EARNINGS
(12 Mo's Ended)**

PRICE New line reflects
Monthly change of holding
Ranges company status

**DIVIDENDS
Annual Rate**

**RATIO-CATOR
Monthly**

12/31/63
ICC approved
merger of SBD
and AX on a
share for share
basis, Federal
Court approved
6/18/66

THOUSANDS OF SHARES

'59   '60   '61   '62   '63   '64   '65   '66   '67   '68   '69   '70   '7

85

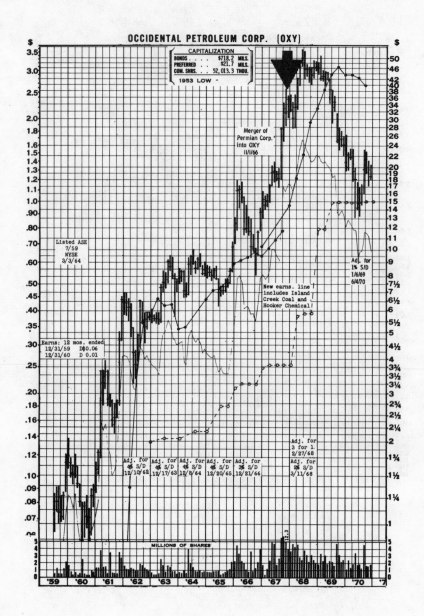

OCCIDENTAL PETROLEUM CORP. (OXY)

CAPITALIZATION	
BONDS	$718.2 MILS.
PREFERRED . .	$21.7 MILS.
COM. SHRS. . .	52,013.3 THOU.

1953 LOW -

Listed ASE
7/59
NYSE
3/3/64

Merger of
Permian Corp.
into OXY
11/1/66

Adj. for
1½ S/D
1/6/69
6/4/70

New earns. line
includes Island
Creek Coal and
Hooker Chemical

Earns: 12 mos. ended
12/31/59 D$0.06
12/31/60 D 0.01

Adj. for
3 for 1
2/27/68

Adj. for
4% S/D
12/10/62

Adj. for
4% S/D
12/17/63

Adj. for
4% S/D
12/8/64

Adj. for
4% S/D
12/20/65

Adj. for
3% S/D
12/31/66

Adj. for
2% S/D
3/11/68

MILLIONS OF SHARES

12.3

'59 '60 '61 '62 '63 '64 '65 '66 '67 '68 '69 '70 '7

86

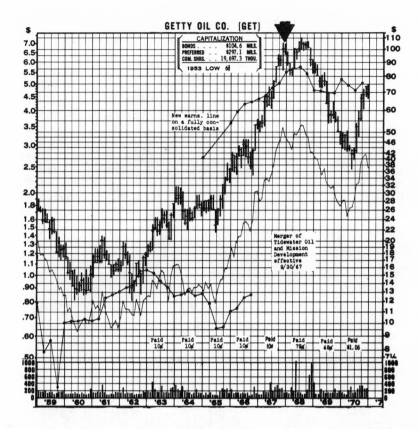

GETTY OIL CO. (GET)

CAPITALIZATION
BONDS . . . . . $104.6 MILS.
PREFERRED . . . $297.1 MILS.
COM. SHRS. . . 19,697.3 THOU.

1953 LOW 6⅛

New earns. line
on a fully con-
solidated basis

Merger of
Tidewater Oil
and Mission
Development
effective
9/30/67

Paid 10¢ Paid 10¢ Paid 10¢ Paid 10¢ Paid 10¢ Paid 7½¢ Paid 68¢ Paid $1.06

'59 '60 '61 '62 '63 '64 '65 '66 '67 '68 '69 '70 '7

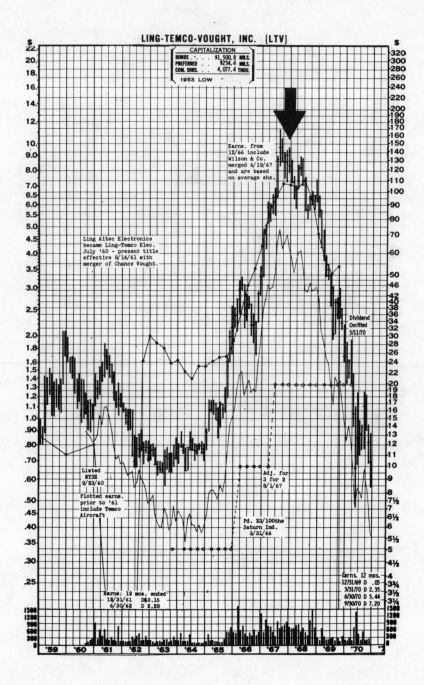

LING-TEMCO-VOUGHT, INC. (LTV)

CAPITALIZATION

BONDS	$1,500.8 MILS.
PREFERRED	$234.4 MILS.
COM. SHRS. . .	4,077.4 THOU.

1953 LOW -

Earns. from 12/66 include Wilson & Co. merged 6/19/67 and are based on average shs.

Ling Altec Electronics became Ling-Temco Elec. July '60 - present title effective 8/16/61 with merger of Chance Vought.

Dividend Omitted 3/11/70

Listed NYSE 9/23/60

Plotted earns. prior to '61 include Temco Aircraft

Adj. for 3 for 2 8/1/67

Pd. 23/100ths Saturn Ind. 3/31/66

Earns: 12 mos. ended 12/31/61 D $3.15 6/30/62 D 2.28

earns. 12 mos. 12/31/69 D .05 3/31/70 D 2.35 6/30/70 D 5.44 9/30/70 D 7.20

'59 '60 '61 '62 '63 '64 '65 '66 '67 '68 '69 '70 '7

TELEDYNE, INC. (TDY)

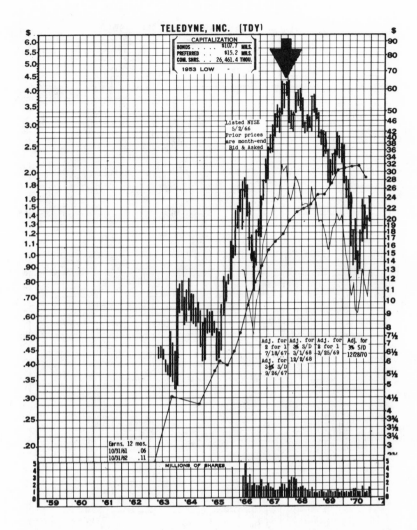

CAPITALIZATION

BONDS	$107.7 MLS.
PREFERRED . . .	$15.2 MLS.
COM. SHRS. . . .	26,461.4 THOU.

1953 LOW -

Listed NYSE
5/2/66
Prior prices
are month-end
Bid & Asked

Adj. for 2 for 1 7/18/67	Adj. for 3% S/D 3/1/68	Adj. for 2 for 1 3/25/69	Adj. for 3% S/D 12/28/70
Adj. for 3½% S/D 9/26/67	12/2/68		

Earns. 12 mos.
10/31/61   .06
10/31/62   .11

MILLIONS OF SHARES

'59   '60   '61   '62   '63   '64   '65   '66   '67   '68   '69   '70   '7

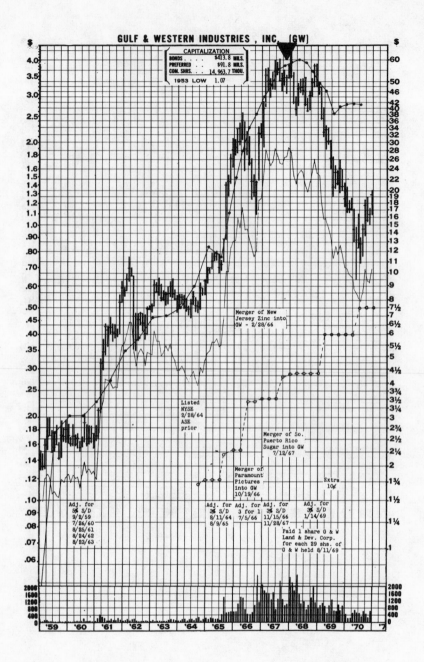

GULF & WESTERN INDUSTRIES , INC. (GW)

CAPITALIZATION	
BONDS	$413.8 MILS.
PREFERRED . . .	$91.8 MILS.
COM. SHRS. . .	14,963.7 THOU.
1953 LOW 1.07	

Merger of New
Jersey Zinc into
GW - 2/28/66

Listed
NYSE
2/28/64
ASE
prior

Merger of So.
Puerto Rico
Sugar into GW
7/12/67

Merger of
Paramount
Pictures
into GW
10/19/66

Extra
10¢

Adj. for
5% S/D
9/2/59
7/26/60
8/25/61
8/24/62
8/23/63

Adj. for
3% S/D
8/11/64
8/9/65

Adj. for
3 for 1
7/5/66

Adj. for
3% S/D
11/15/66
11/28/67

Adj. for
3% S/D
1/14/69

Paid 1 share G & W
Land & Dev. Corp.
for each 29 shs. of
G & W held 8/11/69

'59 '60 '61 '62 '63 '64 '65 '66 '67 '68 '69 '70 '7

90

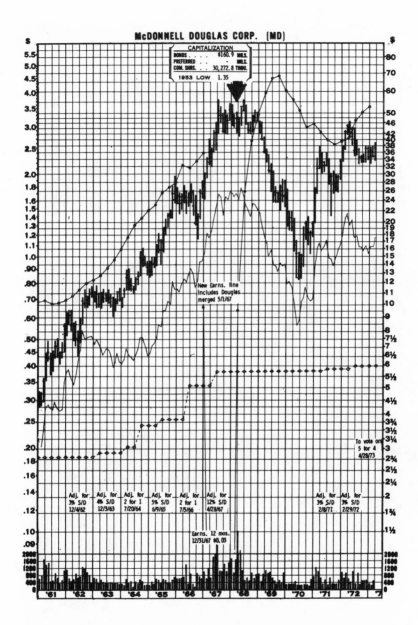

McDONNELL DOUGLAS CORP. (MD)

CAPITALIZATION
BONDS . . . . $160.9 MILS.
PREFERRED . . . - MILS.
COM. SHRS. . . . 30,272.8 THOU.
1953 LOW 1.35

New Earns. line
Includes Douglas
merged 5/1/67

To vote on
5 for 4
4/28/73

Adj. for Adj. for Adj. for Adj. for Adj. for Adj. for   Adj. for Adj. for
3% S/D   4% S/D   2 for 1   5% S/D   2 for 1   12% S/D   3% S/D   3% S/D
12/4/62 12/3/63 7/20/64 6/9/65   7/5/66   4/28/67   2/8/71   2/29/72

Earns. 12 mos.
12/31/67 $0.03

91

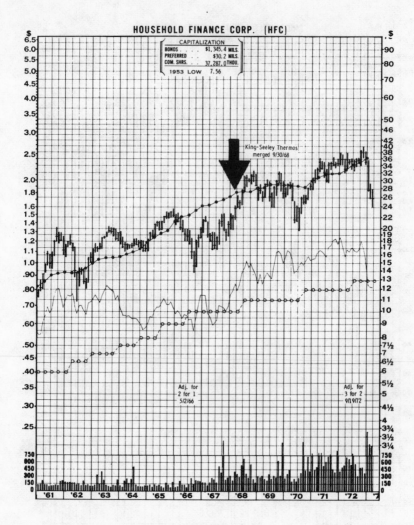

HOUSEHOLD FINANCE CORP. (HFC)

CAPITALIZATION

BONDS	$1,345.4 MILS.
PREFERRED . .	$30.2 MILS.
COM. SHRS. . .	37,287.0 THOU.

1953 LOW 7.56

King-Seeley Thermos merged 9/30/68

Adj. for
2 for 1
5/2/66

Adj. for
3 for 2
9/19/72

92

NORTHWEST INDUSTRIES, INC. (NWT)

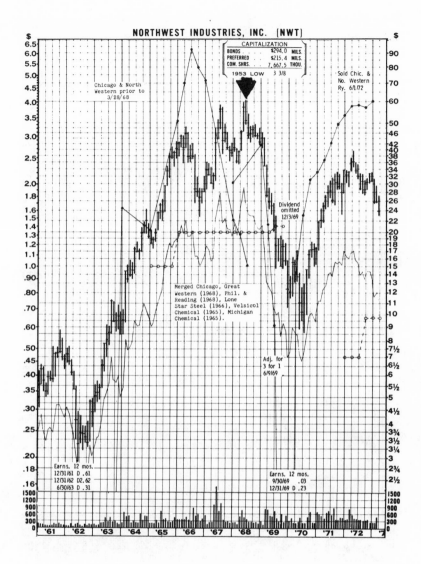

CAPITALIZATION

BONDS	$294.0	MILS.
PREFERRED	$215.4	MILS.
COM. SHRS.	7,667.5	THOU.

1953 LOW   3 3/8

Chicago & North
Western prior to
3/28/68

Sold Chic. &
No. Western
Ry. 6/1/72

Dividend
omitted
12/3/69

Merged Chicago, Great
Western (1968), Phil. &
Reading (1968), Lone
Star Steel (1966), Velsicol
Chemical (1965), Michigan
Chemical (1965).

Adj. for
3 for 1
6/9/69

Earns. 12 mos.
12/31/61 D .61
12/31/62 D2.62
6/30/63 D .31

Earns. 12 mos.
9/30/69   .03
12/31/69 D .23

93

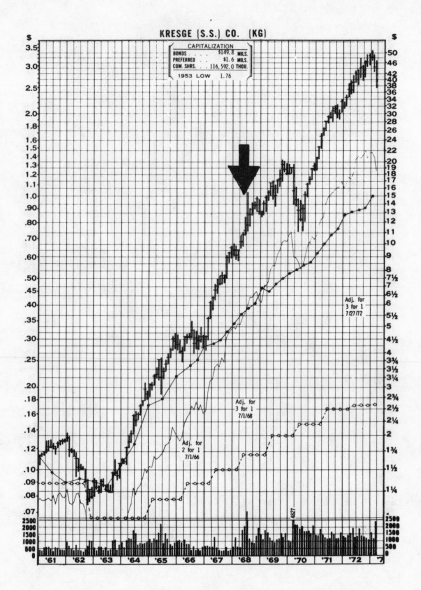

KRESGE (S.S.) CO. (KG)

CAPITALIZATION
BONDS . . . . $149.8 MILS.
PREFERRED . . . $1.6 MILS.
COM. SHRS. . 116,592.0 THOU.
1953 LOW 1.76

Adj. for
3 for 1
7/27/72

Adj. for
3 for 1
7/1/68

Adj. for
2 for 1
7/1/66

94

AETNA LIFE & CASUALTY CO. (AET)

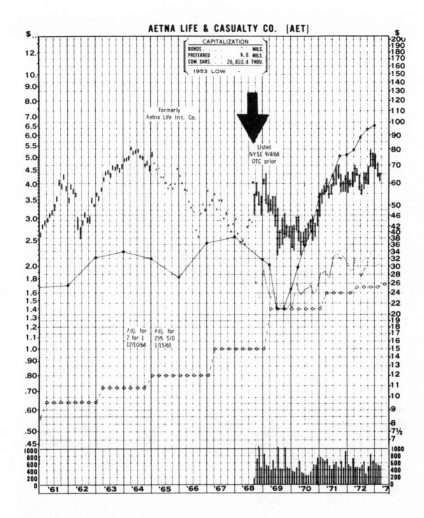

CAPITALIZATION
BONDS . . . . . MILS.
PREFERRED . . . $.8 MILS.
COM. SHRS. . . . 26,810.4 THOU.

1953 LOW -

Formerly
Aetna Life Ins. Co.

Listed
NYSE 9/4/68
OTC prior

Adj. for
2 for 1
12/10/64

Adj. for
25% S/D
1/15/65

'61 '62 '63 '64 '65 '66 '67 '68 '69 '70 '71 '72 '7

95

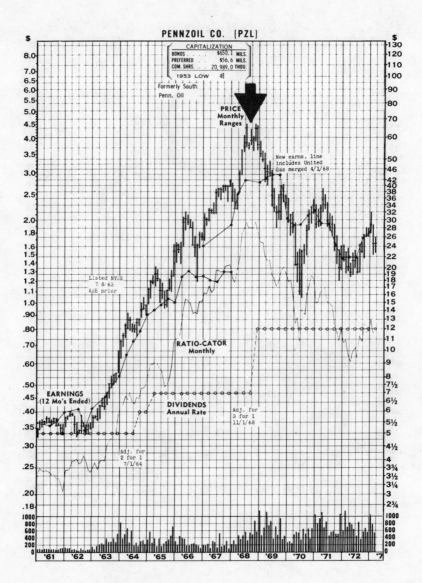

PENNZOIL CO. (PZL)

CAPITALIZATION
BONDS . . . . $650.1 MILS.
PREFERRED . . . $56.6 MILS.
COM. SHRS. . 20,989.0 THOU.

1953 LOW 4⅛

Formerly South
Penn. Oil

PRICE
Monthly
Ranges

New earns. line
includes United
Gas merged 4/1/68

Listed NYSE
7/8/63
ASE prior

RATIO-CATOR
Monthly

EARNINGS
(12 Mo's Ended)

DIVIDENDS
Annual Rate

Adj. for
3 for 1
11/1/68

Adj. for
2 for 1
7/1/64

'61 '62 '63 '64 '65 '66 '67 '68 '69 '70 '71 '72 '7

CITIES SERVICE CO. (CS)

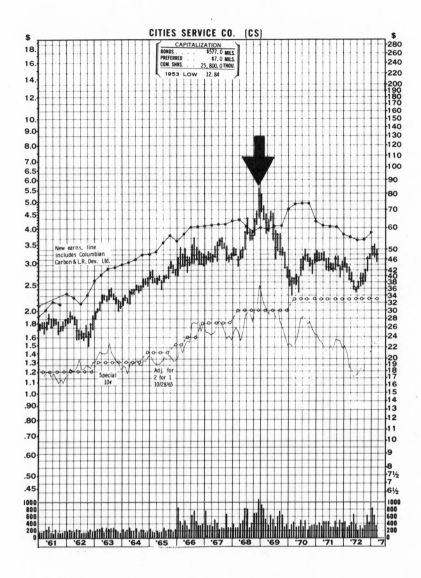

CAPITALIZATION	
BONDS	$577.0 MILS.
PREFERRED . . .	$7.0 MILS.
COM. SHRS. . . .	25,800.0 THOU.

1953 LOW 12.84

New earns. line
includes Columbian
Carbon & L.R. Dev. Ltd.

Special
10¢

Adj. for
2 for 1
10/28/65

'61 '62 '63 '64 '65 '66 '67 '68 '69 '70 '71 '72 '7

97

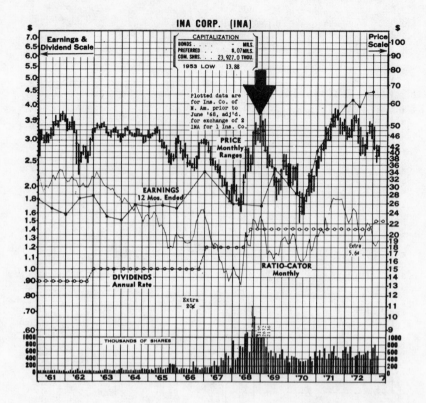

INA CORP. (INA)

CAPITALIZATION
BONDS . . . . - MRS.
PREFERRED . . . $.07 MRS.
COM. SHRS. . . 23,927.0 THOU.

1953 LOW 13.88

Plotted data are
for Ins. Co. of
N. Am. prior to
June '68, adj'd.
for exchange of 2
INA for 1 Ins. Co.

PRICE
Monthly
Ranges

EARNINGS
12 Mos. Ended

RATIO-CATOR
Monthly

DIVIDENDS
Annual Rate

Extra
5.6¢

Extra
20¢

THOUSANDS OF SHARES

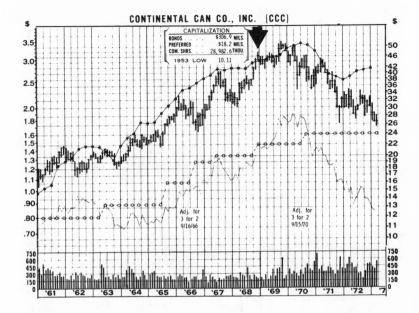

CONTINENTAL CAN CO., INC. (CCC)

CAPITALIZATION
BONDS . . . . $306.9 MILS.
PREFERRED . . $18.2 MILS.
COM. SHRS. . . 28,982.6 THOU.

1953 LOW   10.11

Adj. for
3 for 2
9/16/66

Adj. for
3 for 2
9/15/70

CITY INVESTING CO. (CNV)

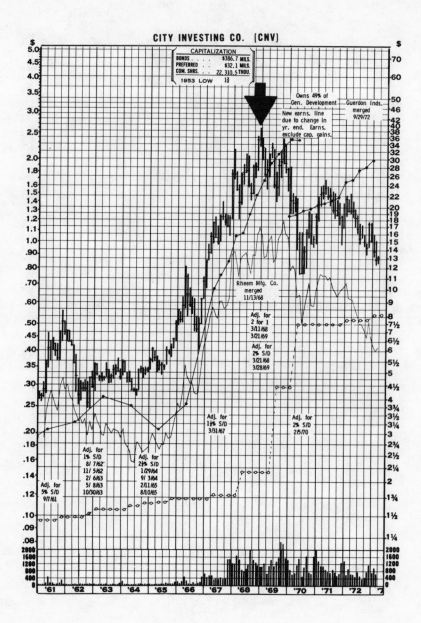

CAPITALIZATION
BONDS . . . . $386.7 MILS.
PREFERRED . . $32.1 MILS.
COM. SHRS. . . 22,310.5 THOU.

1953 LOW 1¾

Owns 49% of
Gen. Development

Guerdon Inds.
merged
9/29/72

New earns. line
due to change in
yr. end. Earns.
exclude cap. gains.

Rheem Mfg. Co.
merged
11/13/68

Adj. for
2 for 1
3/11/68
3/21/69

Adj. for
2% S/D
3/21/68
3/28/69

Adj. for
1½ S/D
3/31/67

Adj. for
2% S/D
2/5/70

Adj. for
1% S/D
8/ 7/62
11/ 5/62
2/ 6/63
5/ 8/63
10/30/63

Adj. for
2½% S/D
1/29/64
9/ 3/64
2/11/65
8/10/65

Adj. for
5% S/D
9/7/61

100

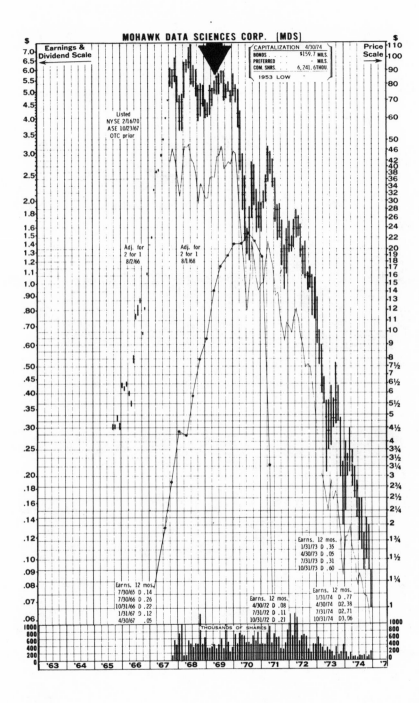

MOHAWK DATA SCIENCES CORP. (MDS)

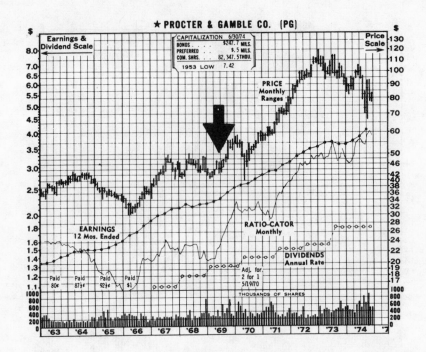

★ **PROCTER & GAMBLE CO. (PG)**

Earnings &
Dividend Scale

Price
Scale

CAPITALIZATION 6/30/74
BONDS . . . $247.7 MILS.
PREFERRED . . $.5 MILS.
COM. SHRS. . .   82,347.5THOU.

1953 LOW   7.42

PRICE
Monthly
Ranges

EARNINGS
12 Mos. Ended

RATIO-CATOR
Monthly

DIVIDENDS
Annual Rate

Paid   Paid   Paid   Paid
80¢   87½¢   92½¢ $1

Adj. for.
2 for 1
5/19/70

THOUSANDS OF SHARES

'63 '64 '65 '66 '67 '68 '69 '70 '71 '72 '73 '74

102

TRAVELERS CORP. (TIC)

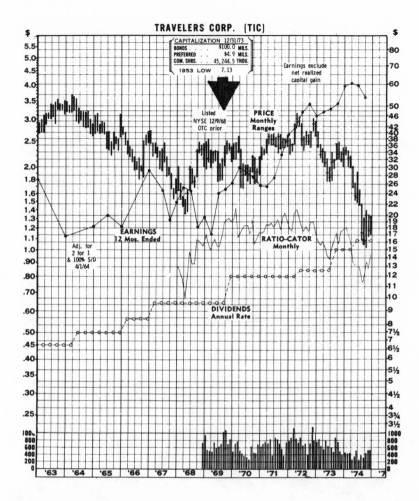

Earnings exclude
net realized
capital gain

Listed
NYSE 12/9/68
OTC prior

PRICE
Monthly
Ranges

EARNINGS
12 Mos. Ended

Adj. for
2 for 1
& 100% S/D
4/1/64

RATIO-CATOR
Monthly

DIVIDENDS
Annual Rate

'63 '64 '65 '66 '67 '68 '69 '70 '71 '72 '73 '74 '7

103

WARNER-LAMBERT CO. (WLA)

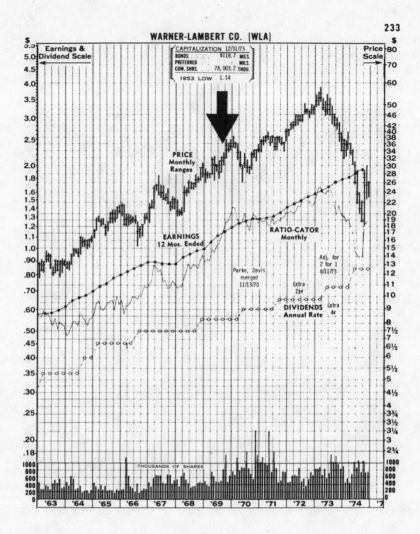

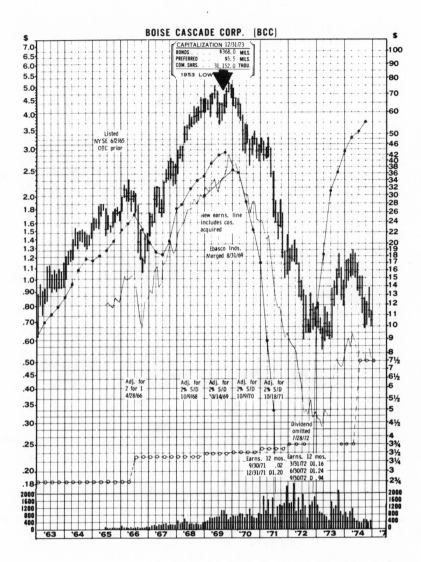

BOISE CASCADE CORP. (BCC)

CAPITALIZATION 12/31/73
BONDS . . . . $368.0 MILS.
PREFERRED . . $5.5 MILS.
COM. SHRS. . . 31,152.0 THOU.

1953 LOW

Listed
NYSE 6/2/65
OTC prior

New earns. line
includes cos.
acquired

Ebasco Inds.
Merged 8/31/69

Adj. for
2 for 1
4/28/66

Adj. for
2% S/D
10/9/68

Adj. for
2% S/D
10/14/69

Adj. for
2% S/D
10/9/70

Adj. for
2% S/D
10/18/71

Dividend
omitted
7/28/72

Earns. 12 mos.
9/30/71   .02
12/31/71 D1.20

Earns. 12 mos.
3/31/72 D1.16
6/30/72 D1.24
9/30/72 D .94

'63 '64 '65 '66 '67 '68 '69 '70 '71 '72 '73 '74 '7

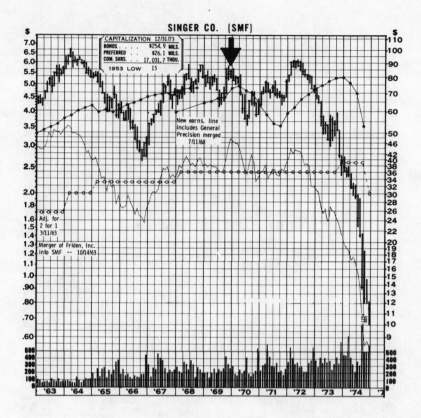

SINGER CO. (SMF)

CAPITALIZATION 12/31/73
BONDS . . . . $254.9 MILS.
PREFERRED . . $26.1 MILS.
COM. SHRS. . . 17,031.7 THOU.

1953 LOW   15

New earns. line
includes General
Precision merged
7/11/68

Adj. for
2 for 1
3/11/63

Merger of Friden, Inc.
into SMF -- 10/14/63

'63   '64   '65   '66   '67   '68   '69   '70   '71   '72   '73   '74

106

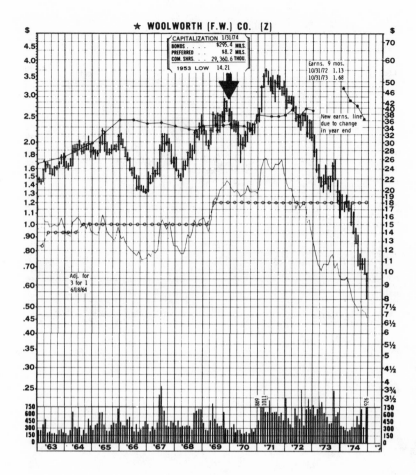

★ **WOOLWORTH (F.W.) CO.** (Z)

CAPITALIZATION 1/31/74
BONDS . . . . $295.4 MILS.
PREFERRED . . $8.2 MILS.
COM. SHRS. . . 29,360.6 THOU.

1953 LOW 14.21

Earns. 9 mos.
10/31/72 1.13
10/31/73 1.68

New earns. line
due to change
in year end

Adj. for
3 for 1
6/18/64

'63 '64 '65 '66 '67 '68 '69 '70 '71 '72 '73 '74 '7

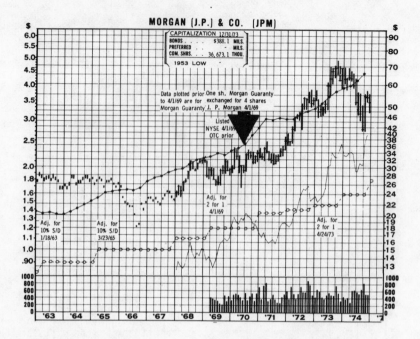

MORGAN (J.P.) & CO. (JPM)

CAPITALIZATION 12/31/73
BONDS . . . . $388.1 MILS.
PREFERRED . . . - MILS.
COM. SHRS. . . 36,673.1 THOU.

1953 LOW

Data plotted prior One sh. Morgan Guaranty
to 4/1/69 are for exchanged for 4 shares
Morgan Guaranty J. P. Morgan 4/1/69

Listed
NYSE 4/1/69
OTC prior

Adj. for
10% S/D
1/18/63

Adj. for
10% S/D
3/23/65

Adj. for
2 for 1
4/1/69

Adj. for
2 for 1
4/24/73

56

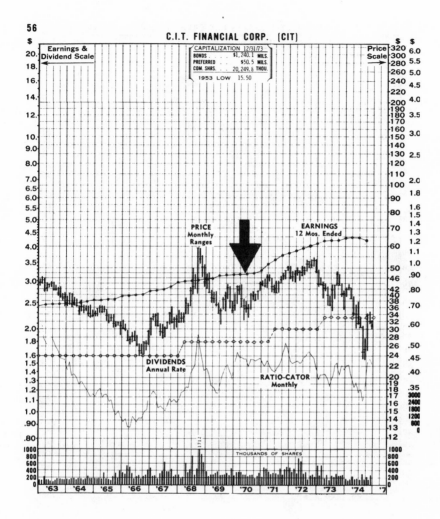

C.I.T. FINANCIAL CORP. (CIT)

CAPITALIZATION 12/31/73
BONDS . . . . $1,240.1 MILS.
PREFERRED . . . $50.5 MILS.
COM. SHRS. . . . 20,249.6 THOU.
1953 LOW 15.50

PRICE
Monthly
Ranges

EARNINGS
12 Mos. Ended

DIVIDENDS
Annual Rate

RATIO-CATOR
Monthly

THOUSANDS OF SHARES

'63 '64 '65 '66 '67 '68 '69 '70 '71 '72 '73 '74 '7

109

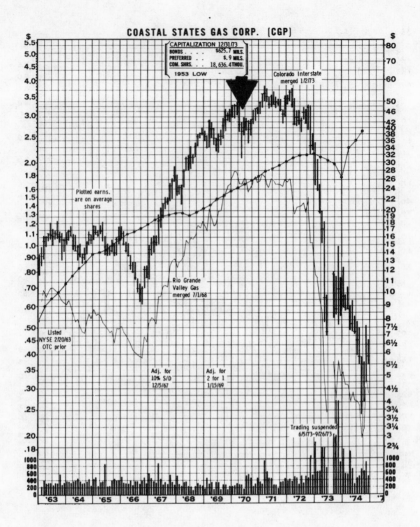

COASTAL STATES GAS CORP. (CGP)

CAPITALIZATION 12/31/73
BONDS . . . . $625.7 MLS.
PREFERRED . . . $. 9 MLS.
COM. SHRS. . . 18,636.4 THOU.

1953 LOW   –

Colorado Interstate
merged 1/2/73

Plotted earns.
are on average
shares

Rio Grande
Valley Gas
merged 7/1/68

Listed
NYSE 2/20/63
OTC prior

Adj. for
10% S/D
12/5/67

Adj. for
2 for 1
1/15/69

Trading suspended
6/5/73-9/26/73

'63 '64 '65 '66 '67 '68 '69 '70 '71 '72 '73 '74

LILLY (ELI) AND COMPANY (LLY)

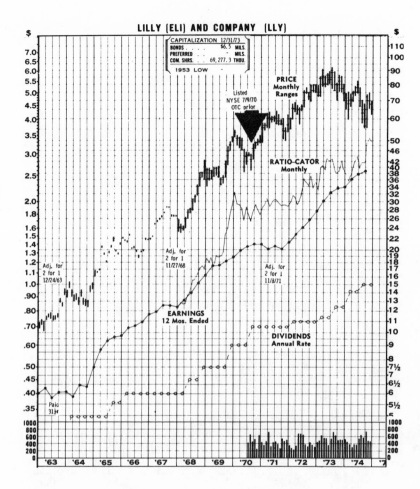

CAPITALIZATION 12/31/73
BONDS . . . . $6.5 MILS.
PREFERRED . . - MILS.
COM. SHRS. . . 69,277.3 THOU.

1953 LOW -

Listed
NYSE 7/9/70
OTC prior

PRICE
Monthly
Ranges

RATIO-CATOR
Monthly

Adj. for
2 for 1
11/27/68

Adj. for
2 for 1
11/8/71

Adj. for
2 for 1
12/24/63

EARNINGS
12 Mos. Ended

DIVIDENDS
Annual Rate

Paid
31¢

'63 '64 '65 '66 '67 '68 '69 '70 '71 '72 '73 '74

111

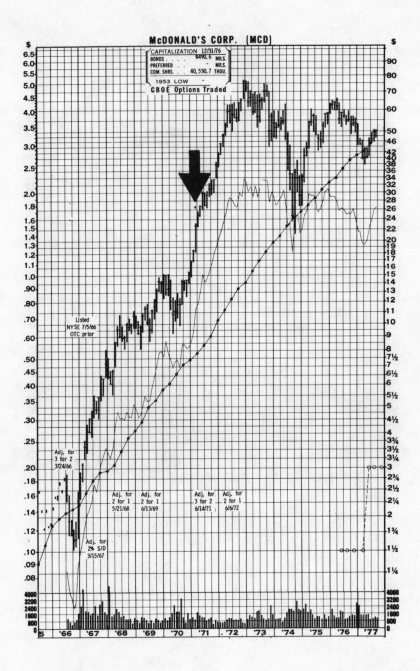

McDONALD'S CORP. (MCD)

CAPITALIZATION 12/31/76
BONDS . . . . $490.6 MILS.
PREFERRED . . . — MILS.
COM. SHRS. . . . 40,530.7 THOU.
1953 LOW
CBOE Options Traded

Listed
NYSE 7/5/66
OTC prior

Adj. for
3 for 2
3/24/66

Adj. for
2% S/D
3/15/67

Adj. for
2 for 1
5/21/68

Adj. for
2 for 1
6/13/69

Adj. for
3 for 2
6/14/71

Adj. for
2 for 1
6/6/72

112

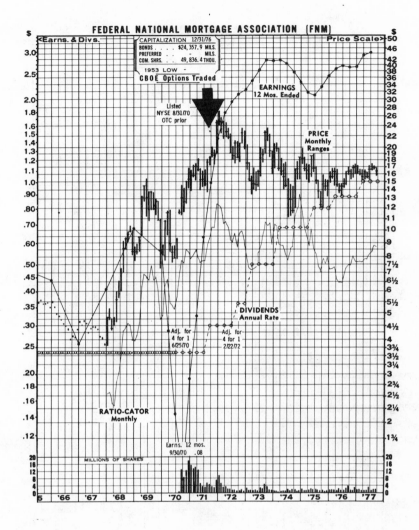

FEDERAL NATIONAL MORTGAGE ASSOCIATION (FNM)

CAPITALIZATION 12/31/76
BONDS . . . . $24,357.9 MILS.
PREFERRED . . . - MILS.
COM. SHRS. . . 49,836.4 THOU.

1953 LOW -

CBOE Options Traded

Listed
NYSE 8/31/70
OTC prior

EARNINGS
12 Mos. Ended

PRICE
Monthly
Ranges

DIVIDENDS
Annual Rate

Adj. for
4 for 1
6/25/70

Adj. for
4 for 1
2/22/72

RATIO-CATOR
Monthly

Earns. 12 mos.
9/30/70   .08

MILLIONS OF SHARES

'66 '67 '68 '69 '70 '71 '72 '73 '74 '75 '76 '77

113

MGIC INVESTMENT CORP. (MGI)

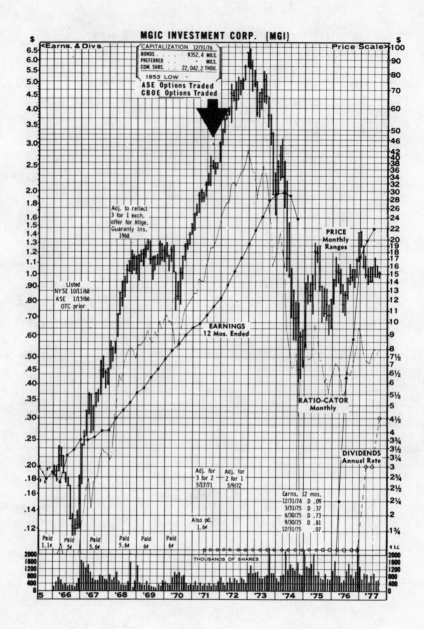

$ ‹Earns. & Divs.›   **Price Scale›** **$**

CAPITALIZATION 12/31/76
BONDS . . . . $352.4 MILS.
PREFERRED . . . — MILS.
COM. SHRS. . . 22,042.2 THOU.
1953 LOW —
ASE Options Traded
CBOE Options Traded

Adj. to reflect
3 for 1 exch.
offer for Mtge.
Guaranty Ins.
1968

Listed
NYSE 10/11/68
ASE 1/13/66
OTC prior

PRICE
Monthly
Ranges

EARNINGS
12 Mos. Ended

RATIO-CATOR
Monthly

DIVIDENDS
Annual Rate

Adj. for
3 for 2
5/17/71

Adj. for
2 for 1
5/9/72

Earns. 12 mos.
12/31/74 D .09
3/31/75 D .37
6/30/75 D .73
9/30/75 D .81
12/31/75 .07

Also pd.
1.6¢

Paid
1.1¢
Paid
5¢
Paid
5.6¢
Paid
5.6¢
Paid
6¢
Paid
6¢

THOUSANDS OF SHARES

'66 '67 '68 '69 '70 '71 '72 '73 '74 '75 '76 '77

114

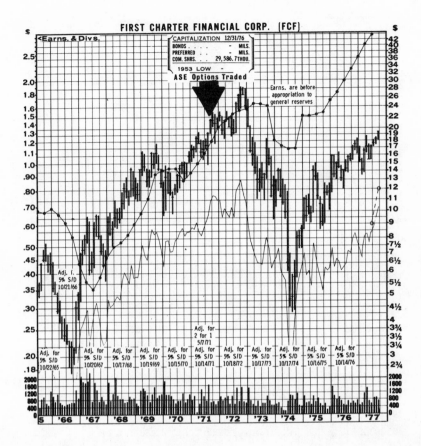

FIRST CHARTER FINANCIAL CORP. (FCF)

Earns. & Divs.

CAPITALIZATION 12/31/76
BONDS . . . .   - MILS.
PREFERRED . . .   - MILS.
COM. SHRS. . . .   29,586.7 THOU.

1953 LOW   -
ASE Options Traded

Earns. are before
appropriation to
general reserves

Adj. for
5% S/D
10/21/66

Adj. for
2 for 1
5/7/71

Adj. for
5% S/D
10/22/65

Adj. for
5% S/D
10/20/67

Adj. for
5% S/D
10/17/68

Adj. for
5% S/D
10/19/69

Adj. for
5% S/D
10/15/70

Adj. for
5% S/D
10/14/71

Adj. for
5% S/D
10/18/72

Adj. for
5% S/D
10/17/73

Adj. for
5% S/D
10/17/74

Adj. for
5% S/D
10/16/75

Adj. for
5% S/D
10/14/76

'66 '67 '68 '69 '70 '71 '72 '73 '74 '75 '76 '77

115

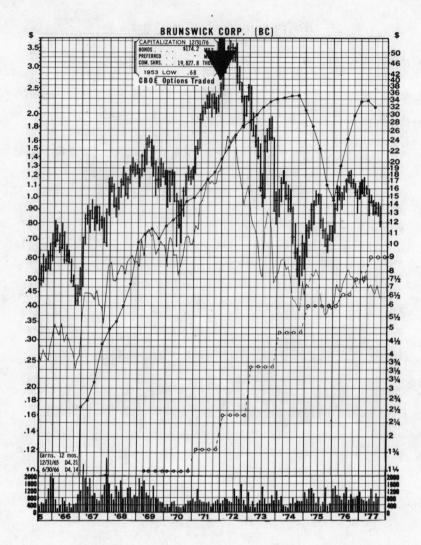

BRUNSWICK CORP. (BC)

CAPITALIZATION 12/31/76
BONDS . . . . $174.2 MILS
PREFERRED . . . - M
COM. SHRS. . . 19,827.8 THOU
1953 LOW .68
CBOE Options Traded

Earns. 12 mos.
12/31/65 D4.21
6/30/66 D4.14

116

LEVITZ FURNITURE CORP. (LEV)

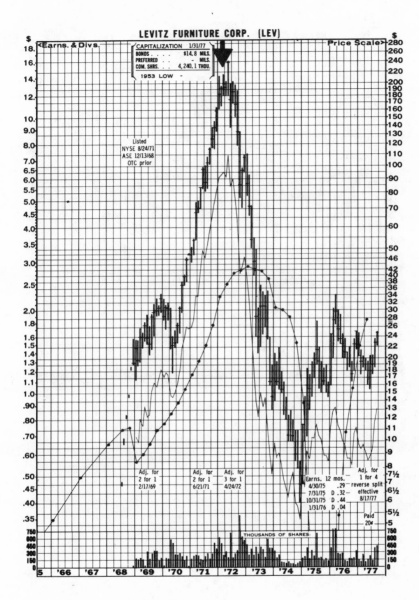

‹Earns. & Divs.

Price Scale›

CAPITALIZATION 1/31/77
BONDS . . . . $14.8 MILS.
PREFERRED . . — MILS.
COM. SHRS. . . 4,240.1 THOU.

1953 LOW -

Listed
NYSE 8/24/71
ASE 12/13/68
OTC prior

Adj. for
2 for 1
2/17/69

Adj. for
2 for 1
6/21/71

Adj. for
3 for 1
4/24/72

Earns. 12 mos.
4/30/75 .29
7/31/75 D .32
10/31/75 D .44
1/31/76 D .04

Adj. for
1 for 4
reverse split
effective
8/17/77

Paid
20¢

THOUSANDS OF SHARES

'66 '67 '68 '69 '70 '71 '72 '73 '74 '75 '76 '77

117

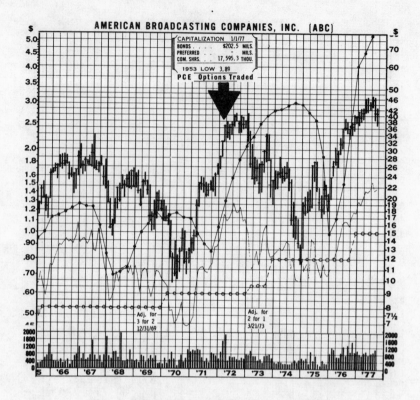

AMERICAN BROADCASTING COMPANIES, INC. (ABC)

CAPITALIZATION 1/1/77
BONDS . . . . . $202.5 MILS.
PREFERRED . . . — MILS.
COM. SHRS. . . 17,595.3 THOU.

1953 LOW 3.89

PCE Options Traded

Adj. for
3 for 2
12/31/69

Adj. for
2 for 1
3/21/73

'66 '67 '68 '69 '70 '71 '72 '73 '74 '75 '76 '77

118

MATSUSHITA ELECTRIC INDUSTRIAL CO., LTD. (MC)

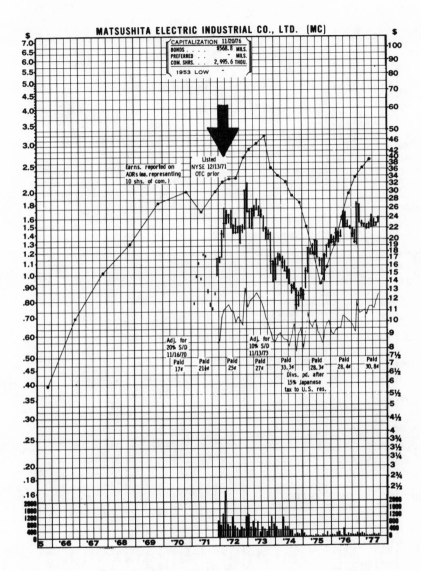

CAPITALIZATION 11/20/76
BONDS . . . . $568.8 MILS.
PREFERRED . . . - MILS.
COM. SHRS. . . 2,995.6 THOU.

1953 LOW -

Earns. reported on
ADRs (ea. representing
10 shs. of com.)

Listed
NYSE 12/13/71
OTC prior

Adj. for
20% S/D
11/16/70
Paid
17¢

Adj. for
10% S/D
11/13/73

Paid
21½¢

Paid
25¢

Paid
27¢

Paid
33.3¢

Paid
28.3¢

Paid
28.4¢

Paid
30.8¢

Divs. pd. after
15% Japanese
tax to U.S. res.

119

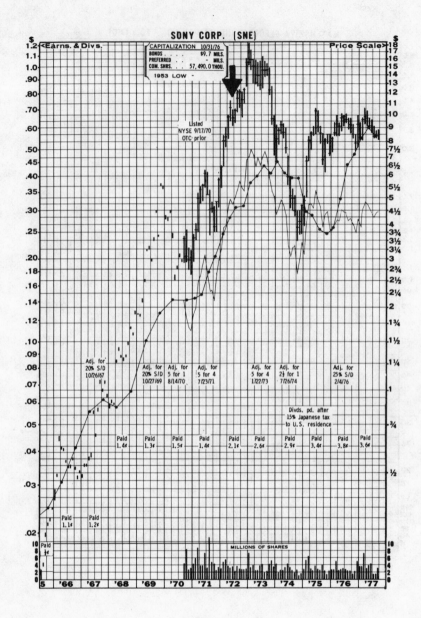

SONY CORP. (SNE)

Earns. & Divs.

CAPITALIZATION 10/31/76
BONDS . . . . $9.7 MILS.
PREFERRED . . — MILS.
COM. SHRS. . . 57,490.0 THOU.

1953 LOW -

Price Scale

Listed
NYSE 9/17/70
OTC prior

Adj. for
20% S/D
10/26/67

Adj. for
20% S/D
10/27/69

Adj. for
5 for 1
8/14/70

Adj. for
5 for 4
7/23/71

Adj. for
5 for 4
1/22/73

Adj. for
2½ for 1
7/26/74

Adj. for
25% S/D
2/4/76

Divds. pd. after
15% Japanese tax
to U.S. residence

Paid
1.4¢

Paid
1.3¢

Paid
1.5¢

Paid
1.4¢

Paid
2.1¢

Paid
2.6¢

Paid
2.9¢

Paid
3.4¢

Paid
3.8¢

Paid
3.6¢

Paid
1.1¢

Paid
1.2¢

Paid
¼¢

MILLIONS OF SHARES

5 '66 '67 '68 '69 '70 '71 '72 '73 '74 '75 '76 '77

120

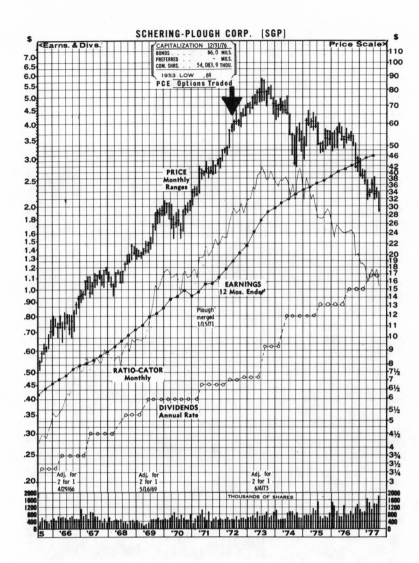

SCHERING-PLOUGH CORP. (SGP)

Earns. & Divs.

Price Scale

CAPITALIZATION 12/31/76
BONDS . . . . $6.0 MILS.
PREFERRED . . - MILS.
COM. SHRS. . . 54,083.9 THOU.
1953 LOW .69
PCE Options Traded

PRICE
Monthly
Ranges

EARNINGS
12 Mos. Ended

Plough
merged
1/15/71

RATIO-CATOR
Monthly

DIVIDENDS
Annual Rate

Adj. for
2 for 1
4/29/66

Adj. for
2 for 1
5/16/69

Adj. for
2 for 1
6/4/73

THOUSANDS OF SHARES

'66 '67 '68 '69 '70 '71 '72 '73 '74 '75 '76 '77

121

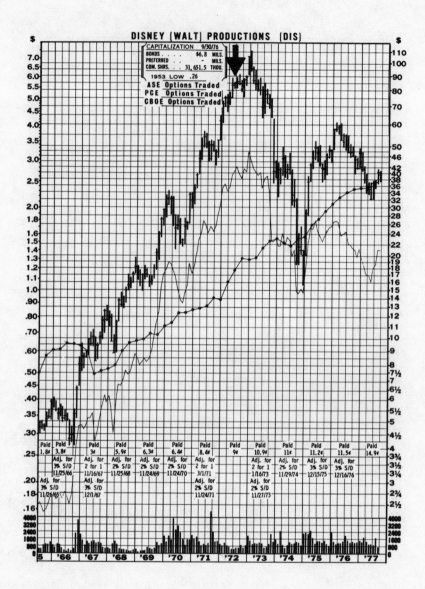

DISNEY (WALT) PRODUCTIONS (DIS)

CAPITALIZATION 9/30/76
BONDS . . . . $6.8 MILS.
PREFERRED . . - MILS.
COM. SHRS. . . 31,651.5 THOU.

1953 LOW .26

ASE Options Traded
PCE Options Traded
CBOE Options Traded

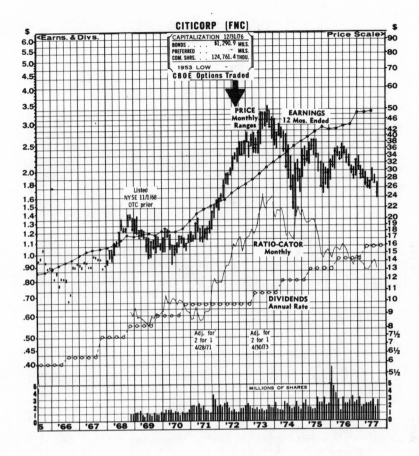

CITICORP (FNC)

Earns. & Divs.

Price Scale

CAPITALIZATION 12/31/76
BONDS . . . . $1,290.9 MILS.
PREFERRED . . . " MILS.
COM. SHRS. . . . 124,761.4 THOU.

1953 LOW -

CBOE Options Traded

PRICE
Monthly
Ranges

EARNINGS
12 Mos. Ended

Listed
NYSE 11/1/68
OTC prior

RATIO-CATOR
Monthly

DIVIDENDS
Annual Rate

Adj. for
2 for 1
4/28/71

Adj. for
2 for 1
4/30/73

MILLIONS OF SHARES

'66 '67 '68 '69 '70 '71 '72 '73 '74 '75 '76 '77

DIGITAL EQUIPMENT CORP. (DEC)

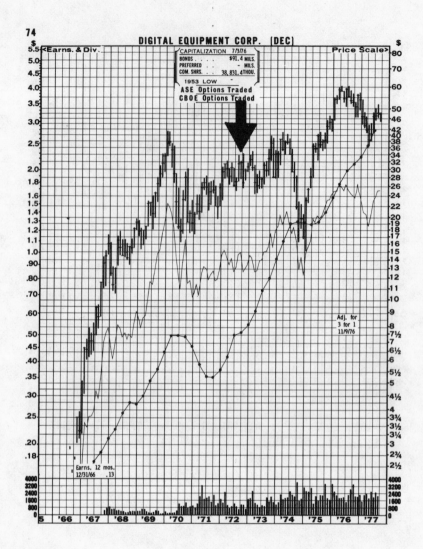

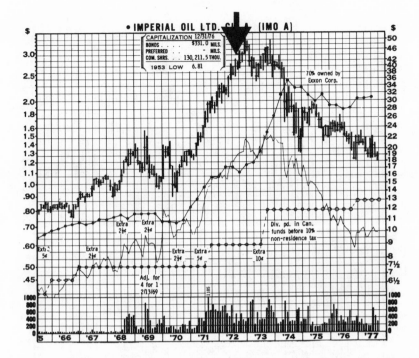

• IMPERIAL OIL LTD. C.... (IMO A)

CAPITALIZATION 12/31/76
BONDS . . . . $331.0 MILS.
PREFERRED . . . - MILS.
COM. SHRS. . . 130,211.5 THOU.
1953 LOW   6.81

70% owned by
Exxon Corp.

Div. pd. in Can.
funds before 10%
non-residence tax

Extra
2½¢   Extra
           2½¢

Exth
5¢   Extra
       2¼¢   Extra-   Extra
                       2¼¢   5¢   Extra
                                                10¢

Adj. for
4 for 1
2/13/69

'66 '67 '68 '69 '70 '71 '72 '73 '74 '75 '76 '77

125

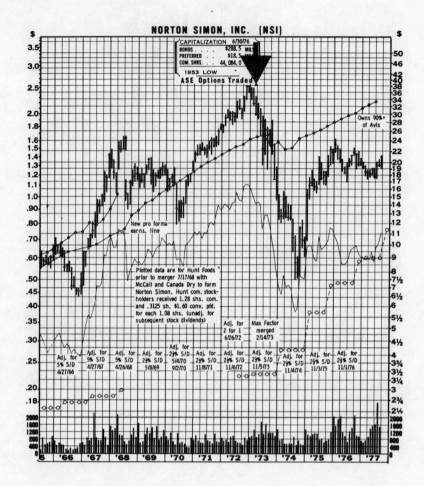

NORTON SIMON, INC. (NSI)

CAPITALIZATION 6/30/76
BONDS . . . . $288.5 MIL.
PREFERRED . . $18.5 MIL.
COM. SHRS. . . 44,084,0

1953 LOW
ASE Options Traded

Owns 90%+
of Avis

New pro forma
earns. line

Plotted data are for Hunt Foods
prior to merger 7/17/68 with
McCall and Canada Dry to form
Norton Simon. Hunt com. stockholders received 1.28 shs. com.
and .3125 sh. $1.60 conv. pfd.
for each 1.08 shs. (unadj. for
subsequent stock dividends)

Adj. for
2 for 1
6/26/72

Max Factor
merged
2/14/73

Adj. for
5% S/D
4/27/66

Adj. for
5% S/D
4/27/67

Adj. for
5% S/D
4/26/68

Adj. for
2½% S/D
5/8/69

Adj. for
2½% S/D
9/2/70

Adj. for
2½% S/D
11/8/71

Adj. for
2½% S/D
11/6/72

Adj. for
2½% S/D
11/5/73

Adj. for
2½% S/D
11/4/74

Adj. for
2½% S/D
11/3/75

Adj. for
2½% S/D
11/1/76

'66 '67 '68 '69 '70 '71 '72 '73 '74 '75 '76 '77

126

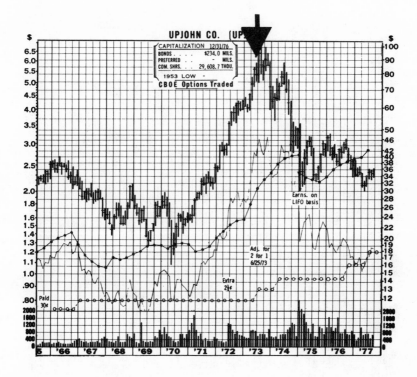

UPJOHN CO. [UP

CAPITALIZATION 12/31/76
BONDS . . . . $234.0 MILS.
PREFERRED . . - MILS.
COM. SHRS. . . 29,608.7 THOU.

1953 LOW -
CBOE Options Traded

Earns. on
LIFO basis

Adj. for
2 for 1
6/25/73

Extra
2½¢

Paid
30¢

'66 '67 '68 '69 '70 '71 '72 '73 '74 '75 '76 '77

127

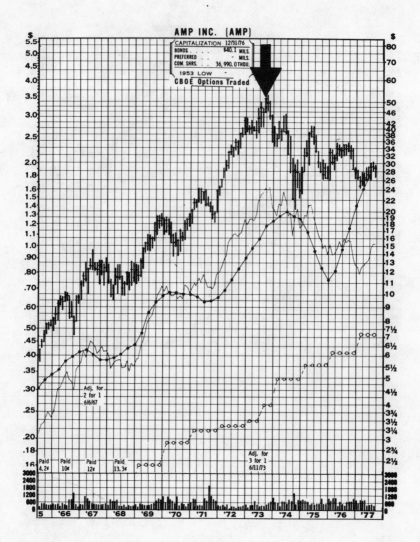

AMP INC. (AMP)

CAPITALIZATION 12/31/76
BONDS . . . $40.1 MILS.
PREFERRED . . " MILS.
COM. SHRS. . . 36,990.0 THOU.
1953 LOW -
CBOE Options Traded

Adj. for
2 for 1
6/6/67

Adj. for
3 for 1
6/11/73

Paid
4.2¢ Paid
10¢ Paid
12¢ Paid
13.3¢

128

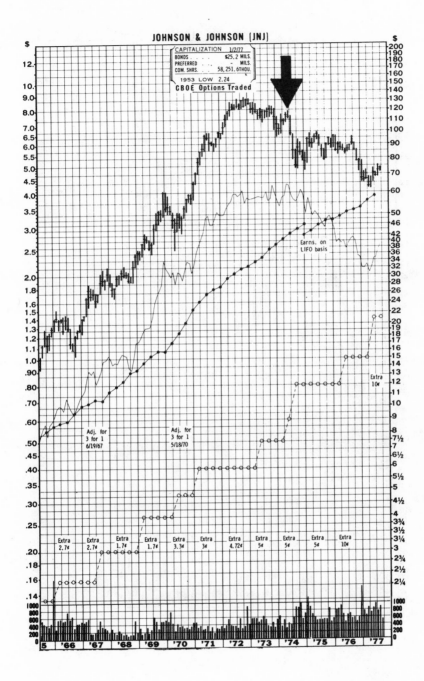

JOHNSON & JOHNSON (JNJ)

CAPITALIZATION 1/2/77
BONDS . . . . $25.2 MILS.
PREFERRED . . . - MILS.
COM. SHRS. . . 58,251. 6THOU.
1953 LOW 2.24
CBOE Options Traded

Earns. on
LIFO basis

Adj. for
3 for 1
6/19/67

Adj. for
3 for 1
5/18/70

Extra
10¢

| Extra 2.7¢ | Extra 2.7¢ | Extra 1.7¢ | Extra 1.7¢ | Extra 3.3¢ | Extra 3¢ | Extra 4.72¢ | Extra 5¢ | Extra 5¢ | Extra 5¢ | Extra 10¢ |

'5 '66 '67 '68 '69 '70 '71 '72 '73 '74 '75 '76 '77

129

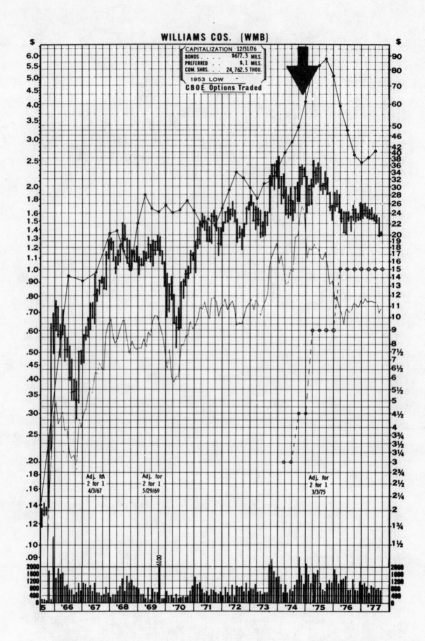

WILLIAMS COS. (WMB)

CAPITALIZATION 12/31/76
BONDS . . . . $677.3 MILS.
PREFERRED . . . $.1 MILS.
COM. SHRS. . . 24,762.5 THOU.

1953 LOW
CBOE Options Traded

Adj. for
2 for 1
4/3/67

Adj. for
2 for 1
5/29/69

Adj. for
2 for 1
3/3/75

AIR PRODUCTS & CHEMICALS, INC. (APD)

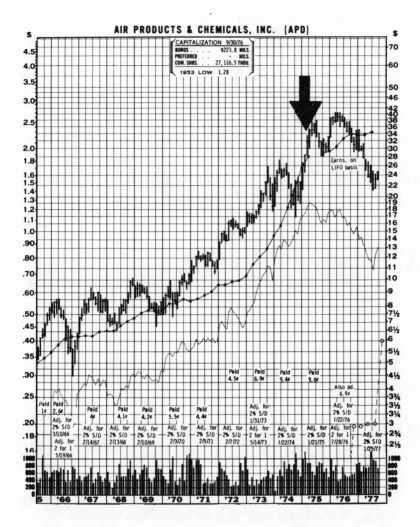

CAPITALIZATION 9/30/76
BONDS . . . . $223.8 MILS.
PREFERRED . . . — MILS.
COM. SHRS. . . . 27,116.5 THOU.

1953 LOW 1.28

Earns. on
LIFO basis

131

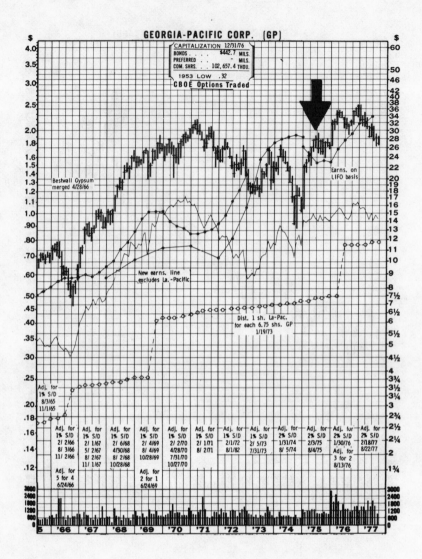

GEORGIA-PACIFIC CORP. (GP)

CAPITALIZATION 12/31/76
BONDS . . . . $442.7 MILS.
PREFERRED . . . — MILS.
COM. SHRS. . . 102,657.4 THOU.
1953 LOW .32
CBOE Options Traded

Bestwall Gypsum
merged 4/28/66

Earns. on
LIFO basis

New earns. line
excludes La.-Pacific

Dist. 1 sh. La-Pac.
for each 6.75 shs. GP
1/19/73

Adj. for
1% S/D
8/3/65
11/1/65

| Adj. for 1% S/D 2/ 2/66 8/ 3/66 11/ 2/66 | Adj. for 1% S/D 2/ 1/67 5/ 2/67 8/ 2/67 11/ 1/67 | Adj. for 1% S/D 2/ 6/68 4/30/68 8/ 2/68 10/28/68 | Adj. for 1% S/D 2/ 4/69 8/ 4/69 10/28/69 | Adj. for 1% S/D 2/ 2/70 4/28/70 7/31/70 10/27/70 | Adj. for 1% S/D 2/ 1/71 8/ 2/71 | Adj. for 1% S/D 2/1/72 8/1/82 | Adj. for 1% S/D 2/ 5/73 7/31/73 | Adj. for 2% S/D 1/31/74 8/ 5/74 | Adj. for 2% S/D 2/3/75 8/4/75 | Adj. for 2% S/D 1/30/76 Adj. for 3 for 2 8/13/76 | Adj. for 2% S/D 2/18/77 8/22/77 |

Adj. for
5 for 4
6/24/66

Adj. for
2 for 1
6/24/69

'66 '67 '68 '69 '70 '71 '72 '73 '74 '75 '76 '77

132

HEWLETT-PACKARD CO. (HWP)

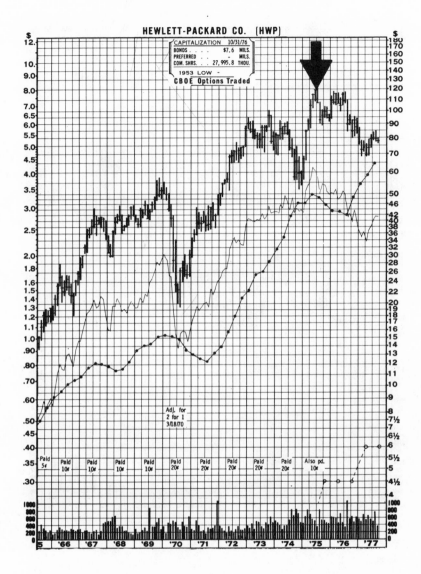

CAPITALIZATION 10/31/76
BONDS . . . . $7.6 MILS.
PREFERRED . . - MILS.
COM. SHRS. . . 27,995.8 THOU.
1953 LOW -
CBOE Options Traded

Adj. for
2 for 1
3/18/70

| Paid 5¢ | Paid 10¢ | Paid 10¢ | Paid 10¢ | Paid 10¢ | Paid 20¢ | Paid 20¢ | Paid 20¢ | Paid 20¢ | Paid 20¢ | Also pd. 10¢ |

'66 '67 '68 '69 '70 '71 '72 '73 '74 '75 '76 '77

133

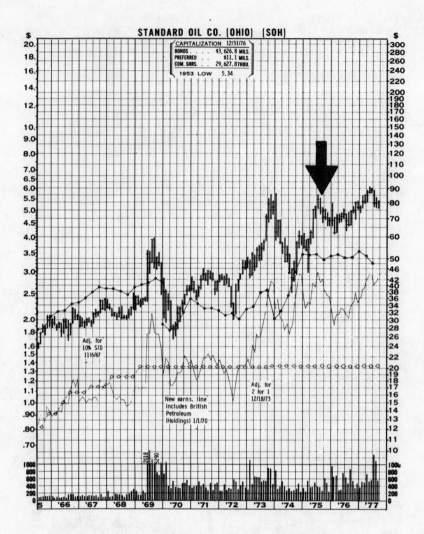

STANDARD OIL CO. (OHIO) (SOH)

CAPITALIZATION 12/31/76
BONDS . . . . $3,626.8 MILS.
PREFERRED . . $11.1 MILS.
COM. SHRS. . 29,627.8 THOU.

1953 LOW 5.34

Adj. for
10% S/D
11/6/67

New earns. line
includes British
Petroleum
(Holdings) 1/1/70

Adj. for
2 for 1
12/18/73

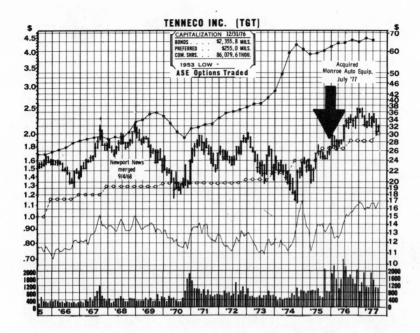

TENNECO INC. (TGT)

CAPITALIZATION 12/31/76
BONDS . . . . $2,355.8 MILS.
PREFERRED . . $255.0 MILS.
COM. SHRS. . . 86,079.6 THOU.

1953 LOW -
ASE Options Traded

Acquired
Monroe Auto Equip.
July '77

Newport News
merged
9/4/68

135

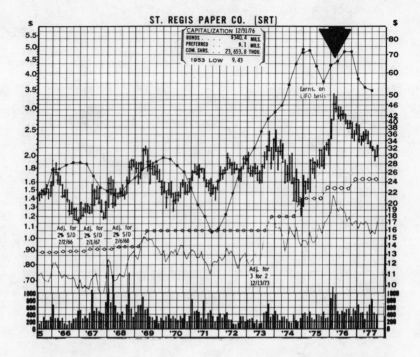

ST. REGIS PAPER CO. (SRT)

CAPITALIZATION 12/31/76
BONDS . . . . . $340.4 MILS.
PREFERRED . . . $.1 MILS.
COM. SHRS. . . 23,653.8 THOU.
1953 LOW 9.43

Earns. on
LIFO basis

Adj. for
2% S/D
2/2/66

Adj. for
2% S/D
2/1/67

Adj. for
2% S/D
2/6/68

Adj. for
3 for 2
12/13/73

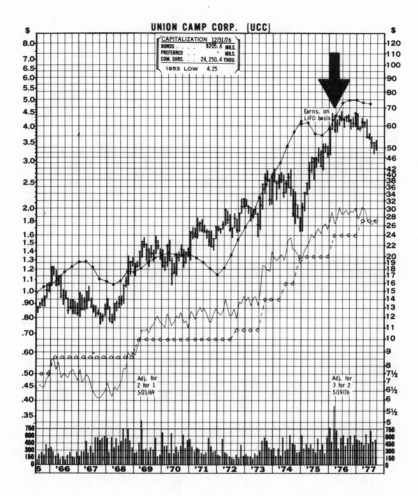

UNION CAMP CORP. (UCC)

CAPITALIZATION 12/31/76
BONDS . . . . $205. 6 MILS.
PREFERRED . . . - MILS.
COM. SHRS. . . 24, 250. 4 THOU.
1953 LOW 4. 25

Earns. on
LIFO basis

Adj. for
2 for 1
5/21/69

Adj. for
3 for 2
5/19/76

137

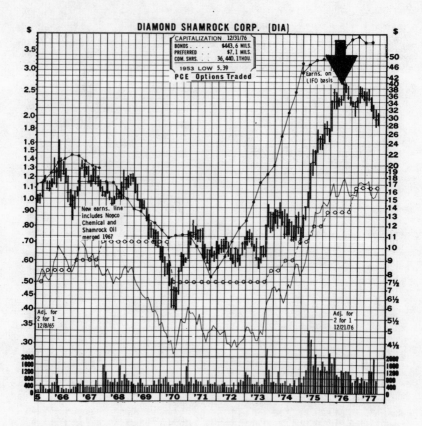

DIAMOND SHAMROCK CORP. (DIA)

CAPITALIZATION 12/31/76
BONDS . . . . $443.6 MILS.
PREFERRED . . $7.1 MILS.
COM. SHRS. . . 36,440.1 THOU.

1953 LOW 5.39

PCE Options Traded

Earns. on
LIFO basis

New earns. line
includes Nopco
Chemical and
Shamrock Oil
merged 1967

Adj. for
2 for 1
12/8/65

Adj. for
2 for 1
12/21/76

'66 '67 '68 '69 '70 '71 '72 '73 '74 '75 '76 '77

138

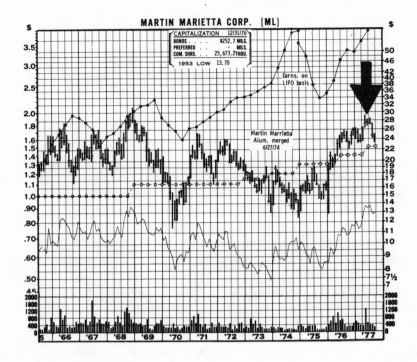

MARTIN MARIETTA CORP. (ML)

CAPITALIZATION 12/31/76
BONDS . . . . $252.7 MILS.
PREFERRED . . - MILS.
COM. SHRS. . . 25,673.2THOU.

1953 LOW 13.70

Earns. on
LIFO basis

Martin Marrietta
Alum. merged
6/27/74

The New Options Market

Something of a Darwinian nature has come along to help the individual investor. This species had become one of the smallest struggling in the Wall Street wilderness. His environment was becoming less and less hospitable and his survival more precarious as forces beyond his power shaped the marketplace. Finally, he found himself vulnerable to being whipsawed by volatility, without any means for counterattack beyond his traditional defense: to try to guess the direction of the market and, with luck, to "win."

Obviously, the individual had to discover a new way to adapt if he were to survive/succeed. And just as he faced up to this challenge, the markets spawned, almost as if by natural evolution, a solution.

This solution involves a new way of using an old investment technique: the option. The change, which is both evolutionary and revolutionary, is the advent of the new standardized options markets. Because of options, the investor is no longer constrained to make the right guesses, while he *is* increasing his return and reducing his vulnerability to volatility.

With the new techniques and new attitudes that we will describe, he may even reap greater rewards than his larger, professional competitors. This is because the standardized options markets allow the individual investor to learn to manage his "stock inventory" the way a businessman manages his product inventory—with discipline, flexibility, and the investment tools to capitalize on probabilities.

But let us back up a little, to the basics of options themselves.

Options are not a new form of investment. They date back, some historians say, to the 1600s. In the United States, stock options have been available for at least 100 years in the over-the-counter market. Other forms of contractual options, involving such things as real estate, professional services, and commodities, are commonplace today.

In any form, an option is a way of permitting the transfer of risk and opportunity among investors. We shall primarily be concerned with the former function—earning a return by transferring risk to someone who is willing to pay you for the opportunity to possibly make a profit.

The essential components of an option follow:

■ A description of the item the option buyer may purchase from the seller (writer).

■ The price at which the item may be purchased.

■ The time period during which the buyer of the option must exercise— or lose—his right to purchase. (The potential buyer must be able to pay the whole purchase price between the beginning and the end of the contractual time period. If the buyer chooses not to exercise his purchase rights during the allowed time—usually because he deems it not to his advantage to do so—the option expires. It ceases to exist.)

■ A sum of money (called a premium) which the option buyer pays for the rights granted, and which the option seller receives. The seller keeps the premium whether or not the option is exercised.

The option has certain advantages for both parties. For a relatively small capital investment, the buyer locks up an opportunity to have exclusive call on some asset for a specific time period, during which he may decide if he wants to risk more capital by exercising his option to purchase that asset. Perhaps he may find a more attractive asset to purchase during that time period. He might even be able to find another buyer for the asset at a price greater than the total of his option price and premium, thereby turning a quick profit on a small investment. The seller, meanwhile, has earned extra income on his investment to offset his risk of ownership (and to effectively reduce his cost of ownership).

Options on stocks are useful tools for investors. Even before the advent of the new standardized options markets (which, as you will see below, greatly added to options' liquidity and flexibility), investors used options to achieve two general objectives:

■ The opportunity to realize a potentially large profit from a relatively small investment—with a known and predetermined "downside" risk (that is, the cost of the premium). Buyers of options are motivated by this possibility.

■ The opportunity to increase—often substantially—the income derived from securities investments. Sellers (writers) of options are motivated by this objective.

Let us look at this transfer of risk and opportunity among investors in a specific example:

Suppose Texas Instruments (TXN) is trading at $100 on the New

York Stock Exchange. Suppose, also, that an owner of 100 shares of the stock chooses to sell to a buyer an opportunity (by means of an option) to purchase his shares of the stock at a specific price (called the "striking price") any time up to a prearranged expiration date. Let us say the owner told the buyer he could buy his 100 shares of TXN stock at $100 anytime between now and 6 months from now, but for that privilege he must pay $8 per share, or $800. The buyer agrees. The money that changes hands is the premium, in this case an $8 premium per share.

The premium is what options trading is all about. An options buyer hopes to purchase an option when the premium is low and later to be able to sell it at a higher premium, realizing a profit on the increase. This would occur, in our example, if TXN moved up over $100, say to $108, in one month. At that point, the option has an "intrinsic" (market price less striking price) value of 8 (108 minus 100) and perhaps a "time" and "leverage" value of 4, for a total value of 12.

Thus the option tool gives the speculator the chance to play a stock's price action without the capital exposure he would risk if he bought the stock outright. His only risk is predetermined and entirely known to him: it is the $8 premium.

Moreover, since the options buyer has purchased the right to call away the stock from the seller, he might alternatively decide to exercise his option and own the stock outright by paying an additional $10,000 (100 shares at $100 per share) to the seller (according to the terms of the original contract).

The seller has given up his stock for $100 per share, but has in effect sold his shares for $108 apiece, since he has already received $8 per share in premiums. Normally, the buyer will not exercise while the option is selling for more than intrinsic value, because he would be economically better off selling the option than calling the stock at the exercise price and selling it at the market price. For example,

*Buy call for	$ 800	*Buy call for	$ 800
*Exercise call	10,000	*Sell call	1200
Cost	$10,800		
*Sell stock	10,800		
Profit	$ 0	Profit	$ 400

*There is a commission cost for each of these transactions not included in this calculation.

Of course, the seller has not received this additional return on his investment without giving up something. What he has sacrificed is the profit that would have accrued to him had the stock risen more than the amount he received in premiums—more than 8 points, in this example.

Before the introduction of standardized options markets, investors who wanted to use these handy options tools were faced with an awkward and illiquid marketplace. They had to make deals through any number of put and call brokers, each of whom had to find the other side of a customer's desired option purchase or sale. Each buy and sell thus involved a contractual agreement between a particular buyer and a particular seller. If either the buyer or the seller wished to liquidate his side of the agreement, he had to negotiate with the other party—who was free to refuse.

What is new—and what has opened up a whole new world of opportunity for the individual investor—is the introduction in 1973 of stock options with standardized terms trading on national regulated securities exchanges. The existence of standardized options on national exchanges means that secondary markets now exist in options, allowing buyers and sellers to deal with thousands of other buyers and sellers on a continuing basis. Now options can be bought and sold with the same ease and in the same manner as securities on the major stock exchanges.

A standardized options marketplace offers even more advantages in terms of liquidity and flexibility to the investor using options. Now buyers of options may sell their contracts at any time prior to expiration. And sellers of options may "buy in" options they have previously written, thus terminating their obligation to deliver the stock.

What is more, now that standardized options markets have eliminated the put and call brokers' procedure of writing contractual agreements between each buyer and each seller, the ability of a seller to terminate his obligation to deliver the stock in no way affects the buyer's right to exercise the option he has bought; with the standardized options markets, the Options Clearing Corporation acts as the guarantor to every buyer and every seller. When a buyer elects to exercise his option, the Options Clearing Corporation "assigns" that exercise to a seller selected at random. Rather than the one-to-one contractual relationship that operated in the obsolete over-the-counter market, there is no longer a continuing relationship between any buyer/seller pair.

The inception of national options trading exchanges has also brought the creation of a much wider variety of options than existed in the put and call brokers' day. This means that investors now have an abundance of ways of expressing themselves about each of the hundreds of optionable stocks. If you can buy or sell options on TXN, to use our example, with striking prices of $90, $100, and $110 and with expiration dates in 3 different months, you have an opportunity to express yourself quite precisely regarding that stock. Do you think it will go up or down short term? Up or down long term? Will it stay near the same price?

Options offer infinite possibilities to use your judgment to position yourself to profit (if that is a game you still wish to play).

In a larger sense, exchange-traded options appeared on the scene, again almost as though foreordained by Darwinian evolution, just at a time when the sophisticated markets of the 1970s were showing a growing awareness of the desirability for:

- Mechanisms for transferring risk.

- Increased liquidity.

Risk transference, not only in stocks and commodities, but also in the short- and long-term money markets, has been the predominant motivation behind the development of options and futures markets. The rapidly growing volume of these markets attests to the fact that they meet this need.

The risk that the securities shareholder wishes to transfer is *price volatility*. The idea that options perform a valid economic function in helping the investor "lay off" this risk is overlooked and misunderstood in some circles, probably because the risk itself is misunderstood. As we noted in previous chapters, too often investors think of stock ownership as "owning a share of America," or owning assets, or owning earnings. In fact, all the investor really owns is price action.

The "merger mania" so evident in the stock market of the late 1970s brings this point home. Unless a shareholder owns *all* the stock of a corporation, he has no way to exercise any rights to the assets or earning power of that corporation. The specter of corporations bidding substantially above market prices to own all the shares of other corporations points out that the value of owning a company. The minority shareholder *may* benefit from the underlying company's success through dividends, and, *if* the market recognizes the company's success, through his shares' price appreciation. But what he *owns* is property *valued at what other investors think it is worth*. Hence he owns price volatility—and risk—and in the current risk-averse market environment, he welcomes mechanisms for transferring that risk.

The options markets bring together investors with many different risk-averse objectives (e.g., call buyers want appreciation potential with downside volatility limited to their premium costs; call writers desire downside protection in exchange for upside volatility, etc.) and allow them to achieve the risk transference they seek.

In performing this function options also add to the liquidity of capital markets. How is this possible? Statistical proof is difficult because of the many variables involved and the lack of control elements. But let us look at the logic of the situation. In a free market system, capital flows where the greatest returns are offered *commensurate with the perception of risk involved*. It can be argued that the infinite combinations of puts and calls now available allow investors so much more flexibility than in the days before exchange-traded options (when the only choice was "own the stock" or "not own the stock"), and so many more chances to create offsetting transactions, that these new stock-and-option markets are attracting added capital. How else could option volume have grown from about 1600 contracts per day in 1973 to 126,000 by June 1976, and annual contract volume from 1,119,177 in 1973 to 32,373,927 in 1976, unless the market was satisfying the needs of both buyers and sellers?*

Some observers fear that the options markets will become so pervasive that investors will no longer trade stocks. This is difficult to imagine, since options have a derivative value, and the relationship between stocks and options is so intertwined that option trading can create stock trading.

Trading in options will translate into stock trading. For example, if everyone were to trade in Xerox (XRX) calls rather than in XRX stock, it seems there would be no movement in the stock. Nevertheless, since the same number of shares of XRX would still be outstanding, if an existing shareholder should decide to sell his stock, he would create a price change. Moreover, there would be a price at which someone would be willing to buy shares, since not everyone is legally or psychologically prepared to own only calls. If the price of the stock were to decline and the call price were to remain stable, the calls would become overvalued and attractive to

---

*Another question argued in academic circles these days is whether options attract money that might otherwise be going into such other areas as venture capital or new issues. This simplistic query overlooks the interrelationships and competition for capital within the capital markets and on an international scale. Capital flows where the rewards are greatest and the risks smallest. New issues compete with old, stocks with bonds, American securities with foreign , savings banks with money market investments, real estate with oil and gas properties, and so forth, and they all compete with each other. No segment of the capital market is guaranteed a share of that market. Shifts are always taking place, and cycles repeat themselves. The new issue and venture capital markets had gone into the doldrums long before option trading came along, because investors were disappointed in their returns. Their day will return in the future. Historically, pension funds have shifted out of bonds and into stocks, and now back to bonds. From time to time there are shifts from corporate bonds to government bonds, depending on yield spreads. When these shifts take place, people do not argue the "role of bonds versus stocks" or "corporate bonds versus government bonds" as they now question "the role of options." One can only hope that options, now in their infancy, will someday graduate from the kind of intellectual abuse that once plagued common stocks earlier in this century.

sell relative to the stock, and the stock would be purchased in order to write calls against it. Conversely, if there was a demand for the stock that was expressed by purchasing calls, then the calls would become overvalued, and to buy XRX stock and sell the overvalued options against it would become an attractive proposition.

Adding puts to the equation only intensifies these relationships and makes it more likely that the demand or supply in one of the XRX securities (stock, puts, calls) will find its way into the others. This is a very positive development for securities markets.

But what does all this have to do with the strategy we propose for surviving/succeeding in the new stock market? This tactic involves removing yourself from the position of having to make the right guesses in a volatile marketplace, changing your concept of investing from "putting your eggs in the right basket" to capitalizing on the most likely occurrences, and managing your stock inventory as if it were a business.

The point will become clearer if we look first at the commodities exchanges from which the options exchanges were conceived. Commodities exchanges bring together the users of commodities and speculators, both of whom fulfill their needs through commodity futures markets. A user (for example, Hershey's Chocolate) would employ this market to reduce the risks inherent in fluctuating cocoa prices by laying off its exposure to short-term price volatility through the purchase of cocoa futures—since these insure its supply of cocoa at a known price. Or, if the company has too heavy an inventory, it could elect to sell cocoa futures. The speculators, who absorb the other side of a big commodities users' purchases and sales of futures, accept these risks for the opportunity of making money by anticipating price changes. Thus, for a big business like Hershey's Chocolate, commodity futures becomes a sensible business procedure for reducing risk.*

You can use your stock inventory similarly in the options market. By buying stocks and selling options on them, you will be laying off some of your market risk (that is, your vulnerability to volatility) by "renting out" that volatility to   speculators   and/or investors. These options buyers are

---

*There is a major difference between an option and a futures contract: an option limits liability, because an option buyer has the *right* to purchase. A futures contract leaves the owner or seller essentially liable for fulfillment of his contract, because a futures buyer has an *obligation* to purchase. The future he has bought or sold is merely a deposit, and the buyer or seller may be called for additional deposits, depending on price changes. Another disadvantage of futures-markets is that the markets may close when price changes exceed a prescribed maximum. Liquidity is thus lost. The unlimited liability on futures contracts will change shortly, as the commodities markets begin to introduce options on futures.

willing to pay you for the privilege of possibly profiting from correctly anticipating future market moves or for their own hedging purposes.

At the same time, you will choose the stocks you buy and the options you sell against them in such a way that you will be capitalizing on the stock's volatility rather than falling victim to it. And, since you will be selecting options that are already selling at prices higher than they are worth, you can be making money if the market goes up . . . or if it stays flat . . . or even if it goes down. And you will be making a good return as long as the stocks in which you are involved do not trade outside their historical ranges. Even if they do, by intelligent adjustment you can survive even the most unlikely series of market events. The most important point to remember is that, with options, you are not joining the hordes who are fecklessly trying to predict the direction of the market; you are reacting to the reality of it.

CHAPTER SIX

Options: The Jargon and the Behavior Patterns

Options provide many ways to capitalize on stock market moves. But before you can take advantage of the flexibility and profitability they can add to your stock "business," you will need to understand options' behavior patterns relative to stocks. To follow the mechanics we discuss later, you will also need to digest this simple glossary, since options trading involves a language all its own:

■ *Call Options:* The right to purchase 100* shares of a specific, usually widely held and actively traded common stock, known as the *underlying security*.

■ *Put options:* The right to sell 100*shares of a specific stock at a fixed price for a specified time period.

■ *Exercise price* (also called the *striking price*): The price at which the call buyer may purchase the stock from (or the put buyer may sell to) the seller of the option.

■ *Expiration date:* The last day on which the buyer of a call option may exercise his right to buy or, in the case of puts, to sell the stock.

Generally, on the national exchanges options expire quarterly, on either a January-April-July-October cycle, a February-May-August-November cycle, or a March-June-September-December cycle. The January cycle is by far the most active, because this was the original cycle, and more of the most active stocks are on it. The exchanges offer trading in the nearest three of the four expiration months in a cycle—for instance, if it is now March, options in the former cycle are available for April, July, and October, while options in the latter cycles are available for May, August, and November, and June, September, and December. (The specific op-

---

*When companies declare stock splits or stock dividends, the exercise price and number of shares are adjusted to reflect this. If a stock splits two for one, an option to buy/sell 100 shares at $50 per share becomes an option to buy/sell 200 shares at $25 per share.

tions' expiration date of each period is the Saturday following the third Friday of the expiration month.) Trading in expiring options usually ends at 3 o'clock (New York time) that Friday, but instructions to exercise can be given until 5:30. (This is why seemingly worthless options are repurchased. At 3 o'clock, a stock with an expiring option at $50 may be trading at $49, but it may rise to $51 between 3 o'clock and 4 o'clock, when the New York Stock Exchange closes.)

Each underlying security will have options trading for three different expiration periods; at the same time, they will have a number of exercise prices available, so that the investor using options may express his opinion about a particular stock in a variety of ways. Generally, new options with higher or lower exercise prices will become available as the underlying security experiences significant price changes. Exercise prices usually exist at 5-point intervals for stocks trading below $50, at 10-point intervals for stocks trading between $50 and $200, and at 20-point intervals for stocks trading over $200. For example, you might be able to buy or sell the following options in Xerox (XRX), now selling at $50 during March: XRX April 40, 45, 50, and 60; XRX July 40, 45, 50, and 60; and XRX October 40, 45, 50, and 60. Sometimes, however, not all of these are available for all currently trading expiration periods, since an option with a particular exercise price is introduced for a given month only if a close relationship exists between the exercise price and the current market price of the stock. It may not be introduced for the nearest expiration month.

■ *Premium:* The money (the price) the buyer pays to acquire a call (or a put) option and the money the seller (writer) receives. (It is always expressed in the price per 100 shares, so that one option in XRX April 60 quoted in the newspapers at $5 will cost the buyer $500 plus commissions.)

The seller or "writer" receives this sum of $500 less commissions. Another usage of the term "premium" is the excess over intrinsic value of the option price. For example: if an option is exercisable at $40, the stock's market price $44, and the option price $6, then the intrinsic value of the option is $4, and its premium (excess) is $2.

Market price of stock	$44
Exercise price of option	40
Intrinsic value of option	$ 4
Market price of option	6
Premium	$2

At any time before the end of an expiration period, an option buyer may sell his option (closing sale), thus realizing either a profit or loss, depending on the increase or decrease in the market value of the option. Similarly, unless his previously sold option is exercised, an option writer may "buy in" his option, thus effecting a "closing purchase" transaction which terminates his obligation to deliver stock. His profit or loss is the difference between the premium he received on the original sale (called an opening sale) and the premium he must pay for buying it back, or, if it expires, the total amount of the original sale.

Since premiums are to options what market prices are to stocks, it is necessary for the investor to have knowledge of what factors combine to determine the fair value of a particular option at a particular time. Option valuation is an integral part of our survival/success technique.

What do we mean when we say an option is overvalued? Option valuation is an entirely different matter from stock valuation. The former is much more precise. The "true" value of a stock is much more difficult to ascertain than the value of an option, because a stock has, for all practical purposes, an infinite life.

Over the long term, a stock's value depends on its underlying company's earnings and dividends, the aggregate of all its investors' hopes and expectations, the merits of alternate investments, and the mood of buyers and sellers. The latter is a variable that can be a function of any factor, discernible or not.

One investor may think that he can assess a particular security's future worth by applying certain yardsticks and assumptions to the underlying company's business. Based on his evaluation of this business, he will translate to the stock a discounted value for the company's future earnings. If his assumptions are right, he will eventually realize a profit on his stock investment as the price of the stock increases to reflect the company's rising earnings. But, even if his fundamental assumptions are correct, the investor is operating in a marketplace where the price of his holding is determined by a multitude of variables, including many that are entirely external to the business of the underlying company. Shrewd as he may be, he may not have the financial patience to wait for his stock's market price to reflect his subjective judgments. What is more, if the underlying company's prospects improve but his stock's price deteriorates, he will not know whether to be more patient or to question his own judgment.

In contrast to stocks, options have a finite life. Their value runs out with time, which is why some people refer to options as "wasting assets" (they are, of course, also wasting liabilities). The day after the expiration date, an option's value is zero. Unequivocally. During its lifetime, an option's true value is not easy to calculate, but it is a function of factors that are more measurable than those influencing stock prices.

These factors include some that are *known* quantities: the *time* left in the option and the *market price* of the stock relative to the *exercise price* of the option. Let us examine these:

- *Time left to run in an option.*

All else being equal, the more time remaining until the expiration date, the higher an option's value will be. For instance, if we compare an April and a July option with the same exercise price, the July option would ordinarily command a higher premium, since the buyer will be securing more time—he will be purchasing the opportunity for an additional 3 months in which the price of the underlying stock may rise.

- *Market price of the stock and the exercise price of the option.*

When the market price of a stock is greater than the exercise price of a call option, that option is said to have "tangible," "real," or "intrinsic" value. In more common parlance, that option is "in the money." An example would be a call option on XRX common stock with an exercise price of $40, when the stock is selling at $45. Obviously, the right to purchase a $45 stock at $40 has a tangible value of $5. Such an "in-the-money" option will tend to move in tandem with the stock. Just how closely a one-point movement in the option price correlates with a one-point movement in the stock's market price is called the option's "*sensitivity*." This sensitivity will approach 1.00 as the option nears expiration.

When the market price of a stock is less than the exercise price of a call option, that option is commonly referred to as being "out-of-the-money." An example would be a call option on XRX common stock with an exercise price of $50, when the stock is selling at $45. Since such an option has no "intrinsic" value, it will tend to have a lower sensitivity— that is, it will move less per one-point move in the stock, but its sensitivity will increase as the stock moves closer to the exercise price. If there is no such move, the sensitivity of an out-of-the-money option will decline as a result of the passage of time. While an in-the-money option tends toward a sensitivity of 1.00 (point for point) with the stock as it nears the expiration date, an out-of-the-money option will tend toward zero as it approaches expiration.

Sensitivity can more precisely be defined as the expected price movement of an option per $1 change in the price of the underlying stock. An option theoretically cannot have a sensitivity greater than 1.00 relative to the stock.

Sensitivity changes as time passes and, also, as the relationship between the striking price of one option and the market price of its underlying stock is altered. For example, an option to buy a stock at $50 per share, when it is selling at $40, will be more sensitive when there are 6 months left in the option than when there are 6 days left. This is because the time left has value, and the probabilities that the stock might sell for well over $50 are greater for a 6-month period than for a 6-day period. As the stock rises in price, that probability increases. If four days pass and the stock has risen to $45, the chances for the 6-month option have increased considerably, while in the case of a shorter option the stock has only two days left to sell at $50—so that the time factor has negated the price factor, and the sensitivity has, if anything, declined. For a graphic illustration of how sensitivity changes with time and price fluctuations, see Table 9-1.

Sensitivity also reflects the fact that, the deeper in the money an option is, the less premium over intrinsic value there will probably be. The less this premium, the greater the sensitivity. This is because, the deeper in-the-money, the more capital must be employed to purchase an option; thus the buyer gets less leverage and, therefore, the buyer is not willing to pay much of a premium (excess over intrinsic value). So, a very deep in-the-money option with no premium will move almost point for point with the stock.

In addition to these two objective qualities—time, and the relationship of market price of stock to exercise price of option—there are other, more subjective, factors that enter into the option valuation:

One is the *rate of return available elsewhere*. This involves the current cost of money and dividends to be paid during the option period, both contributing to the premium an owner of the stock "expects" for assuming equity ownership, rather than the risk-free return available elsewhere. The cost of money (interest rates) is a factor because the buyer of an option is getting the price volatility of the stock without tying up capital. Therefore, the investor who is tying up capital (that is, the options seller, the investor who already owns the stock long or has committed collateral in some other form) has to be compensated for interest he is not earning as well as the risk of ownership and/or obligation. Dividends also figure into the rate of return the stock owner enjoys (in contrast to the options buyer, who is not entitled to dividends), and dividend yield must also be weighed versus the "risk-free" (usually defined as short-term Treasury bill) rate available alternately. Then there is the very subjective part of options premiums that involves the *price the stock owner expects for being in stocks at all*. For some investors a 5% rate of return is an acceptable increment to the risk-free rate, whereas for others a 3% rate may be acceptable. The higher the expectation, the higher the standard for option overvaluation.

The final (and equally subjective) determinant of options valuation is *trading volatility*, or the tendency of the underlying stock to fluctuate in price. The higher the volatility of the underlying stock, the higher the premium that stock is likely to command. This is because a buyer will be more willing to pay a higher option price in a situation in which he knows that the underlying stock has the capability (by historical standards) to make considerable moves in short time periods. Sellers are also aware of the volatility so they expect higher premiums to offset the risk of ownership.

(However, the arithmetically calculated rate of return from buying volatile stocks and selling options will most likely be high, even if the option is undervalued. This is a dangerous lure, since the undervaluation is telling you that the rate of return, although high by normal standards, is not high enough to compensate for the possible losses inherent in the ownership of the stock.)

How can you take all these factors into account and determine whether an option is overvalued or undervalued? Using common sense, you can grasp the principle: Take a stock with which most investors are familiar—General Motors. Suppose someone were to offer you a 6-month call option to buy GM at $70 with the stock selling for $70 and the option priced at ⅛ (that is, for $12.50 you have the opportunity to purchase 100 shares of GM for $7000 at any time in the next 6 months). You would undoubtedly consider that a cheap option. Even if you expect GM to decline, you would recognize this as a good deal. Your chances of succeeding and the rewards for success are so great relative to the small investment risked that this seems like "an offer you can't refuse." Even a peripheral knowledge of the volatility of GM suggests that it is a good deal.

Conversely, if the price of the option were $20 (that is, for $2000 you have the opportunity to purchase 100 shares of GM for $7000 at any time in the next 6 months), it would seem very expensive. The chances of making money on this transaction are low, and the option is particularly unattractive when an alternative is to buy GM stock on 50% margin. Buying the stock on margin entails an expenditure of $3500 (plus interest on the debit balance); for that you may collect dividends, you have no time limit on your ownership, and you have not increased your risk of ownership by very much, since you have spent only $1500 more than you would have for the option. Although your total exposure is greater, the probability of GM declining more than 35 points, or 50%, in 6 months is very low.

Obviously, somewhere between ⅛ and 20 is the fair value of the 6-month option at $70. Although the true fair value of an option cannot be determined exactly, it can be established closely enough to be able to avoid buying the upside potential at too high a price or selling the potential upside too cheaply.

Computer pricing models that perform this function of calculating the fair value of options are in use today. They attempt to quantify mathematically, using actual data, the potential risks and rewards of every tradeable option—that is, to quantify the instinctive conclusions we drew in the GM comparison. It is important that you have access to such a facility—most commonly, through your broker—if you are serious about being in the business of options. Note that you will require more than just a computer that can figure yields or returns on covered writing; you will need one that provides options valuations based on probabilities.

A probability model generates the most likely distribution of prices for any stock for any specific time period. The basic assumption for all probability models is that future volatility (that is, in the immediate future) will closely approximate past volatility. Although this is not always true, it is true often enough to use it as a basis for options valuations. For example, assume that over the past 3 years a stock has demonstrated that for 90-day periods (starting a new period every day) the price of the stock has been:

Up 20–30%	averaging	out	to	25%	gain	5%	of the time
Up 10–20%	"	"	"	15%	"	10%	"
Up 0–10%	"	"	"	5%	"	15%	"
Unchanged	"	"	"	0%	"	40%	"
Down 0–10%	"	"	"	5%	loss	15%	"
Down 10–20%	"	"	"	15%	"	10%	"
Down 20–30%	"	"	"	25%	"	5%	"

Theoretically, someone who bought 100 3-month calls one at a time would get back (assuming a $100 stock):

$2500	5	times	out	of	100,	or	$12,500
$1500	10	"	"	"	"	"	15,000
$ 500	15	"	"	"	"	"	7,500
Total							$35,000

All other occurrences (70 out of 100) would produce nothing for a call buyer. Therefore, if 100 calls were purchased for $350 each, the cost would equal the proceeds. The "fair value" of each call in this simple case would be $350, or 3½. Anything more than that would produce a loss for the buyer. The option would be "overvalued," since the buyer clearly paid too much for the volatility. An option now selling for less than $350 (3½) would produce a profit and would therefore have been "undervalued." However, the seller of these calls would not be interested in selling calls just to get his money back. He wants to earn a return on the risk of owning the stock or, if he did not own the stock, for incurring the obligation to deliver. Therefore, the fair value calculated above on a pure probability basis must be adjusted upward somewhat to reflect the cost of money. This is one example of the sophistication that computerized pricing models employ in order to more precisely calculate the fair value of an option.

Suppose that the other factors combine to give us a fair value for this option of $375(3¾). If the option is selling for $425(4¼), it might not look like it is overvalued by very much, because we are only talking about $50 per option or 50¢ per share of stock. But this represents a 13% ($425/$375) overvaluation—which *is* meaningful.

It is very important for you to have access to the most accurate available computer pricing model to determine overvalued and under-valued options—for your return is based upon consistently capitalizing on the "spread" between an option's fair value and its market value.

Think of an insurance company. The difference between the actuarial value and the premium the company may charge is not great (after allowance for profit and other costs) relative to the face amount of the policy, but if an insurance company were to sell "undervalued" insurance long enough, you can be sure that it would fail, since the law of averages would be working against it. Option values work out in the aggregate, but not necessarily in every individual situation. That is why it is important to manage an option writing program as a "business." The more cases over which the activity is spread, the more the possibility of successful results. Diversification, continuity, and discipline are essential ingredients when depending on probabilities.

We are not saying flatly that the buyer of overvalued options and the seller of undervalued options will always lose money. We are talking about probabilities. If you continually buy overvalued options, the odds strongly suggest that you will be a loser. The converse is true for sellers. The differential from fair market value is an edge one would like to get, not give.

Some investors do not consider overvaluation when selling options. They merely look at the rate of return. That is a mistake. One does not purchase bonds when they have high yields without looking at the quality of the credit behind the bonds. In this world, there is a relationship between risk and reward. Many sadder-but-wiser investors have purchased stock and sold (written) calls on high volatility stocks because the rate of return on the investment was high—only to find that the risk of ownership was even higher. Their mistake was in selling undervalued options.

CHAPTER SEVEN

Various Options Strategies: The Advantages and Disadvantages of Each

We have explored some of the reasons why individuals choose to be either buyers or sellers of options.

Obviously, an individual's decision to be either a buyer or a seller depends on his financial objectives and requirements and his analysis of future stock market moves. At one point in time he may decide to, be an options buyer; at another, he may elect to be an options seller—or he may decide to hedge himself by being both a buyer and a seller.

Now let us look at various options strategies—buying puts/calls outright; selling "covered" puts/calls; selling "uncovered" puts/calls; and using spreads, straddles, and combinations—describing the advantages and disadvantages of each.

Why Buy Call Options: Some Strategies and Cautions

As we have discussed, leverage (the ability to play a stock's price action with an investment much smaller than that needed to buy the stock itself) and limited risk (your loss being limited to the money spent on the option premium) are the two major attractions in buying options.

For example, suppose that today Xerox (XRX) is selling at $50 per share, and that a call option with a $50 exercise price expiring 4 months from now can be brought for $4 per share. Now suppose that 2 months from today the price of XRX has risen to $56, and the option at $50, since it is also more valuable, has risen to $8. If you had bought 100 shares of stock at

$50 for $5000 and sold it at $56 for $5600, you would have realized a gain of $600, or 12%, on your investment. However, if you had instead bought the option for $4 (or a $400 investment) and had sold it for $8 (or proceeds of $800), you would have realized a gain of $400 on your $400 investment, or 100%—considerably greater leverage than you had obtained through stock ownership. As an options investor, you had far less risk than the stock owner. Your risk was limited to the price of your option premium—$400—while the stock owner's risk was, at least in theory, as much as $5000.

Not all buyers purchase options in order to resell them later. Every options holder has the privilege, before expiration, of exercising his option and calling for delivery of the stock. He accomplishes this simply by notifying his broker that he wishes to exercise the option, and then paying the purchase price of the exercised stock, plus commission. Obviously, exercise of an option is not worthwhile unless the price of the underlying stock is high enough above the exercise price to cover commissions. Even if it is not, it is normally cheaper to sell the option rather than to exercise it, because there are more transaction costs involved in exercise and there is usually a ready market for options—at a slight discount—among professional traders whose cost of exercise is lower than the call owner's. The trader, who is a broker and does not pay commissions, will buy the call, exercise it, and sell the stock, making a small profit.

Some call buyers who intend to exercise may do so for the following reasons:

- To "nail down" in advance the maximum price they would have pay to for a stock that may be selling for a higher price in future months.

- To secure the price of a stock now for purchases to be made at a future date when the investor expects to have increased cash flow. An options buyer may expect to have increased cash in upcoming months from the maturation of fixed income securities or the sale of property. He would buy options now with an eye toward exercising them at a set price when his cash situation improves.

- To cover a short sale. If an investor opts to sell a particular stock short, he can protect himself against the otherwise unlimited liability of that short sale if, through buying call options, he fixes the maximum price he will have to pay to cover.

- To accumulate a larger position without moving the price—since there may be more shares available in the options market than in the stock market.

Buying call options is a practice generally regarded as highly speculative by the public. Actually, with the proper precautions, it can be more conservative than buying stocks. If you follow two simple precepts, you can employ options in such a way as to increase your opportunity for profit and reduce your risk of loss.

- *The first is to buy options "with insurance."*

This means that, instead of entailing the capital risk of spending X amount of money on the purchase of 100 shares of stock, you spend only the percentage of X required to buy an option on that stock and invest the difference in a fixed income security, such as Treasury bills or bonds. This gives you the double-barreled advantage of leverage on your option position and limited risk in the equity market (your risk being limited to the price of your option).

For example, let us say that the investor is interested in taking a position in XRX stock. To buy the stock outright at $50, where it is currently trading, would entail a capital commitment of $5000 and a risk, at least in theory, of $5000. As an alternative, then, he might wish to buy a 6-month option on 100 shares with an exercise price of $50 and pay that option's current premium—for example, $4—thus spending only $400. The "insurance" angle comes into play when he takes the difference between the stock purchase and the option purchase—$4600—and invests it in Treasury bills for 6 months at a 5% return. His $4600 would thus earn interest of $115, and this return can be considered to have reduced his option cost from $400 to $285 ($400 less $115). Therefore, his risk is commensurately reduced, although he is foregoing any dividends the company might pay. If the stock rises in price, his profit will be $285 less than it would have been had he owned it; conversely, if the stock declines, his potential loss as an option owner will not exceed $285.

Another way of comparing stock ownership with call ownership and

	Stock Ownership	*Call Arithmetic*
A rises 30 points	+ 3000	+ 2715
B is unchanged	−	− 285
C declines 30 points	− 3000	− 285
Net change	−0−	+ 2145
A rises 20 points	+ 2000	+ 1715
B unchanged	−	− 285
C declines 20 points	− 2000	− 285
	−0−	+ 1145

the "arithmetic of losing" would be to watch three stocks (A, B, and C), instead of one, and see what happens if one stock, A, rises, C declines, and B remains unchanged. This is compared with the purchase of a call for $285 on each. See Table/page 159.

Perhaps these examples are loaded, but you can set up any combination, and the principle will hold. The more the stocks rise, the less the percent disadvantage of the call buyer; the more they decline, the greater the advantage of the call buyer. Let's return to the XRX example and construct a table of comparisons, Table 7-1.

Remember the arithmetic of losing? In this example the higher the stock rose, the less the percentage disadvantage of the call buyer. But look at the loss column. If the stock declines, the percentage appreciation required by the stock owner to get to where the call buyer is becomes larger and larger.

	%Appreciation Required For:	
Stock Price	Call Buyer to Catch Up with Stock Buyer	Stock Buyer to Catch Up With Call Buyer
80	80/7715 or 3.69%	
70	70/6715 or 4.24%	
60	60/5715 or 4.99%	
50	50/4715 or 6.04%	
40		4715/4000 or 17.88%
30		4715/3000 or 57.17%
20		4715/2000 or 135.75%

■ *The second—and much more important—precept is to choose which options you will buy based on option valuation and sensitivity, not on the more common rationale that "this stock is going up and I can make a bundle buying the options."*

The latter is one of those self-defeating habits we discussed in the last chapter—putting oneself in the risky business of having to guess correctly whether or not the stock will rise. The former is an example of getting into the options business as a business.

It is important to remember that if you are going to be in options at all—outside of just being a speculator betting on your stock going up—you will need access to the options valuation computer models we discussed previously.

You will want to be able to identify undervalued options, so that you can buy their volatility for less than it is worth.

You will want to be aware of sensitivity, so that you can decide which

TABLE 7-1 Total Assets from Buying Stock versus Buying Calls and Investing the Difference

	Buys Stock			Buys Call & Invests Difference				
Stock Price	Beginning Assets	+ Profit =	Total Assets After	Beginning Assets	Cost of Call	+ Profit =	Total Assets After	Advantage Of call Buyer
80	5000	+ 3000 =	8000	5000	– 285	+ 3000 =	7715	(–285)
70	5000	+ 2000 =	7000	5000	– 285	+ 2000 =	6715	(–285)
60	5000	+ 1000 =	6000	5000	– 285	+ 1000 =	5715	(–285)
50	5000	– =	5000	5000	– 285		4715	(–285)
40	5000	– 1000 =	4000	5000	– 285		4715	+715
30	5000	– 2000 =	3000	5000	– 285		4715	+1715
20	5000	– 3000 =	2000	5000	– 285		4715	+2715

options will give you the "most bang for the buck" relative to the amount of capital you wish to put up. Most options buyers are inclined to buy in-the-money options, because in-the-money options move more per one-point move in the stock; this higher sensitivity, versus out-of-the-money options' lower sensitivity, can be quantified by a computer valuation model.

Sometimes it is smarter to buy a larger position (for the same dollars) in out-of-the-money options. Suppose you were to buy a call for $500, and the sensitivity on that particular option is .8 (that is, for each one-point move in the underlying stock, the option is expected to move 8/10 of a point). If you could also buy, for the same amount of money, four times as many out-of-the-money options (at $125 apiece), each with a .4 sensitivity, you would be wise to choose the latter, since the sensitivity to a price advance would be 1.6 (4 x .4) rather than .8 (1 x .8); to put it another way, you would own the volatility equivalent of 160 shares, rather than 80 shares. Making money in out-of-the-money options does not necessitate that the underlying stock rise to the exercise price of these options. The options will increase in value as the stock goes up, even if the stock does not reach the exercise price, as long as there is a reasonable amount of time left.

Buying calls is a strategy that can result in some spectacular percentage gains, as well as many strike-outs. In fact, the call buyer will probably lose most of the time, but that does not mean he must lose money on balance. If he uses a reliable valuation model to avoid buying overvalued options and to identify undervalued options, he should do much better than if he purchases the same stocks at the same time. The reason for this is that his advantage over the stock purchaser in declining markets is greater than his disadvantage in rising markets—again, the arithmetic of losing.

Selling "Covered" Call Options: More Strategies and More Cautions

The seller of call options is motivated by considerations opposite to those of call buyers. Rather than gain leverage, the seller seeks to reduce his exposure to the stock market. He is willing to give up some of his upside potential, which is uncertain, for the certainty of the premium. This premium will also cushion him against declines and increase his return in flat markets. In essence, he is reducing the volatility of his portfolio.

These objectives can be realized by selling options against securities he already owns (a practice known as "covered writing," since the option sales are "covered" by long security positions). A simple illustration shows how this works:

Suppose an investor owns 100 shares of Xerox (XRX) which is selling at $50 per share. He sells a 6-month option on XRX at $50 for a $4 premium and receives $400 on which he can earn interest. Although he has given up any appreciation XRX might enjoy, the $4 premium has increased his return from XRX considerably, and he suffers no opportunity loss unless XRX rises above $54. Moreover, his option sale in no way affects other income from his stock, because he retains cash dividends earned on his XRX during the time his option remains unexercised.

At the same time, this investor has protected himself from a decline in the market value of his XRX to the extent of his premium. If, for example, XRX declines to $47, he is better off than the investor who only owns XRX stock long, because even though they both have lost $3 in market value the option writer has collected $4 in premiums (which he will keep if XRX remains below $50)—for a net gain of $1. He will not incur a net loss until his XRX drops below $46 at expiration, since his $4 premium has in effect given him $4 worth of "downside" protection.

The options writer has not gained all these advantages, however, without giving up something. His risks are twofold:

- That the option he has sold will be exercised and his stock "called."

As an options seller he has obligated himself to deliver 100 shares of the underlying stock for each option sold if and when the option is "called." He will, of course, receive the exercise price agreed upon in his option contract ($50 per share, or $5000). And, regardless of whether his option is "called," he is entitled to keep the premium he was paid upon sale of his option. He may, of course, repurchase the option at any time prior to being called. This is one of the major advantages of the options exchanges. He may repurchase the option—in a marketplace of many buyers and sellers of that identical option—for more or less than the price at which he sold it, depending largely on the price of XRX common and the time left until expiration of the option.

- That he will not be able to participate in the profits he might otherwise realize if the stock were to rise in value.

Again, this would be an opportunity loss, but the transaction itself would be profitable. (In our example, the investor profited on the stock's move between 50 and 54.) This is true whether or not the covered writer buys back his previously sold options before expiration. If the underlying stock rises significantly and he chooses to buy back the options he has sold (existing obligation) to avoid being called, he will probably have to pay a higher price than he received for selling it, since the options premiums would probably be increasing along with the rising stock price. If he does not buy back his options, he will probably have his stock called away at the exercise price, leaving him with the proceeds at exercise price ($50 per share) plus the proceeds of the premium he received for selling ($4 per share)—but without the profits he would otherwise have enjoyed as the stock rose above that combined level. For example, if he were to sell an October 50 option for $4 on his position when the stock was $50, and the stock were to rise to $60, he would receive the equivalent of $54 for his stock; however, he will have given up 6 points' profit. The most a covered writer can expect to realize is the total of the exercise price plus the premium.

The seller therefore has the risk of ownership, but he also has sold an unknown upside potential for a "certain" premium.

In order to keep the odds in his favor, the writer should always look to sell options only when they are "overvalued." Then he will be selling his upside potential for more than it is statistically worth and at the same time reducing his risk of ownership. If he consistently sells undervalued calls, he will not offset his risk of ownership enough, nor will he benefit from a rising market enough to be better off than if he just owned the stock.

Sensitivity plays a part, too, in covered writing. As previously noted, options almost always have a sensitivity of less than 1.00. Therefore, if a writer is long 100 shares of XRX and against that has sold one call option with a sensitivity of .6, he is in effect long 100 and short 60 shares. He is thus still net long rather than perfectly hedged, so that any price decline in the underlying stock will reduce his stock's market value more than a compensating profit from the decline in his liabilities—that is, the options he has written.

For these reasons, covered writing will always be a bullish posture, and maximum returns will be realized if the underlying stock stays at the same price or rises. Nevertheless, since the covered writer collects premiums as "downside protection," even if the underlying stock goes down, he is still better off than if he merely owned the stock.

Over the years since the creation of national standardized options exchanges, the strategy of "covered writing" has gradually gained respectability and acceptance as a conservative investment technique.

In 1974 the Insurance Department of the State of New York amended a portion of the state's insurance rules and regulations to allow New York-licensed insurance companies to write options on their stock portfolios. In the language of the ruling, the department took the position that "the sale of exchange-traded call options through an exchange, on stock which is already owned by an insurer, provides the insurer with a conservative money management tool by which it can minimize the risks inherent in the ownership of stock.''

In mid-1976 the Mikva Bill passed both houses of Congress and was signed into law as part of the Tax Reform Act, enabling tax-exempt institutions such as pension funds, foundations, and university endowment funds to write call options on common stocks in their portfolios without risking their tax-exempt status or paying taxes on those transactions. Previously, the Internal Revenue Service had not ruled on whether or not it would treat options' premium income as "unrelated business income," so that tax-exempt funds decided to steer clear of the options market rather than risk paying taxes or filing tax returns. The Tax Reform Act also characterized all gains or losses on options as capital transactions.

Today, many financial institutions (including bank trust departments, insurance companies, pension funds, mutual funds, endowments, and charitable foundations) are engaged in covered writing programs. Will increased institutional participation (particularly since institutions tend to be sellers) mean a secular downtrend in options premiums, as some observers contend?

Of course, the options market, like the stock market, responds to supply and demand. When the stock market is rising, options premiums generally rise. This is because buyers are willing to pay more and sellers are not so interested in offsetting the risks of their securities' holdings. Conversely, in a declining market, options buyers are not so anxious to "pay up" for a "right to purchase" that has a limited life span. Sellers will be more anxious to collect premiums and thus cushion the effects of a market decline. Since most buyers and sellers of options are expressing opinions, they will probably be bullish or bearish at the same time, thereby causing over- and undervaluation in options. Some people argue that when the Chicago Board Options Exchange first opened for trading in the spring of 1973, option premiums were quite high relative to subsequent years because of the market's "inefficiency." Option volume was a fraction of what it is today. As participants became more sophisticated, they contend, and particularly as more institutional sellers entered the option markets, premiums declined and will continue at low levels forever. What they overlook is that:

- In the spring of 1973 we were at the top of a bull market that most "experts" thought would go higher.

- The 1973–1974 bear market was a very volatile period.

- Since then, market volatility has receded from those peaks.

- Interest rates were higher then.

All these factors have caused option premiums to be lower today than in 1973. This author's prediction is that when the next wave of enthusiasm engulfs the stock market, there will not be enough sellers to meet the demand for calls, and premiums will expand dramatically to levels of extreme overvaluation, as they always have.*

The investor who elects to try covered writing on his own portfolio must keep in mind the distinctions between writing on a diversified versus an undiversified portfolio.

Covered writing in a *diversified* portfolio makes eminent sense if the investor follows the options-as-a-business principles we have discussed. He must not allow himself to become trapped into the common practice of selling options on the basis of his own judgment that the market, or one stock in particular, is going down or staying flat. Then his results will be only as good as his short-term market judgment. (There have been very few investors, institutional or individual, who have demonstrated consistent skill in timing short-term market swings.) He should instead use a pricing model to identify overvalued options. This method allows him to sell his upside potential for more than it is statistically worth. At the same time, he is gaining an edge in protecting himself against a decline in his underlying stock. But, because options do not have a sensitivity greater than 1.00, he is not fully hedged; thus he is risking losing more in the market value of his underlying stock than he will be collecting in premiums in a declining market.

Nevertheless, because he has reduced the impact of losses, and his disadvantage in rising markets will be less than his advantage in stable or declining markets, he should be able to improve his overall performance. Covered writers who are continuously selling options regardless of valuation will not do nearly as well, because they will frequently sell their upside too cheaply.

Covered writing in an *undiversified* portfolio, however, is often unrewarding. An investor who owns a large block of stock that he does not want to sell because of tax considerations may be tempted to sell options on that stock in order to improve his income. This, however, puts him in an inflexible position.

Since he has a large percentage of his assets tied up in this one stock and its options, he cannot enjoy a rise or protect himself from a decline in the market. If his underlying stock declines, he will be losing more in capital value than he gains in premiums, because the sensitivity of the options is less than 1.00. If his underlying stock rises, in order to avoid getting called, he will have to buy back the previously sold options for cash at higher prices than he received. Of course, he can then sell more

---

*In the explosive spring 1978 rally, this occurred.

options with a higher striking price. But his option-hedged posture means that psychologically he cannot enjoy a price rise in his one, beloved stock. What is more, the whole strategy of selling only overvalued options does not work as well when there is only one position to write against, since he is dealing with probabilities that cannot be expected to produce results in any one instance.

Nevertheless, writing on an undiversified portfolio can be made profitable with sufficient adjustments. Naturally, in flat or declining markets the program would generate substantial additional income. The problem comes when the stock rises in price during the option period; then the option will have to be repurchased, perhaps at a loss and a net cash outlay. The cash outlay can be reduced by selling new options at a higher striking price.

For example, assume that XRX is $50, and that a 90-day call at $50 expiring in April is sold for $350. The stock then rises to $58 in the next 60 days. The investor decides to repurchase the $50 option he sold and is able to do this for $850. At the same time, he sells a new call expiring in July at $60 for $275. At this point he has $800 of unrealized appreciation in the stock, while receiving $625 in premiums and paying out $850 repurchase costs. The net result is a cash outlay of $225, against an unrealized gain of $800, or $575 net ahead before deducting the market value of his liability (the $60 option). There is, therefore, a small opportunity loss and the possibility that the stock might now decline. If it does decline back to $50, say, there is no unrealized benefit, but a cash outlay has been made (the $60 option will expire in this case). For the program to make sense, there must be enough occurrences where the premiums sold do not have to be repurchased. Unless a stock is in a strong uninterrupted uptrend, the odds are good that the investor will be a net beneficiary over the course of a market cycle, repurchases notwithstanding.

One way to reduce the possibility of a cash outlay is to start out by selling options on a small percentage of the position and increasing the percentage as the stock rises. In this way, you are selling more options than you are repurchasing. You will not earn as many dollars if the stock stays flat or declines initially, but you will be able to keep the cash flow positive in a greater number of situations. For example, suppose you own 1000 shares of XRX, which is selling at $50. It is your judgment that the chances of XRX rising above $75 in the next 6 months are remote. You decide to sell two options at $50 for $350 each. If the stock rises to $58, as in the previous example, you may repurchase these two options for $850 each, or $1700, and sell five $60 options at $275 each, or $1375. The net cash flow so far is $700 + $1375 − $1700, or $375. Should the stock run to $68, you are in a position to repurchase those options and sell eight or ten options and still keep a positive cash flow. The account would probably very rarely be fully optioned, and a positive cash flow will almost always be possible. In the instance where the stock runs up so far so fast that you are faced with a repurchase outlay, you can derive some comfort from the fact that the net worth of the account has increased substantially (although not as much as if there had been no option sales). Of course, there is no formula for the rate at which options should be sold. That is a judgment, but an intelligent, high probability range can be established and adhered to, with excellent results. For example:

When R is
Selling at:

			Debit ($)	Credit ($)
$50	Sell	2 options @ 50 for $350 each		700
$58	Buy	2 options @ 50 for $850 each	1,700	
$58	Sell	5 options @ 60 for $300 each		1,500
$68	Buy	5 options @ 60 for $850 each	4,250	
$68	Sell	10 options @ 70 for $400 each		4,000
		Subtotal	5,950	6,200
$78	Buy	10 options @ 70 for $900 each	9,000	
$78	Sell	10 options @ 80 for $450 each		4,500
		Total	14,950	10,700

It is clear that, with the stock at $68 at expiration, there would be an unrealized gain of $18,000 and a profit on the options transactions of $250. If the stock were $78 at expiration, there would be an unrealized gain of $28,000 and a loss on options transactions of $4,250.

As you can see, this technique results in your being better off in all but the lowest probability situations. Not only does the stock have to rise substantially; it has to do it in a limited time period. When a series of options expires, the entire process can begin again at the new price level. If the stock were to rise to $58 and the $60 option were to expire, then the two, five, and ten-option selling program would take you up to $80 rather than $70.

Another possibility is to just sell, if available, way out-of-the-money options on the theory that most of the time they will expire. In that way you can write on the entire position.

Covered writing in either a diversified or undiversified portfolio has one major disadvantage that is inherent in its one option per 100 shares of stock structure: inflexibility. Such inflexibility forces the investor to make "massive retaliation" decisions when the price of the underlying stock(s) declines. A simple example illustrates:

Suppose you own 100 XRX, now selling at $50. Against that you have sold one July 50 XRX at $4, thus collecting $400 and protecting yourself against a decline to the extent of 4 points (at expiration); that is, to $46 on your stock. Now suppose the market declines and your stock goes to $45. You choose to buy back your July 50 XRX, which is now selling at $1. You have made a 3-point profit on your option sale and have lost 5 points in the market value of your stock, so that you are now behind 2 points. What do you do?

If you fear a further decline in the market, you might now sell one XRX July 45 against your stock position. Let us say you collect a $3 premium on that sale. Now you are protected against further deterioration in your stock by 3 points, or to $42. The stock declines to $40. Again, you repurchase the $45 option for $1 (you had sold it for $3) and sell a $40 option for $2½. (These options have different amounts of time to run, so the premiums are not proportional.) So far you have sold options for $4, $3, and $2½ and have repurchased options for $2 and $1, for a net premium of $6½, while the stock is down 10 points.

The stock now rallies to $49, and the $40 option must be repurchased for $10½. The result to date is a 4-point loss in options and a one-point loss in the stock. This is not good. At some point, perhaps, it might work out favorably. Or, you could rationalize the first decline and just let the option expire, consoling yourself by thinking that at $40 you would have held the stock anyway, so that you are better off to the extent of the original premium.

But rationalizations are not realities. The point is that covered writing offers only a partial hedge. The lower the stock, the less the hedge. As you follow the stock down with lower strike options, you increase the chance of whipsaw. You cannot recover your losses point for point unless you sell such a deep in-the-money option that you have neutralized the position. In that case, you would have been better off selling the stock. Or, you could have repurchased the original $50 option and sold another $50 option of a more distant month. This procedure would eliminate the chance of whipsaw, but it would not offer the same downside protection, since, with the $50 option now out of the money, you will receive fewer dollars' premium. You are depending on the stock to rise in price in order to come out whole.

Conversely, if the stock were to rise to $58 and you were to repurchase the option you originally sold at $4 for $10 and sell a new $60 option for $3, and if the stock retreated back to $50, you would be even on the stock and have a 3-point loss in option transactions before commissions. If you were willing to earn just the original premium, you would let the stock be called and not run the risk of whipsaw that is part of the covered writing adjustment process.

What is more, one-to-one writing gives you limited downside protection—limited to the amount of premium you can collect. If your stock position has lost 10 points and you have collected 4 points in premiums from option sales, you are better off than the investor who only owns the stock; however, you have still lost money in the stock's decline.

The pricing model which you use to calculate premium values can also be used to calculate risk reduction—that is, the reduction in the probability of loss from selling the option. This can be an important figure. It is not the arithmetic division of premiums by market price, but a probability calculation of how much protection is really given by the sale of a call option. For example, a $4 premium on a $50 stock that is not volatile gives considerably more risk reduction than the same $4 on a highly volatile $50 stock. Therefore, the level of risk reduction should be a consideration, along with overvaluation and return when entering into a covered writing position.

Covered writing can earn excellent returns in a rising market. If losses can be kept to a minimum in declining markets, the overall results can be good. One way to accomplish this is to own stocks and sell options only when premiums are overvalued and to have the discipline to stay out of the market when the numbers are not there.

"Uncovered" or "Naked" Call Writing

A covered call option means that the writer owns the stock or a security convertible to the stock against which it is written. In the case of "naked" call writing, the writer does not own the stock; the option is written against cash or against collateral consisting of Treasury bills or bonds, or against other common stocks, warrants, convertible bonds or convertible preferreds—any security but the one on which the option was sold. In any case, a naked call writer must deposit and maintain with his broker sufficient funds or other collateral to assure that the stock can be purchased for delivery if and when the option is exercised.

As long as the underlying stock does not rise above the striking price plus the premium at expiration, it is possible for a naked call writer to realize profits. *At expiration* is emphasized, because the further the stock is from expiration, the more premium the naked call writer may have to pay to repurchase. Even if the striking price is above the market price, he can suffer losses on repurchases. For example: if XRX is at $50 and a $60 option is sold for $1½, the option may rise to $3 if XRX goes to $58 and not too much time has passed.

The naked writer is, in fact, the reverse of the call buyer. He is putting his money on the line on a bet that a particular stock will decline or not rise very much. But, unlike the call buyer (who can limit his losses to the amount of premium he pays and who can let his profits run), the naked call seller has limited profits (limited to the premiums he has collected) and potentially unlimited losses. This risk stems from the possibility of a sharp rise in the market price of the stock, leading to the potential threat of exercise of his option. In order to then satisfy his delivery obligations, he might have to buy the stock in the marketplace at a price well above the exercise price. Even if he sought to avoid exercise by buying back his previously sold option, he might, in a rising market, have to buy the option back at a loss, perhaps a substantial one.

The naked call writer's risks in a rising market are exacerbated by options' sensitivity, since out-of-the-money options' sensitivity increases as the price of the stock rises toward and above the exercise price. Suppose a naked writer sold 10 XRX July 60s when the stock was trading at $50. At the time, each XRX July 60 had a sensitivity of .15; thus the writer was in effect short the equivalent of 150 shares at $60. However, as XRX subsequently rose in price, the July 60 options became more sensitive (that is, they tended to move more per 1-point move in the stock). By the time XRX had risen to $60, the options had a sensitivity of .8, so that the naked call writer was effectively short 800 shares. Options' sensitivity characteristic therefore increases the naked writer's upside exposure as the stock rises.

However, the major disadvantage of naked call writing is not so much the risk of a rising market as the burdens imposed by exchange and brokerage house collateral requirements. The mechanics of collateral requirements will be explained in detail in Chapter 9, "Constructing and Adjusting Your Variable Hedge." Suffice it here to say that collateral requirements rise faster than the price of the underlying security. Thus while at expiration the underlying stock theoretically has to go up a certain amount before the naked call writer of an out-of-the-money option begins to lose money, collateral requirements have been rising before the stock reaches that point, resulting in a situation in which the writer might be forced to buy back his naked call, even before the stock gets to the exercise price. What is more, there is no distinction made for collateral purposes between an option that has 6 months to run and one that has one day to run. Thus it is possible to have a margin call even if the position is still potentially profitable.

For example, if an April $60 call with 6 months to run is sold for $2 when the stock is at $50, the collateral requirement will be 30% of $50, or

$1500 less the $200 premium, or $1300 less the difference between 60 and 50 ($1000), for a requirement of $300. If the stock rises to $56 one week before expiration and the option is selling for ¼, the collateral required to support this position is now 30% of $56, or $1680 less $400 (60–56), or $1280. The amount on deposit is the original $300 plus the premium of $200, so a call may be issued for the difference, $1180.

One way the uncovered writer can reduce his increasing collateral requirements as the underlying stock rises is to buy back his originally sold option and sell a higher priced option. This, however, will usually require an additional cash outlay, since he is probably paying more for his existing obligation than he would be receiving for his new one. Moreover, it is sometimes not possible to do this, because the exchanges may not yet have created the higher-strike-price option if the stock has not traded there recently.

Spreads

Another widely practiced option strategy is spreading. Briefly, spreading is the simultaneous purchase and sale of calls (or puts) on the same underlying stock. Thus one might create a spread with the same striking price, but with different expiration months (for instance, buying XRX July 40s and selling XRX April 40s). This is called a *calendar spread* (and is also referred to as a "time spread" and a "horizontal spread").

Please note that it is important to be purchasing the more distant option, since that collateralizes the nearer one. The reverse is not true. Suppose that the investor notes that XRX common stock is selling for $52, and that the XRX April 50 is selling at $4 and the XRX July 50 at $5½. Since he believes XRX will stay flat over that time period, he gives his broker an order to "buy one July 50 and sell one April 50 for a 1½ debit." His buy order may be filled at $5¾ and his sell order at $4¼. A spreader would ordinarily establish his two positions by giving his broker an order without price limits, but simply with "1½ debit" or "2 credit" or whatever spread he desires. This gives the broker maximum flexibility in filling the order.

By the middle of April the price of XRX has declined to $48. The April 50 no longer has any intrinsic value, but is trading at ⅛. The July 50 (which has also lost intrinsic value) is trading at $2¾ because of the value of the remaining time (it still has 3 months to run). The spread has now widened to 2⅝. The spreader can buy back his April 40 at ⅛, sell the July 40 at 2¾, and realize a 2⅝ "credit." That credit less his original 1½ investment (debit) leaves him with a net profit of 1⅛, or $112.50 (4⅛ profit on the April 40 less a 3-point loss on the July 40).

Another type of spread is the *price spread* (also called "vertical spread''), which involves the simultaneous purchase and sale of calls (or puts) on the same stock with the same expiration date, but with different striking prices. The price spread is either a bull or bear spread. The bull spread is so called because the profitability is a result of the stock rising.

For example, if the XRX April 45 is selling for $3 and the April 50 is selling for $1, the spreader is paying $2 (3–1) for the spread. If the stock rises to $55 by expiration, then the April 45 will be selling for $10 (55–45) and the April 50 for $5 (55–50), for a differential of 5 (10–5). No matter how high the stock goes, the differential will not exceed 5 (the difference between 45 and 50). However, the spreader had paid only $2 and can close out the spread for $5, so he earned a very high return (150%). The bear spread is the opposite. If he sells the April 45 for $3 and buys the 50 for $1, he receives a ''credit'' of $2. If the stock declines, the option he bought for $1 will expire for a loss, but he can buy back the one he sold for less than $3. If the stock declines below $40, it will expire worthless, and he will earn the 3 points he sold it for, less the 1 he lost on the April 45 for a 2-point profit. Since he would have had to put up 3 points in order to sell the spread (45–40 less the credit of 2 he received for the spread) he will have made a profit of $2 on an investment of $3 (See Table 7–2).

The disadvantages of spreading are threefold: the transaction costs eat quickly into profit margins, since establishing and closing a spread can involve four transactions (buying and selling 40s; buying and selling 45s) (see Table 7-2). The ''overhead'' created by these transactions' costs means that the investor must be very accurate in predicting the market action of the underlying stock and its options if he is to come out ahead. Finally, and most important, the ordinary investor is competing with professional arbitrageurs. As much as half the volume on the option exchanges is done by market makers and brokerage firm traders, many of whom are spreading or creating the markets. Not only do such professional spreaders enjoy higher profit margins, since they are non-commission paying accounts, but they also spend the whole trading day watching each price change and communicating with the floor traders (if they are not actually there themselves) at the various options exchanges. The outsider obviously has a problem beating them at their own game.

Puts

In June 1977 puts were introduced to exchange trading. They offer a whole new investment dimension. Thanks to exchange-traded puts, you have many more avenues of expression about optionable stocks, much more flexibility in profiting from the new stock market's volatility, and an entirely new set of weapons against the arithmetic of losing.

TABLE 7-2 Comparison of Commission Costs of Spreads of Different Quantities (CBOE Schedule)

Investment	# Options	Buy @ 4	Sell @ 10	Profit on Long	Sell @ 2	Buy @5.	Loss on Short	Net Profit
	1 no comm.	400.00	1,000.00	600.00	200.00	500.00	300.00	300.00
250.01	1 w/comm.	425.00	974.95	549.95	174.99	525.00	350.01	199.94
	5 no comm.	2,000.00	5,000.00	3,000.00	1,000.00	2,500.00	1,500.00	1,500.00
1,123.04	5 w/comm.	2,068.00	4,902.83	2,834.83	944.96	2,574.50	1,629.54	1,205.29
	10 no comm.	4,000.00	10,000.00	6,000.00	2,000.00	5,000.00	3,000.00	3,000.00
2,216.07	10 w/comm.	4,118.00	9,827.66	5,709.66	1,901.93	5,127.00	3,225.07	2,484.59
	25 no comm.	10,000.00	25,000.00	15,000.00	5,000.00	12,500.00	7,500.00	7,500.00
5,419.17	25 w/comm.	10,232.00	24,647.16	14,415.16	4,812.83	12,754.50	7,941.67	6,473.49
	50 no comm.	20,000.00	50,000.00	30,000.00	10,000.00	25,000.00	15,000.00	15,000.00
10,754.34	50 w/comm.	20,422.00	49,501.33	29,079.33	9,667.66	25,452.00	15,784.34	13,294.99

Puts are easy enough to understand on the surface. But if you are used to thinking in terms of calls, you will find that you need to literally turn 180 degrees mentally before you can deal comfortably with puts' mechanics, risks, and opportunities. After a while, however, you will find that puts become second nature, like driving a standard transmission car.

Puts are the right to sell a stock at a fixed price and for a fixed period of time. Therefore, puts increase in value as a stock declines (in contrast to calls, which increase in value as a stock rises). The buyer of a put benefits from a decline in the underlying stock, and a put seller's cost to cancel out his obligation increases as a stock declines—both cases again exactly opposite to that of calls.

Why Buy Puts

Put buyers are usually motivated either by the desire to profit from a declining market or the desire to protect an existing position.

Profit from a declining market has heretofore been the province of short sellers. However, puts offer the potential short seller more leverage and less risk. A short seller of 100 shares of XRX at $50, for example, would be required to borrow the stock (his broker can do that for him), deposit a margin of 50% (this can be changed by the Federal Reserve Board) of the market value of the stock ($2500), and hope to be able to purchase the stock at a lower price to cover his short position. However, if XRX were to rise instead of fall, he would be faced with additional margin calls as well as an unlimited upside liability (since, theoretically, a stock can rise without limit but can only decline to zero). The short seller is also required to pay dividends during the period he is short.

In contrast, the buyer of a put to sell 100 XRX at $50 can profit from the stock's decline at only a fraction of the cost involved in shorting the stock itself, with a limited liability and no dividend payout. Let us say that in January XRX was selling at $50 in the marketplace, and a July 50 put was selling for a premium of $3. The buyer of such a put could lose no more than the $3 premium he had paid, if the stock rises. Should the stock decline to $40, his July 50 put will increase in value to at least $10, and he can sell the put itself on the options exchanges, thus reaping a profit; of, if he chooses, he can purchase the stock for $4000 and deliver it against payment of $5000, for a gain of $1000 less the $300 cost of the put and transaction costs.

Put buying can also provide long-term investors with a kind of low cost "disaster insurance." Suppose you own 100 shares of XRX bought at a cost of $20, and XRX is now selling at $50. Suppose, too, that you are concerned about the possibility of an unforeseen market dip substantially reducing the value of your stock. (Most declines are unforeseen by most everybody; otherwise, no one would ever lose money in stocks.)

You are reluctant to sell your low-cost basis stock because of the capital gains tax liability such a sale would incur. How can you protect yourself from a decline in your existing position? Like the homeowner who is concerned about his risk of unaffordable financial loss through fire, tornados, or other disasters, you want to be able to buy inexpensive protection against a loss you cannot afford to suffer. The answer is an undervalued out-of-the-money put. In this case, you might be able to buy a put at $40 which, for a cost of ½ or ¼ point ($50 or $25), will protect you for 6 to 9 months.

At this low cost you can continue to buy "disaster insurance" each time your put expires, if another is available. A put with a higher striking price gives you more protection, but it may be too expensive to carry. Thus while you might be willing to endure a 10-point decline in your XRX (from 50 to 40)—as in a deductible casualty policy—you would pay for a low cost means of shielding yourself from what could conceivably be an almost total loss.

Over the past few years, declines of 75% or more in "good" stocks were not unusual.

Put buying thus offers investors a more complete hedge against market declines than one-to-one covered writing, where your downside protection is only as great as the premiums received.

Why Sell Puts

Put sellers are motivated by the potential to:

■ Purchase stock at lower than the current market price (current price less the premium).

■ Profit from a rise in the stock which would allow the seller to keep the premium while his put remains unexercised.

■ Repurchase the put for less than he sold it.

In exchange for the premium he is paid, a put writer agrees to purchase the underlying stock at the exercise price if, at any time prior to expiration of his put, the stock is "put" to him. For example, let us say that when XRX is selling at $50, you sell a put on the stock with an exercise price of $50 and an expiration 6 months hence, and receive a $3 premium. If the market price of XRX stays at $50 or rises above that during the succeeding 6 months, you will not be "put" stock. Therefore, you would keep the $3 premium. If, however, XRX were to decline to $45 before expiration, you might be "put" stock; that is, you might be required to buy it at the stipulated exercise price of $50. Your net cost, however, would be $47 ($50 reduced by your $3 premium already collected). Should XRX decline to $40 in the marketplace and you were "put" the stock at $50, you would be paying a net cost of $47 per share for stock you could have bought in the open market for $40. Of course, like call writers, put writers can terminate their contractual obligations at any time prior to exercise by entering into closing purchase transactions.

Straddles and Combinations

More sophisticated options strategies include using straddles and combinations. A straddle is a put and call on the same stock, with a common strike price and expiration date. If puts and calls on the same stock have different features (terms), the package is called a combination. These combinations can be of infinite variety.

Buyers of straddles generally expect that the underlying stock will be volatile in either direction. Thus they are motivated by the opportunity to make a profit—with a limited risk—if the stock rises and/or declines substantially.

A specific example of a straddle purchase is this:

If XRX is currently selling at $50 and you expect it to fluctuate widely in the next 6 months, you might buy a 6-month call with a $50 exercise price for a premium of $5 and a 6-month put with a $50 exercise price for a premium of $3 (for a total straddle premium of $8). Therefore, you would make money if Xerox were to trade more than 8 points up (or over $58) or more than 8 points down (under $42). You would only lose all your premium money if XRX were to stay at $50 for 6 months. If the stock were to rise to, say, $60 at expiration, your profit would be 10 points less your premium, or $2. (In this case, your $50 call could be exercised at $60, for a 10-point profit, and your put would have expired.)

If XRX declines to $40, you could buy the stock, exercise your put to sell at $50, and your call would expire (again for a 10-point profit less your premium, or a net of $2).

Between the time you buy the straddle and the time it expires, you may, of course, trade against it as market conditions change. If the price of the underlying stock goes down, for example, you could sell the put at a profit and keep the call in the hope that your stock will rally before expiration.

Sellers of straddles generally expect the stock to trade in a narrow range. If they are right, they can collect and keep premiums from both their puts and calls. But if they are wrong, and the stock both rises and falls substantially before expiration, they could conceivably have both their puts and calls exercised and incur substantial loss. (They might also benefit substantially from such an occurrence. It would depend on the time sequence and what action would be taken.)

A specific straddle sale might look like this: If XRX is selling at $50 and you expect it to fluctuate only slightly during the next 6 months, you could write (sell) a $50 call for a premium of $5 and write (sell) a $50 put for a premium of $3 (or a total straddle premium of $8). If the stock stays close to $50 for 6 months, you may be able to keep both premiums, for an 8-point profit (which is very unlikely). If it rises only to $55, your call would be exercised, creating a $5 loss, which, subtracted from your $8 of premiums collected, would net a profit of $3. If it declines only to, say, $45, your put would be exercised, creating a $5 loss, but your premiums of $8 would mean your net profit would be $3.

A straddle seller may also trade against his straddle during its lifetime. If the underlying stock declines, for example, he could repurchase the call and keep the put liability in hopes of a subsequent rise. However, more than a straddle buyer, he faces the risk of being whipsawed if the stock both rises and falls before expiration, e.g. the stock rises substantially above the striking price, his call is exercised, and he covers; the stock then declines substantially below the striking price, the put is exercised, and he sells. He has experienced the worst of all possible worlds! If the straddle seller attempts to protect himself from whipsaw by remaining short the stock which was called (and putting up the necessary collateral) he can still suffer additional loss if the stock continues to move higher. Remember that the seller has no control over when he is exercised.

Comparing Puts and Calls

The relationship between buyers and writers of calls and buyers and writers of puts invites some interesting comparisons. The seller of a call who owns stock is in a position comparable to the short seller who writes a put (except that the short seller has unlimited upside liability, while the stock owner's risk is limited to the difference between the stock's market price and zero).

The other distinction between the covered call writer and the short seller who writes puts is that the stock owner receives dividends while the short seller pays them. The uncovered writer of a put has obligated himself to buy the stock at exercise price, so that his risk is the price of the stock (it can only go down to zero). Since he has the risk of ownership but no upside potential, he is in a position comparable to the covered call writer, except that he does not collect dividends, and the premium he recieves will probably be less than that of the call writer. This is offset by the fact that he can earn interest on the money that is not committed in the stock. The uncovered call writer, like the short seller, has unlimited risk, but he does not have to pay out dividends.

Similarly, the "cross-pollenization" between puts and calls gives us some perspective on which strategies to employ. Since the economic effect of a put can be created by selling a stock short and buying a call (this is a "synthetic put"), the cost of an exchange-traded put will not normally exceed the cost of this "synthetic" transaction.

Why is this so? Arbitrageurs would prevent it from being otherwise. For example, if you were to sell short 100 shares of XRX at $50 and buy a call at $50 for a premium of $4, you are in the same position as a put buyer who pays a premium of $4 for a put at $50. In other words, in both cases you would make money to the extent that XRX declines more than 4 points, and your maximum risk would be 4, assuming there were no dividends to be paid during the period.

The advent of exchange-traded puts has not canceled investors' ability to execute such short-stock/buy call "synthetic puts." If an exchange-traded put were selling at $6 and an investor could create a synthetic put for $5 and sell it for $6 with no risk, arbitrageurs would quickly close the gap. (Only professional arbitrageurs, however, could ordinarily obtain such a profit, since their transaction costs are lower, and they earn interest on short sales.)

This is not to say that puts cannot be overvalued. They can, but they are limited by the price of the call (except, of course, if short sellers cannot borrow stock).

How do overvaluation and undervaluation fit into an investor's perception of puts? The value of a put should theoretically be less than that of a call, because capital market theories assume that stocks have an upward bias—and, in fact, the stocks have, over the long run, demonstrated such an upward bias—and because stock prices can rise more points than they can fall. Another reason would be that calls are a substitute for a cash consuming position (long stock), while puts are a substitute for a cash generating position (short stock).

Furthermore, investors are psychologically oriented toward "things" increasing in value. Accumulation of wealth over the centuries has resulted from ownership of property, rather than from selling in advance of a decline in the value of an asset.

Nonetheless, puts have had higher values than calls at certain times—mainly during bear markets, when the general investor expectation is that prices will continue to go lower. Historically, these periods have not lasted long. In past markets, when puts have become overvalued, it has usually been correct to sell them. This is based on the observation of puts trading in the over-the-counter market, since they have not, until recently, been traded on exchanges.

Comparing Puts, Calls, Straddles, and Stocks

At this point, it might be helpful to summarize the relationships between puts, calls, straddles, and stocks by using a single formu¹⁻

C = Call	**St** = Straddle
P = Put	+ = Long
S = Stock (100 shares)	− = Short

The first relationship is one we have already discussed:

P = C − S   A long put equals a long call and short stock. If you are short stock, you have downside potential, but your upside risk is limited to the premium paid.

S = C − P   Long stock equals a long call and a short put. Being long a call and short a put is the economic equivalent to owning a stock, since you own the upside potential through the long call and have the risk of ownership through the short put, i.e., stock will be put to you if it declines.

C = S + P   A long call equals long stock and a long put. By being long a call, you have the upside potential of the stock, but you have paid a premium to limit loss.

− C = − S − P   A short call equals short stock plus a short put. In this position, your profit is the premium on the call and your liability on the upside is unlimited.

− P = S − C   A short put equals long stock and a short call. Being long a stock and short its call is the covered writing position and is equivalent to a short put, since you have limited your profit to the premium and have incurred the risk of ownership.

− S = P − C   Short stock equals a long put and a short call. In either case, you would profit from a decline in the price of the stock and suffer from a rise in price.

St = P + C   A straddle is equal to a long put and a long call.

St = C + C − S (or 2C − S)   A straddle equals two long calls and short stock. Seeing these two formulas together, one can understand that, since a put is equal to short stock and a long call, then a long straddle (put and call) is equal to short stock and two long calls. In either case, profits are made outside the range of the stock price plus or minus the premium. However, similarly:

St = S + 2P   A straddle equals long stock and two long puts, since the implication remains that profit occurs outside a range.

$- St = - P - C.$ A short straddle equals a short put and a short call.
$- St = S - 2C$ By substitution, we can also see that a short straddle equals long stock and two short calls. Similarly:
$- ST = - S - 2P$ A short straddle is also equal to short stock and two short puts. In each of these three cases, profit is earned when the stock stays within the range created.

It is clear from these three formulas that selling a straddle when one is long stock is a very bullish position. Since the short straddle is equivalent to being long stock and short two calls, then, if you are already long stock, you have the equivalent of a 200 share position and short two calls. This means you have the downside risk on 200 shares, and you therefore need the stock to go up to avoid the double exposure.

The formulas we have used to clarify the various relationships between stock and options do not, for simplicity's sake, take into account such other important factors as dividends and the costs of tying up capital. For example, buying a call and selling a put is equivalent to owning the stock—except that you do not receive dividends. Nevertheless, buying a call and selling a put means that you have less capital tied up than if you were to buy the stock.

The Options Options Create

These descriptions of options strategies have revealed that each has a major disadvanntage:

- The put/call buyer must be right on the stock to win.

- The one-to-one covered writer is constrained by inflexibility, and he needs a flat or a rising market to earn a good return.

- The naked put/call seller faces great collateral and price risks.

- The spreader cannot under most circumstances compete profitably with the professionals.

- The straddle buyer and/or seller has to be correct in predicting volatility.

All of these strategies require that the investor make an odds-against forecast upon which his profitability is dependent.

And so we turn, in the next chapter, to our recommended strategy for surviving/succeeding in the new stock market: the variable hedge.

CHAPTER EIGHT

The Variable Hedge

At last, there is an investment technique that tips the odds in the investor's favor.

Variable hedging is a conservative approach, characterized by low volatility and relatively small fluctuations in net worth, that operates on a principle completely at odds with conventional investment techniques. Rather than depending on the market or on the rising value of his assets, the investor who uses variable hedging depends only on the most likely occurrences—that stocks will continue to trade with approximately the same volatility as in the recent past; that is, volatility changes slowly, especially in the efficent market stocks.

What is more, if the unlikely happens, and volatility increases abruptly (if it decreases, it is a positive development for the variable hedger), variable hedging allows for temporizing moves that adapt the hedge to the unexpected.

Meanwhile, the investor who uses variable hedging is consistently earning more than a market rate of return. Thus it is an excellent technique for making money and, particularly, for keeping it, since a characteristic of this investment technique is the reduction of the investor's exposure to the volatility of today's stock market.

Stated as simply as possible, variable hedging involves:

- Identifying overvalued options (where buyers are paying more for volatility than it is worth);

- Selling combinations of those options against a long stock position in such a way as to create wide profit ranges—which are the most likely price ranges in which the underlying stocks will be selling in the time up to the options' expiration date.

Thus variable hedging provides a "band" within which the options writer will realize a profit. At the same time, it solves covered writing's biggest problem—inflexibility. Because the variable hedger is willing to be short more than one option per 100 shares of long stock, he may sell additional options and/or substitute other options with or without repurchasing those initially sold in order to adjust to changing realities.

The following is a simplified example of a variable hedge, to illustrate how this technique works:

Buy XRX at $50
Sell 4 October 60 at $2   (180 days until expiration)

In creating this particular hedge, the decision to use these options and their underlying stock was a deliberate one, based on a computer pricing model that showed (1) the options to be overvalued, (2) their sensitivity to be .25, so that the investor knew how many to sell in order to match the pricing model's parameters for a neutral hedge, and (3) the probability of achieving a 20% (or any other acceptable) return, by calculating the width of the band in which the underlying stock can trade and still earn that return and (4) the reduction of risk in owning the stock.

In other words, the discipline required by the variable hedging technique forces the investor to manage his stocks, as we have discussed, as if they were a business—he must stifle his ego, and, instead of guessing which way the market will go, he must make choices based on probabilities, with the objectives of earning good returns and reducing risks. *Thus he starts out with the odds in his favor.*

(One sometimes-heard objection to the variable hedging concept is, "Why should I have to buy stocks I don't like just to sell options on them?" This reflects another self-defeating attitude similar to the idea that you "win" in the marketplace by divining the market's future direction. There is little relationship between an investor's affection for a stock and that stock's market appreciation since, to paraphrase Adam Smith, the stock you love does not love you. It does not even know you own it. The most beloved stocks in most investors' portfolios are those that are down from their cost. Since the investor cannot admit to himself that he has made a mistake, he keeps the stock in the hope that his dreams will come true. With variable hedging, we approach investing as a discipline— buying stocks that are already efficiently priced and selling their over-valued options—not just hopes and dreams. We are capitalizing on others' quixotic tendencies.)

The profit range created by this particular hedge is $42 to $66 at expiration. This is easily figured. The sale of the 4 XRX October 60s at $2 creates a total premium of $8. This hedge would therefore still be profitable until XRX declines to $42, because at that point the investor has lost 8 points in the stock, but he would have made 8 points in premium. On the upside, $66 is the point at which the hedge is no longer profitable, because at $66 the investor had already made 16 points on his long position, has collected 8 points in premiums for a total of 24 points, and is now obligated to sell 400 shares of stock at $60 (which has a market value of $66), resulting in a 24-point loss.

The investor's vulnerability to volatility is greatly diminished, since the pricing model shows that XRX is unlikely to trade outside a range of $42 to $66 (24 points) within any 180-day period. Keep in mind, too, that we are recommending a variable hedging approach to an entire portfolio of, say, ten stocks, so that while three or four might conceivably exceed their profit ranges in any period, the rest will probably remain in the high profitability area (see Table 8-1).

Maximum profitability for this hedge is 18 points, and maximum annualized rate of return is 18 (profit)/42 (investment) $\times$ 2 (to annualize 180 days), or 85.7%. While this is not likely (since it would require XRX to be exactly $60 at expiration), the wide band of profitability created by this hedge makes an attractive rate of return possible, even though the stock fluctuates quite widely. Table 8-1 shows how this is possible and compares it to a covered write (1:1) of the same option:

TABLE 8-1   Comparative Rates of Return (Not annualized) Covered Write vs. 4:1 Variable Hedge

Stock Price	Covered Write (1:1) % Rate of Return	Variable Hedge (4:1) % Rate of Return	
65	25.0	7.1	less likely price for
62½	25.0	25.0	XRX
60	25.0	42.9	
57½	19.8	36.9	
55	14.6	30.9	more likely price for
50	4.2	19.0	XRX
45	(6.3)	7.1	
42½	(11.5)	1.2	
40	(15.6)	(4.8)	less likely price for XRX

Maximum profitability occurs if the stock is at $60 at expiration, because at that point it would not be called away, and the options would expire worthless. Therefore, the investor keeps the stock, on which he has a 10-point profit, as well as his premiums received (8 points), for a total profit of 18 points. This is the ideal result, but a very unlikely one. However, it is clear that the variable hedge yields a superior return to the covered write (at $60) at every price from zero up to $62½.

We can also make the comparison of selling one $50 option at $5 vs. two at $5. Similar results are observed, but the price at which the return is equal is lower ($55.60).

TABLE 8-2   Comparative Rates of Return (not annualized) Covered Write vs. 2:1 Variable Hedge

Stock Price	Covered Write (1:1) % Rate of Return	Variable Hedge (2:1) % Rate of Return	
65	11.1	(12.5)	less likely price for
62½	11.1	(6.3)	XRX
60	11.1	0	
57½	11.1	6.3	more likely price for
55	11.1	12.5	XRX
50	11.1	25.0	
45	0	12.5	
42½	(5.6)	6.3	
40	(11.1)	0	less likely price for XRX

Keep in mind too that XRX is just one of a portfolio, and that this hedge as originally constructed need not stay the same if the market changes direction. As stocks approach their breakeven points, adjustments to the breakeven points can be made by substituting other options, which would move the entire range for that position up or down.

CHAPTER NINE

Constructing and Adjusting Your Variable Hedge

Suppose that you have found the concept and the discipline of variable hedging attractive, and that you wish to undertake running your stocks as a business. How do you get started?

Step 1: Identify a Number of Overvalued Options

What are overvalued options?

As you will recall from earlier chapters, the concept of option valuation involves many more measurable factors than that of stock valuation. These factors are:

- Time left in the option.

- Market price of the underlying stock.

- Exercise price of the option.

- The cost of money (level of interest rates).

- Dividends to be paid during the option period.

- Trading volatility of the underlying stock.

Taking all these factors into consideration, one can, with common sense, tell roughly whether a particular option is over- or undervalued—as in our comparison of a 6-month option on GM at $70 when the stock was selling at $70 and the option was priced at ⅛, with an identical option priced at $20.

Far better than common sense, however, are any number of computer pricing models available today that calculate the fair value of every available option. Once you know the fair value, you can see how much the market price of that option represents overvaluation or undervaluation.

Which computer pricing model should you use?

A number of brokers offer such computer access today. Find one which the broker uses for his own arbitraging. If he puts his own money on the computer's calculations, it is good enough for you.

How can you choose the most attractive options for selling from among your list of overvalued possibilities?

It is difficult to compare how much one option is overvalued as opposed to another, since your list will undoubtedly include options on different stocks, with different expirations, different market prices, and different exercise prices. You will need to come up with a common denominator to determine relative overvaluation. Here is how to do it: Subtract an option's fair value from its market value. Express this as a percentage of the underlying stock's market price, and annualize it (if it is a 3-month option you will multiply by 4, if it is a 6-month option you will multiply by 2, etc.) This will give you a "yield" figure which we will call "incremental return from overvaluation." Now you will have one "incremental return" figure for each potential option-writing candidate, and you can compare them.

If your incremental return on a particular option is 5% or more, it is a good candidate, for this means that you can use this option to increase your yield from the stock itself by an additional 5%.

One caveat: Be sure that any overvalued option you are considering has gained its overvaluation in an environment in which at least 20 of those options were traded. This will increase the probability that its high premium is not just an aberration, and that the option is liquid enough to execute your sales.

Here is an example of figuring "incremental return from overvaluation" in order to compare options as writing candidates:

Stock: Ford (F), now selling for $55¼ in May
Option: F July 55
Market price: $3.00
Fair value: $2.50 (as determined by computer pricing model)
Difference: $0.50
"Overvaluation yield" (difference divided by market price of stock): .009497
Time left to run in option: 2 months
Incremental return: 5.42% (.009497 x 12/2)

Here is another example that compares options on the same stock with two different maturities:

Stock: Upjohn (UPJ), now selling for $30¼ in May

Option:	UPJ July 30	UPJ October 30
Market price:	$1.75	$2.50
Fair value:	$1.40	$2.26
Difference:	$0.35	$0.24
Overvaluation yield:	.01157	.00793
Time left:	2 months	5 months
Incremental return:	6.94%	1.90%

With "incremental return" as our common denominator, it is now easy to see that the UPJ July 30 is more overvalued than either the F July 55 or the UPJ October 30, and that the UPJ July 30 offers the greatest potential incremental return.

These examples are based on a one-to-one relationship—that is, covered writing. In order to adjust the figure to reflect the variable hedge, the overvaluation should be adjusted for the number of options that will be sold per 100 shares of stock (the reciprocal of the sensitivity figure) and then compared with other neutral hedges. For example:

Option	(1) Neutral Hedge	(2) Absolute Over- valuation	# Shares × Overvaluation (Col. 1 × Col. 2)	÷ Market Price of Stock	× Annual- ization	= Incremental Annualized Return (%)
UPJ July 30	1.67:1	.35	.5845	1.932	12/2	11.59
UPJ Oct 30	1.64:1	.24	.3936	1.301	12/5	3.12
F July 55	1.85:1	.50	.925	1.674	12/2	10.04

The UPJ July 30 is clearly the most attractive on an incremental return basis.

Of course, if the incremental return turns out to be a minus number, you would not even consider this option as a writing candidate, since it is undervalued rather than overvalued. Were you to purchase this stock and sell this option, you would be selling volatility for less than it is worth while incurring the risk of owning the stock. With such an undervalution you are better off owning this option than the underlying stock itself— since you would be getting the stock's volatility without having the risk of ownership.

Once you have chosen your list of options with the greatest relative overvaluation (by using the common denominator of calculating incremental return),how many should you consider as possible positions when completing the steps outlined below?

It depends on the amount of money you are considering. There is a trade-off among diversification, transaction costs, and flexibility. A guideline might be three to five different stock-and-option positions per $50,000, up to $150,000. Above $150,000 you do not need to add too many, as you will have a minimum of nine positions by then, which is a reasonable level of diversification.

With the process of identifying and comparing overvalued options completed, you can now move on to the next step:

Step 2: Determine a Neutral Hedge

With this step, you will be creating a hedge that should make money no matter what the market or the stock does (although large gaps or air pockets are a risk, since you cannot adjust gradually)—all a part of the philosophy behind variable hedging, which aims to remove you from the "no-win" strategy of having to guess the stock's future direction correctly.

Thus "neutral" does not mean there is no profit and no loss; rather, it is a position with neither a bullish nor a bearish bias, enabling you to capitalize on overvaluation rather than relying on the odds-against forecasting of market moves.

To set up a neutral hedge, you will first need to determine the sensitivity of your chosen overvalued options, in order to know how many options (per 100 shares of stock owned) you need to sell to create neutrality.

An example will illustrate this procedure: Suppose you are long 100 XRX stock at $50, and you have selected as an overvalued option candidate a XRX October option with a striking price of $60 and 90 days to run. The computer pricing model tells you that this particular option has a sensitivity of .33 (that is, for every 1-point move in the stock, the option should move ⅓ point). Stated another way, this sensitivity number means that the option has only ⅓ of the volatility (in absolute terms or points) of the stock for small changes. If you are to be neutral, one side of the stock-option equation should not be out of balance with the other.

Thus if you were to engage in pure one-to-one covered writing, that is, to sell only one option against your 100-share long position, you would, because of the sensitivity factor, effectively be long 100 shares and short only 33 shares, or net long 67 shares. This is not a position that makes money no matter what the market does. Instead it is a bullish position. If the market goes up, you make money on the stock faster than you lose money on the option. If the stock goes down, you lose capital at a greater rate than you profit from the decline in the value of the option.

You would have to sell more than one option—in this case, three options—to be approximately neutral. With a 3:1 hedge you would effectively be long 100 shares and short 99, or about neutral.

To further examine this example, if you were to sell four of this particular option, your hedge would have a bearish bias. You would be long 100 shares and short 4 × 33, or 132 shares, a net short position of 32 shares. You would then make more money if your stock were to go down immediately than if it were to go up immediately. But the passage of time would reduce the sensitivity, thereby reducing the bias.

Remember that your aim is always to stay as neutral as is practicably possible—to lessen your vulnerability to market moves. To construct a hedge with either a bullish or a bearish bias would defeat your purpose. You would then be putting yourself in the same position as an investor who only owns stocks or who is only short stocks: you win if the market heads in one direction, but you lose if it moves the other way.

What is neutral today, however, may not necessarily be neutral tomorrow. Neutrality is constantly changing as the price of the underlying stock changes, and as time passes. Even if the price of the underlying stock stays the same, neutrality changes as time is used up. This is because the sensitivity of options changes over time.

A neutral hedge, for example, will accrue a bullish bias from the passage of time, even though the price of the stock remains the same, because the *sensitivity of an out-of-the-money option decreases* as the option's life runs out. In our XRX example, you would find that after a few weeks the option's sensitivity would have declined to .25, and a few weeks later, to .20. Therefore, to remain neutral you would have to adjust by later selling another option (to be short four options, with a .25 sensitivity), and, at a further point, still another (to be short five options, with a .20 sensitivity). Or, you might reduce the long positions or sell other call options, such as a XRX January 50 with a high sensitivity.

If the price of the underlying stock declines, the sensitivity of an out-of-the-money option also diminishes, because the probabilities of the stock's rising to the exercise price are diminishing; and the hedge becomes more bullish. If the price of the underlying stock rises, the sensitivity of the option increases, making the hedge more bearishly biased. Both instances require adjustments to keep the hedge neutral.

Conversely, *an in-the-money option becomes more sensitive as* time passes and the excess over intrinsic value disappears. Sensitivity begins to approach 1.00. To adjust, you may have to buy back previously sold options.

Just how much sensitivity changes with changes in the underlying stock's price and the passage of time can be seen in the matrix of General Motors options, Table 9-1.

TABLE 9-1   Sensitivity Matrix of General Motors (GM) as of April 28, 1977

	GM 60 Call Option			GM 70 Call Option			GM 80 Call Option	
GM Market Price	July	Oct.	Jan.	July	Oct.	Jan.	July	Oct.
80	.99	.98	.98	.95	.89	.87	.55	.58
78	.99	.97	.95	.92	.86	.82	.42	.51
76	.99	.97	.95	.87	.81	.79	.32	.41
74	.98	.95	.93	.77	.74	.72	.21	.36
72	.98	.93	.91	.66	.66	.66	.13	.29
70	.96	.92	.88	.57	.57	.61	.07	.22
68	.91	.87	.85	.42	.47	.54	.05	.16
66	.88	.82	.80	.29	.39	.47	.03	.11
64	.80	.75	.73	.17	.31	.38	.01	.06
62	.66	.66	.66	.10	.22	.30	.00	.05
60	.55	.57	.60	.05	.17	.24	.00	.01

This matrix illustrates the following points:

- As the price of GM rises, the sensitivity of every option rises.

- As the price of GM causes an option to be in the money, the nearest expiration becomes the most sensitive of that series, although the nearest expiration (when the option was out-of-the-money) had previously been the least sensitive.

This is clearly illustrated by the GM 70 series. Compare the sensitivities when the stock sells for $68 against the sensitivities when it sells for $72. This is consistent with the idea that out-of-the-money options tend toward zero as expiration draws closer, compared with in-the-money options, which tend toward a sensitivity of 1.00.

By now it is obvious that your hedges, once constructed, have to be monitored. They cannot be left to languish, because they are constantly changing, shifting in neutrality as time and market conditions change. Hedges must be adjusted to reflect market conditions in the same way that businessmen adjust inventories to reflect the demands of their customers:

they try to position themselves correctly at the outset, but often they must quickly adjust their reorder rates to reflect what is selling well.

We will discuss the fine points of adjustments later. Suffice it here to make two points:

■ As a practical matter, you cannot always have perfectly neutral hedges for each of your positions. You have to have some tolerance — say, plus or minus 20% of neutrality—with an eye toward netting out neutrality when considering your portfolio as a whole. Commissions and whipsaw possibilities make it too expensive to allow constant small adjustments for each position.

■ You have a great deal of flexibility as to how you may adjust for neutrality. There are more alternatives than simply selling more or buying back some of your existing short options. You can add and/or subtract the same option, add and/or subtract other options, and/or sell or buy stock.

After you have picked your overvalued options and determined your neutral hedge (for this point in time), the next step is to:

Step 3: Calculate Your Profit Range and Decide if It is Reasonable

Along with the next two steps, "Calculate Your Maximum Rate of Return" and "Calculate the Range of Probability of Achieving a 20% Return," this determination will help you decide whether or not a particular variable hedge position is worth constructing. This step answers the question, "Does it give me enough protection from the stock's volatility?" The next two steps answer the question, "How much will it pay me?"

Your profit range involves two determinants:

■ The downside breakeven point: This is easily figured by taking the price you pay for your stock position and subtracting from it the proceeds from your options' sales. Let us say that you buy 100 XRX at $50 and sell three XRX 90-day options with a striking price of $60 and a market price of $2.

Price you paid for stock:	$50
Proceeds of selling 3 options at $2:	−6
Downside breakeven point:	$44

In common sense language, this means that at $44 on the stock you neither make nor lose money, because you have lost $6 in your stock and gained $6 in your options. Above $44 on the stock you make money, and below $44 you lose it. Thus $44 is your downside breakeven point *at expiration*. Since the options will retain some value if the stock declines to $44 prior to expiration, the interim downside breakeven point is somewhat higher. This is because—prior to expiration, with the stock at $44— you would have to pay something for the options previously sold, if you desired to buy them back.

- The upside breakeven point: This calculation involves two steps. First, determine the point of the stock's trading range where your hedge will yield its maximum profit, and then determine how many dollars you make at that point. Second, calculate the rate at which the profit is decreasing until you reach the point where the hedge begins to lose money.

For example, in our XRX position, maximum profitability will occur when the stock trades at $60 at expiration. This is because at that point you will have made 10 points on your long stock position (from 50 to 60) and will have taken in 6 points for options sold, and the options will have expired worthless. Thus, you will make $16 on your hedge.

The formula for figuring maximum profitability is this:

- For out-of-the-money options (as in the case of XRX 60s, sold when the stock was $50), the point of maximum profitability is the options' striking price. There you keep your stock profits, as well as the premiums from previously sold options. The dollar profit is the premiums *plus* the difference between the market price of the stock and the striking price.

- For in-the-money options, the point of maximum profitability is also the striking price, but the maximum profitability is the sum of the premiums *less* the difference between the striking price and the price paid for the stock.

To move on to your upside breakeven point, you must see how many options you are net short. Divide the number of dollars you make at the point of maximum profitability by that number. Then add the result to the point of maximum profitability to find the upside breakeven point.

Let us look again at the hedge with 100 shares of XRX bought at $50 and three XRX 60s sold at $2. We have already determined that the point of maximum profitability is $60, and at that point your maximum dollar profit is $16. With this hedge you have sold three options, but are net short only two options, since one is covered by your 100-share long stock position. So you divide $16 (maximum dollar profit) by 2 (number of net short options). Then you add the resulting $8 to 60, making $68 your upside breakeven point. Thus, the formula for upside breakeven is:

$$
BE = \text{Strike Price} + \frac{\left(\text{Strike Price} - \begin{matrix} \text{Market} \\ \text{Price of} \\ \text{Stock} \end{matrix}\right) + \left\{\begin{matrix} \text{Market} & \text{No. of Options} \\ \text{Price} & \text{Sold Per} \\ \text{of Call} \times 100 & \text{Shares Stock} \end{matrix}\right\}}{\begin{matrix} \text{No. Options Sold Per 100} \\ \text{Shares of Stock} \qquad -1 \end{matrix}}
$$

And, applying this to our example:

$$
BE = 60 + \frac{(60 - 50) + (2 \times 3)}{3 - 1} = 60 + \frac{10 + 6}{2} = 68
$$

To prove your answer, start with the breakeven point and work backwards. At $68, you make $18 on your long stock position and collect $6 in option premiums, for a total of $24. However, you are obligated to deliver 300 shares of stock at $60, resulting in a 24-point loss, (68-60) × 3, or 8 × 3. Thus at $68, your hedge is neither making nor losing money.

The "band" of stock prices between your downside breakeven point and your upside breakeven point is your profit range. (In the case of the XRX example, the range is $44−68). How do you know if this range is a "good" one; that is, if it is wide enough to provide reasonable protection from market volatility? (Your profit range can be adjusted upward or downward if the stock moves substantially in one direction or another, but it is wise to start with a wide enough band to give you protection from ordinary market volatility.)

There are three ways to test whether or not your breakeven range is sufficiently wide:

■ Does common sense indicate that it is a sensible range in light of the underlying stock's historical trading range?

The common sense test would tell you, for example, that a 4-point band for GM is too narrow, while a 40-point band is probably too wide. If you would rather trust statistics than your common sense, move on to the next two tests:

■ Ask your broker for the underlying stock's calculated standard deviation.

Standard deviation is a statistical measure of volatility. In a normal distribution, the standard deviation would include two-thirds of the cases. Stock prices are not "normally" distributed, since they can rise more points than they can decline. Therefore, a "log-normal" distribution that is skewed to reflect this is used, although not everyone agrees that this is correct.

Beta, which is a measure of stock volatility *relative* to the stock market (using the S&P 500), should not be used, because what you are buying is the stock, and what you are selling is that stock's *actual* volatility.

- Look at a stock's semi-log chart.

This is a chart that is on a geometric scale, so that percentage changes are equal; thus the distance between 20 and 40 equals the distance between 40 and 80. If, for example, your proposed hedge creates a profit range that covers 20% of the price action on either side of the stock's current price, the chart will graphically show if this is a wide enough band by historical standards.

Your initially constructed profit range, like your initially constructed neutral hedge, will change as time and the price fluctuations of the underlying stock alter the market values of your stock and written options. Adjustments can easily be made. As with the adjusting process for keeping your hedges neutral, you can change the mix of your options; and thereby lower or raise the entire range by adding and/or subtracting the same options, adding or subtracting other options, and selling or buying the stock.

Keep in mind one very important point: breakeven points (both upside and downside) are calculated as if the options expire *today*. As a practical matter, then, if the stock rises or falls before expiration, any profit range calculated as of expiration date is in fact wider than it appears. This is because the options, before expiration, will still have some time value left in them. If they must be repurchased, the repurchase price would have to be deducted from the point spread between the upside and downside breakeven points.

A return to our XRX example illustrates this point. We initially created a range of $44−68 (as of expiration). If the XRX stock were to decline to $44 before the end of the option period, and you were to choose to buy back your previously sold options with a $60 striking price in order to sell other options to create a lower profit range, you would have to pay something for the privilege of buy-back, even though the price might only be ⅛ or $1/16$. Nevertheless, this narrows your calculated range. Similarly, if XRX were to trade at $68 while there was still time left in the option period, your $60 strike price options would now be in the money, and they would probably have to be repurchased at some premium over their intrinsic value of $8.

More details on how to adjust profit ranges will be found in the section on adjusting. Suffice it here to say that if you are satisfied with your initial profit range, you can now move on to the next step in constructing your variable hedge.

Step 4: Calculate Your Maximum Rate of Return

This step will help you decide, from a return standpoint, if a particular variable hedge is worth doing. You can calculate the largest amount you can expect to make on the hedge as originally constructed. The next step will then tell you the likelihood of your earning a 20% annualized return.

For quick figuring, this calculation of maximum returns does not include commissions or dividends. Therefore, your maximum return should be quite high in order to net out a reasonable return after transaction costs. As a rule of thumb, it is recommended that this calculation produce at least a 40% annualized return to be considered worthwhile. The reason this is so high is that the achievement of this maximum rate of return is unlikely.

The calculation itself is simple. It is a matter of taking the maximum dollar profit you would earn at the point of maximum profitability (a calculation you have already performed, in step 3), expressing it as a percentage of your investment, and then annualizing this percentage:

$$\text{Maximum annualized rate of return} = \frac{\text{Maximum dollar profit}}{\text{Net invested dollars}} \times \frac{12}{\text{\# months remaining in option period}}$$

Again in the XRX case, we determined in step 3 that maximum profitability for this hedge would occur when the stock traded at $60 at expiration. At that point, you will recall, you would have made 10 points on your stock position (bought at $50) and 6 points on option premiums when the options would have expired worthless. Thus your maximum dollar profit would be $16.

Your net investment in the XRX stock was $44, since you paid $50 but received back $6 in option premiums. $16/44$ is a 36% return for 90 days (3 months). Annualized, it is a 144% (36% × 4) rate of return.

Obviously, a 144% return is worth pursuing, although it is extremely unlikely that it would be achieved. But by aiming high, we increase the likelihood of achieving a reasonable return after costs. What is the probability of achieving a 20% return? That calculation occurs in the next step:

Step 5: Calculate the Range of Probability of Achieving a 20% Return

At this point, you have already determined that the variable hedge that you are considering has a reasonably wide profit range to accommodate all but the most unusual trading experiences of the underlying stock within a specific time period. However, you are not in this business merely to break even. You hope to make a respectable return.

At this point, you have also determined that, at the point of maximum profitability within the profit range, the annualized return is high enough to net out a reasonable return after costs. But how about other-than-maximum profitability?

This step will help you determine the width of the band of prices within which the underlying stock may trade and still allow you to achieve a respectable return of 20%.

The simplest way to figure this is to start with the dollars you must earn and work backward, a procedure which goes like this:

■ To have a 20% annualized return, how many dollars must you make? This is 20% of your investment annualized. Figure out how many dollars you must make to achieve an absolute 20% return, and then multiply the answer by the number of months left in the option divided by 12. (For a 3-month option, multiply by $^3/_{12}$, or ¼; for a 6-month option, multiply by $^6/_{12}$ or ½, etc.) The result is the dollar amount you must make on this hedge to achieve your return goal.

■ Calculate down from the upside breakeven point and up from the downside breakeven point the price of the stock at which you are making at least that amount of dollar profit.

1. For each point up from the downside breakeven point you are increasing your profitability at the rate of $1 per point times the number of shares of stock you own.

2. For each point down from the upside breakeven point you are increasing your profitability at the rate of $1 per point times the number of shares you are net uncovered short.

■ Once you have determined the 20% profitability range, which is obviously narrower than the profit range, decide whether this smaller range is wide enough to allow the stock reasonable expectation of continuing to trade within it during a specific time period.

For example, in the XRX case, your profit range has been calculated to be $44-68. To make 20% annualized on this hedge, you must earn 20% per year on your cost, which is $4400. Thus on a cost of $4400 you must make $880 multiplied by $^3/_{12}$ or ¼ (since this is a 90-day option), or a total of $220 (about 2 ¼ points).

The downside of the range in which you can make 20% is therefore your downside breakeven point ($44) plus 2¼, or 46¼. (The proof of this calculation, figured another way, is that at 46 ¼ you have lost 3¾ points on your stock position, but you have made 6 on your option's sales, for a net gain of 2¼.)

The upside of the range in which you can make 20% is figured by taking the top of your profit range ($68) and subtracting 2¼ divided by 2 (2 being the number of options net uncovered short), or 1⅛. This makes the upside of your narrower range 66⅞. (The proof of this calculation, figured another way, is that at 66⅞, you have made 16⅞ on your stock and 6 on your option sales, for a total of 22⅞ points, and you have lost 6⅞ on 3 options, or a total of 20⅝ points, for a 2¼ point profit.)

Now the range in which you make a 20% annualized return has been determined as 46½-66⅞. Is this a reasonable band within which Xerox can be expected to trade within any 90-day period? The computer pricing model can give you the probabilities. As another rule of thumb, we suggest that this range have a 45% probability of being sufficient, if this particular hedge is to be considered applicable to your purposes. (Keep in mind that a 45% probability of achieving at least a 20% return does not mean that there will be a 9% probable return. The extent of the gains greater or less than 20% and the possible losses are not quantified. Therefore, that is a fallacious inference.)

Now that your proposed hedge has passed the above tests, we move on to additional steps that deal with the costs of your whole variable hedge portfolio, some profitability parameters, and some facts you need to know about commissions and collateral requirements.

Step 6: Understand the Mechanics of Collateral Requirements*

Collateral requirements on an uncovered option position are 30% of the market value of the underlying stock plus or minus the difference from the

---

*For simplicity's sake, "option" in this section refers to calls. Put collateral requirements are discussed later.

strike price of the option ($250 minimum per option). The calculation is illustrated in the following example:

Long 100 XRX with a market value of $50 per share, or $5,000
    (assuming the proceeds of the option sales were part of
    the stock purchase funds)
Short 3 XRX options with a $60 striking price

Take 30% of $5000, or	$1,500
Subtract the difference between the striking price of $60 and the market price of $50, or 10 points × 100 shares†	1,000
Collateral requirement is	$ 500 per uncovered option

†If the market price is higher than the striking price, you add the difference rather than subtract it.

In this case there are two uncovered options (you have sold three options, but one is covered by the 100-share long stock position). Therefore, the above requirement is $500 × 2, or $1000.

To see where this collateral requirement will come from, we now look to the loan value of the long stock position. You own 100 shares at $50; thus you have a market value of $5000. Under 50% margin requirements the loan value is $2500. Assuming that there is no money already borrowed against this stock position, you have a loan value of $2,500 less the collateral requirement of $1000 ($500 per option × 2 options), or excess collateral of $1500.

Collateral calculations become more complicated as the price of the underlying stock changes. Suppose your XRX moves to $55. Then the requirement is as follows:

30% of $5500 (market value with stock at $55)	$1650
Subtract difference between striking price of the options ($60) and market price of stock ($55), which is 5 points × 100 shares	500
The collateral requirement is now	$1150 per uncovered option

Thus as the stock rises 5 points, the requirement rises $650, or $130 per point per option.

Since collateral requirements change measurably with each one-point movement in the underlying stock, it is important from the outset that you calculate—for each position in your portfolio—the point at which the underlying stock's loan value will no longer support the uncovered options. This is figured as follows:

Assume we return to our original position of 100 XRX at $50, with the stock at $50 and three options (two of them short) with a striking price of $60.

We determined the requirement was:	$500 per option
Number of uncovered options:	2
Collateral requirement:	$1000
Loan value of 100 shares of XRX long (50% of $5000)	$2500
Excess collateral:	$1500

How far can the stock rise before we run out of excess collateral? We have also seen that the collateral requirement in this case goes up or down $130 per point change in the price of the stock. Since there are two uncovered options, that would be $260 ($130 × 2) per point change in XRX. While the collateral requirement is increasing with the stock rising, the loan value of the long stock is also increasing, at a rate of $50 per point (50% of $100). Therefore, the net additional requirement per point rise in the stock is $260 less $50, or $210 per point. With an excess collateral of $1500, then, the position would have excess to support a rise of 7.142 points ($1500 divided by $210). Thus, XRX could rise to $57.142 per share before we run out of collateral.

To prove this calculation correct, refigure the collateral requirements with the stock at $57.142:

30% of $5714 is:	$1714
Subtract difference between striking price of $60 and market price of $57.14, which is 2.86 × 100 shares:	286
Collateral requirement is:	$1428 per option
Number of uncovered options:	× 2
Collateral requirement:	$2856
Loan value of 100 shares of XRX at $57.14 (50% of $5714)	$2857 (differential due to rounding)

See Table 9-2 for sample collateral problems.

There are some important points to keep in mind when considering collateral requirements:

■ *No matter how low the stock declines, the minimum collateral re-quirement is $250 per uncovered option.* For instance, at $40 the require-ment is technically zero, since 30% of 40 is $1200 less the $2000 differ-ence from striking price. Nevertheless, $250 would be required.

■ *Once the underlying stock rises above the striking price, its loan value ceases to increase.* Thus in our XRX example, once the stock rises above $60, the net requirements increase $260 per point without the offsetting $50 per point rise in the stock.

■ *If there is a debit in the account, it must be deducted from loan value before figuring excess collateral.* For example, if the XRX position were to have a $1000 debit balance, then the new excess collateral would be $500 rather than $1500, since the $2500 collateral value would be reduced by $1000 to $1500.

Collateral requirement		$1000
Loan value	$2500	
Less debit balance	1000	
Collateral value of stock		1500
Excess collateral		$ 500

Conversely, the effect of a debit balance is to lower the point at which additional collateral is required. Since excess is now only $500 and col-lateral requirements are rising at a rate of $210 per point, the price at which XRX common no longer supports the uncovered options is $52.38 (that is, $500 excess divided by $210 = 2.38 points) rather than $57.142.

■ Remember that in a diversified portfolio of several variable hedges, the requirements and values are merged so that some positions may require more collateral at the same time that others may release collateral.

Since you are managing a business, you have to keep track of the excess collateral in the account, so that you can estimate how much of a risk in the market you can experience before having to take action on a collateral basis. You would estimate this by calculating the excess in the account (in most instances, your broker can supply it for you) and dividing that number by the number of uncovered options × $130 which gives you the average number of points your stocks can rise before you have to adjust

TABLE 9-2   Calculating Collateral Requirements on a Portfolio

			Collateral Value		
(1)	(2)	(3)	(4)	(5)	(6)
Stock	Number of Shares	Market Price	Market Value Long (col. 2 × col. 3)	50% Margin Requir- ed[a]	Loan Value (col. 4 − col. 5)
ABC	400	38⅜	15,350.00	7675.00	$ 7,168.75[b]
BGH	200	68⅛	13,625.00	6812.50	6,812.50
FNC	300	21¾	6,525.00	3262.50	3,262.50
DD	100	111½	11,150.00	5575.00	5,500.00[b]
PRD	300	24⅝	7,387.50	3693.75	3,693.75
TXN	200	70	14,000.00	7000.00	7,000.00
WX	500	17¼	8,625.00	4312.50	3,750.00[b]

$ 37,187.50

Add credit balance: 18,598.00

Total loan value: $ 55,785.50

[a] Subject to change by Federal Reserve Board; currently: 50% on marginable securities, 75% on listed bonds, 90% on U.S. Government Securities.
[b] Market value of stock for collateral purposes is limited to the striking price of options outstanding against it.
[c] $250 minimum.

positions or deposit additional collateral. The stocks that support out-of-the-money options will, of course, benefit from a rise in price, because their collateral value is increasing.

Another point to keep in mind is that the requirement for an uncovered option with one day to run is the same as for one with 6 months to run. Therefore, by replacing a near–term option with a longer–term option, the collateral requirement remains the same, but the net cash proceeds of the transaction will generate collateral. Collateral for this account need not be the underlying stock itself. It could be other stocks, bonds, any marginable security, or cash.

TABLE 9-2   Calculating Collateral Requirements *(continued)*

(1)	(2)	(3)	(4)	(5)	(6)
		Collateral Required			
		+Points in-the	*Collateral*		
	Market	*Money × 100*	*Require-*	*Number*	
	Price of	*or*	*ment per*	*of Un-*	
	Underlying	*−Points out-of*	*Uncovered*	*covered*	*Collateral*
Option	*Stock × 100 ×30%*	*the Money × 100*	*Option* [c]	*×Options*	*Requirement*
3 Feb. 35	—	—	—	0	$ 0
4 Feb. 40	1151.25	(162.50)	988.75	3	2,966.25
12 Feb. 45	1151.25	(662.50)	488.75	12	5,865.00
7 Jan. 70	2043.75	(187.50)	1856.25	5	9,281.25
3 Jan. 20	—	—	—	0	—
1 Apr. 110	—	—	—	0	—
1 Apr. 120	3345.00	(850.00)	2495.00	1	2,495.00
4 Apr. 25	738.75	(37.50)	701.25	1	701.25
6 Apr. 30	738.75	(537.50)	250.00	6	1,500.00
2 Apr. 70	—	—	—	0	—
4 Apr. 80	2100.00	(1000.00)	1100.00	4	4,400.00
5 Jun. 15	—	—	—	0	—
5 Jan. 20	517.50	(275.00)	250.00	5	1,250.00

Collateral requirement: $ 28,458.75

Excess: 27,326.75

$ 55,785.50

Beside keeping a vigilant eye on collateral requirements, another part of the job of monitoring your variable hedges is watching the bias of the whole portfolio:

Step 7: Calculate Your Portfolio Bias on an Ongoing Basis

This is a simple calculation that you should perform frequently with a view toward keeping your portfolio as a whole as neutral as possible (that is, neither bullish nor bearish). As we discussed in the section on setting up neutral hedges, your results as a variable hedger will depend on your not playing hunches that the market is going up or down. Trying to outguess the market's immediate future direction is a loser's game, and it has no place in the strategy we are developing here.

Since it is impossible to keep each individual hedge perfectly neutral, the idea is to keep the bias of the portfolio as a whole within a certain range of tolerance, so that it approximates neutrality.

The calculation is done like this:

■ *For each stock-option position, multiply the number of options by today's sensitivity for that option.* This will tell how many shares you are effectively net long or net short for each position.

■ *Translate this net short or long figure for each position into a dollar amount.*

■ *Divide by the equity.* This will tell you your total portfolio's exposure in terms of dollar risks to the stock market's volatility. See Table 9-3 for sample calculations.

■ *Your aim should be to be no more than 20% biased in either a bullish or bearish direction.* The whole portfolio will not, of course, be skewed by 20% if none of your individual positions is more than 20% out of line. This kind of total portfolio calculation is also important in helping you know on a daily basis which of your positions are most vulnerable to the market's volatility.

It is important to monitor on a day-to-day basis the changes in your portfolio's bias by stock, just as it is vital for the businessman to keep a daily tab on his inventory and sales figures. Table 9-3 shows a typical work sheet.

Step 8: Keep in Mind the Dynamics of your Profitability

As you monitor your variable hedges daily and try to keep in mind a rough idea of how profitable your positions are, you must remember that profitability in this operation is different from profitability in simply trading stocks. Just as the attitude of trying to second guess the market's future direction is self-defeating in stock trading, the erroneous notion that profitability depends on your long positions going up or down is self-defeating in a variable hedging program.

Instead, profitability is a result of the differential in the rate of change between your assets (your stocks) and your liabilities (your options—they

TABLE 9-3 Portfolio Bias Calculation Worksheet

(1)	(2)	(3)	(4)	(5)	(6)	(7)	(8)	(9)
	Number of Shares	Number of Options		Equivalent Short Position in Shares	Net Position in Shares (Long-short)	Market Price of Stock	$ Long or (Short)	% of Equity
Stock	Long	Short	× Sensitivity* =	(col. 3 × col. 4)	(col. 2 − col. 5)	=	(col. 6 × col. 7)	
ABC	400	3 Feb. 35	.92	276 ⎫				
		4 Feb. 40	.33	132 ⎬ 420	(20)	38⅜%	(767.50)	(8)
		12 Feb. 45	.01	12 ⎭				
BGH	200	7 Jan. 70	.27	189	+11	68⅝%	+ 749.37	+ .8
FNC	300	3 Jan. 20	.98	294	+ 6	21¾	+ 130.50	+ .1
DD	100	1 Apr. 110	.62	62 ⎫ 90	+10	111½	+1115.00	+1.2
		1 Apr. 120	.28	28 ⎭				
PRD	300	6 Apr. 30	.18	108 ⎫ 328	(28)	24⅝%	(689.50)	(.7)
		4 Apr. 25	.55	220 ⎭				
TXN	200	4 Apr. 80	.18	72 ⎫ 188	+12	70	+ 840.00	+ .9
		2 Apr. 70	.58	116 ⎭				
WX	500	5 Jan. 15	.97	485 ⎫ 490	+10	17¼	+ 172.50	+ .1
		5 Jan. 20	.01	5 ⎭				
						Portfolio Bias	+1550.37	+1.76%

*If options are puts, sensitivity will be negative and should be *added* in column 6, i.e. subtracting a negative yields a positive number.

205

are liabilities, because they represent an obligation to sell stock, if called, at a specific price).

A simple comparison shows why this is so:

An investor who owns $100,000 worth of stocks sees his net worth rise or fall as the price of his stocks fluctuates. An investor with a $100,000 variable hedging program is not so sensitive to market moves; when his assets (stocks) go up, his liabilities (options) increase, too, but hopefully at a slower rate. When his assets go down, his liabilities go down, too, so that the change in his net worth is less than that of the investor who is only long stock, and the change can actually be positive.

The variable hedger can profit handsomely when the market does virtually nothing—a statement that hardly applies to the investor who owns only stock. When the market is not up, or when there are only small changes in stock prices, the probabilities increase that the variable hedger's assets (stocks) will stay within their profit ranges, and that his liabilities (options) will lose value and eventually disappear (that is, expire). Profitability, therefore, comes from the fact that the hedger's assets increase at a faster rate than that of his liabilities; or, the former decline at a slower rate than that of the latter.

Meanwhile, the variable hedger's stock business is also collecting dividends and earning interest and/or additional premium income from new positions created with the proceeds of options sold. Table 9-4, showing a performance report of an actual variable hedging account, shows portfolio transactions, performance, income and profitability over a 6 month period.

Step 9: Learn to Adjust Your Positions to Market Vicissitudes

The most important skill that the variable hedger must develop is to know *when and how to adjust his positions as market conditions change*.

As we have pointed out previously, the latitude for adjustment and the resulting flexibility are two of the major attractions of variable hedging. As your stocks move up or down, you have any number of ways to move your profit ranges upward or downward, so that your hedges remain profitable despite market moves.

However, we have also noted that it is impractical to change everything minute–to–minute to accommodate small market moves, for it is too expensive and time-consuming. There are no ironclad rules that state when to adjust, or how to adjust (since you must usually choose from

TABLE 9-4 Performance Report for Total Account of John Doe

Date	Add. or Withdr. Amount	S&P500 ADJ*	DJIA ADJ*	Value of the Account	Number of Units	Total Value Per Unit	Income Since Inception	Income Value Per Unit	Principal Value Per Unit
12/31/76	60,855.06	107.46	1,004.65	60,855.06	608.55	100.00	.00	.00	100.00
1/17/77		103.91	969.04	62,042.87	608.55	101.95	202.53	.33	101.62
1/31/77		102.36	957.78	61,719.06	608.55	101.42	202.53	.33	101.09
2/15/77		101.53	949.42	61,707.52	608.55	101.40	321.46	.53	100.87
2/28/77		100.44	942.97	62,369.99	608.55	102.49	321.46	.53	101.96
3/15/77		102.78	973.60	63,384.75	608.55	104.16	593.09	.98	103.18
3/31/77		99.38	929.07	63,278.09	608.55	103.98	593.09	.97	103.01
4/15/77		102.21	959.80	64,284.40	608.55	105.64	708.14	1.17	104.47
4/29/77		99.75	940.27	64,401.83	608.55	105.83	708.14	1.17	104.66
5/13/77		100.51	943.41	64,317.33	608.55	105.69	871.14	1.44	103.03
5/31/77		97.78	915.40	63,572.32	608.55	104.47	871.14	1.44	103.03
6/15/77		101.52	936.49	64,766.90	608.55	106.43	1164.54	1.92	104.51
6/30/77		102.58	936.98	65,019.95	608.55	106.84	1164.54	1.91	104.93

*Adjusted for reinvestment of dividends.

Table 9—4 (continued)

ACCOUNT OF JOHN DOE
As of December 31, 1976

ASSETS

LONG STOCK

		MARKET VALUE
200	Burroughs @ 91 5/8	$18,325.00
300	Citicorp @ 32 3/4	9,825.00
100	Dupont @ 135 1/8	13,512.50
200	Eastman Kodak @ 86	17,200.00
500	Westinghouse @ 17 5/8	8,812.50
	Credit balance	2,855.06

TOTAL ASSETS	$70,530.06

LIABILITIES AND NET WORTH

SHORT OPTIONS

		MARKET VALUE
4	Burroughs April 100 @ 2 9/16	$ 1,025.00
1	Burroughs April 90 @ 7 1/8	712.50
5	Citicorp April 35 @ 15/16	468.75
3	Citicorp April 30 @ 3 5/8	1,087.50
3	Dupont April 130 @ 10	3,000.00
1	Eastman Kodak April 90 @ 4 1/8	412.50
1	Eastman Kodak April 80 @ 10	1,000.00
4	Eastman Kodak April 100 @ 1 1/4	500.00
2	Westinghouse April 15 @ 3 1/8	625.00
9	Westinghouse July 20 @ 15/16	843.75

TOTAL LIABILITIES	$ 9,675.00
NET WORTH	60,855.06
TOTAL LIABILITIES AND NET WORTH	$70,530.06

ACCOUNT OF JOHN DOE

SCHEDULE OF TRANSACTIONS

January 1, 1977 through June 30, 1977

SETTLEMENT DATE			TRANSACTION	REALIZED GAIN(LOSS)
1/17/77	Sold	3	Burroughs April 90 @ 2 13/16	
1/19/77	Sold	2	Burroughs April 80 @ 4 1/2	$ 1,018.04
1/21/77	Bought	4	Burroughs April 100 @ 5/16	1,146.25
1/21/77	Bought	4	Eastman Kodak April 100 @ 1/4	
1/26/77	Sold	2	Eastman Kodak July 80 @ 5 7/8	
1/26/77	Sold	2	Burroughs July 80 @ 4 7/8	
1/27/77	Bought	2	Burroughs April 90 @ 5/8	401.02
1/31/77	Bought	1	Burroughs April 90 @ 5/8	569.07
1/31/77	Bought	1	Burroughs April 90 @ 5/8	200.51
2/ 3/77	Bought	1	Eastman Kodak April 90 @ 3/8	672.66
2/ 9/77	Bought	2	Burroughs April 80 @ 1 1/8	616.09
2/ 9/77	Bought	1	Eastman Kodak April 80 @ 15/16	676.22
2/ 9/77	Sold	1	Eastman Kodak July 70 @ 6 1/4	
2/11/77	Bought	5	Citicorp April 35 @ 3/16	456.50
2/11/77	Sold	3	Citicorp July 30 @ 2 11/16	
2/22/77	Sold	1	Eastman Kodak July 70 @ 6 3/8	
3/ 2/77	Bought	3	Dupont April 130 @ 3	874.20
3/ 2/77	Sold	1	Dupont July 130 @ 5 7/8	
3/ 2/77	Sold	2	Dupont July 140 @ 1 15/16	
3/ 9/77	Sold	2	Burroughs July 70 @ 3 1/4	
3/29/77	Sold	2	Eastman Kodak July 70 @ 3 7/8	
3/29/77	Sold	2	Burroughs July 60 @ 5 3/8	

Table 9—4 (continued)

Date	Action	Qty	Description	Amount
3/29/77	Bought	2	Burroughs July 80 @ 3/16	891.92
4/ 1/77	Bought	3	Citicorp April 30 @ 1/16	854.79
4/ 1/77	Sold	3	Citicorp October 30 @ 1 9/16	247.48
4/ 6/77	Bought	2	Dupont July 140 @ 1/2	
4/ 7/77	Sold	2	Dupont July 130 @ 2 1/2	(431.16)
4/14/77	Bought	1	Westinghouse April 15 @ 3 7/8	
4/22/77	Sold	2	Eastman Kodak October 60 @ 7 3/4	1,105.68
4/25/77	Bought	2	Eastman Kodak July 80 @ 1/8	
4/25/77	Sold	2	Burroughs October 60 @ 3 5/8	1,891.66
4/26/77	Bought	4	Burroughs July 70 @ 3/16	1,789.27
5/11/77	Bought	4	Eastman Kodak July 70 @ 3/8	
5/23/77	Sold	3	Eastman Kodak October 60 @ 4 1/4	
5/24/77	Sold	*3	McDermott August 60 @ 1 7/8	
5/27/77	Sold	3	McDermott August 60 @ 1 1/2	
	Bought	*100	McDermott @ 55 1/2	
5/31/77	Bought	100	McDermott @ 54 3/4	
6/ 2/77	Sold	1	McDermott August 50 @ 4 7/8	
6/ 3/77	Bought	3	Dupont July 130 @ 5/16	928.63
6/ 3/77	Sold	1	Dupont October 130 @ 1 9/16	
6/ 3/77	Sold	1	Dupont October 120 @ 5 1/4	
6/ 8/77	Sold	2	Dupont January 130 @ 2	
6/24/77	Bought	3	Citicorp July 30 @ 1/16	741.99
6/29/77	Bought	9	Westinghouse July 20 @ 1 5/8	(868.19)

Total Realized Gains $13,782.65

* Please note that the purchase of the stock and the sale of the options were done simultaneously. The options were sold on May 22nd and settled on May 23rd, (options settle next day). The stock was purchased on May 22nd and settled on May 27th, (stock settles in 5 days).

ACCOUNT OF JOHN DOE

SCHEDULE OF DIVIDENDS AND INTEREST

January 1, 1977 through June 30, 1977

DATE		AMOUNT
1/ 3/77	Eastman Kodak	$ 180.00
1/ 6/77	Interest on Credit Balance	22.53
2/ 1/77	Citicorp	72.00
2/ 7/77	Interest on Credit Balance	12.93
2/ 7/77	Burroughs	34.00
3/ 1/77	Westinghouse	121.50
3/ 7/77	Interest on Credit Balance	25.13
3/14/77	Dupont	125.00
4/ 1/77	Eastman Kodak	80.00
4/ 6/77	Interest on Credit Balance	35.05
5/ 2/77	Citicorp	79.50
5/ 6/77	Interest on Credit Balance	43.50
5/ 9/77	Burroughs	40.00
6/ 1/77	Westinghouse	121.50
6/ 7/77	Interest on Credit Balance	46.90
6/13/77	Dupont	125.00
	Total Income	$1,164.54

Table 9—4 (continued)

ACCOUNT OF JOHN DOE
As of June 30, 1977

ASSETS

LONG STOCK	MARKET VALUE
200 Burroughs @ 62 3/8	$12,475.00
300 Citicorp @ 27 3/8	8,212.50
100 Dupont @ 116	11,600.00
200 Eastman Kodak @ 59 1/2	11,900.00
500 Westinghouse @ 21 1/2	10,750.00
200 J.Ray McDermott @ 57 5/8	11,525.00
Credit balance	5,344.95
TOTAL ASSETS	$71,807.45

LIABILITIES AND NET WORTH

SHORT OPTIONS	MARKET VALUE
4 Eastman Kodak October 60 @ 3 1/2	$ 1,400.00
3 Citicorp October 30 @ 9/16	168.75
1 McDermott August 50 @ 8-1/4	825.00
1 McDermott August 60 @ 1 11/16	1,012.50
2 Burroughs July 60 @ 2 3/4	550.00
2 Burroughs October 60 @ 5 1/4	1,050.00
1 Dupont October 130 @ 13/16	81.25
1 Dupont October 120 @ 3 1/4	325.00
2 Dupont January 130 @ 2	400.00
2 Westinghouse October 20 @ 2 3/8	475.00
10 Westinghouse October 25 @ 1/2	500.00
TOTAL LIABILITIES	$ 6,787.50
NET WORTH	65,019.95
TOTAL LIABILITIES AND NET WORTH	$71,807.45

several possible adjustments). If there were, a computer could adjust. This part of variable hedging requires judgment.

But the judgment you will need for adjustment is not an opinion about the market's movements in the future. On the contrary, you have to suspend all judgments of the market's future direction. Don't be tempted when the market is down, for instance, to create hedges with a bullish bias to take advantage of a hoped-for rebound. Then you are no better off than the trader who is trying to second-guess the market. Your aim is always to remain as neutral as possible. You need to pick the best combinations of options to buy back and/or sell, in order to alter your breakeven ranges at least cost and least risk. You must ask yourself, "What is the least costly way for me to adjust; where is the penalty for being wrong the least, and where is the probability for another adjustment the least likely?"

In answering these questions, you have to consider and calculate the alternatives. You must watch your transaction costs (commissions). You must keep in mind the collateral requirements of each potential adjustment, as well as the situation with collateral in all your other positions.

In terms of general principles, your objective should be to try to bring your hedges' bias back toward neutral by maneuvers that involve:

- The least cost and the fewest options.

- Keeping the number of naked options to a minimum (to avoid collateral hits and rapid changes in neutrality).

Let us look at a typical choice that you may have to make:
You start with a position of

Long 100 Eastman Kodak (EK) at 100
Short 3 EK October 110s at 3½
Your profit range is $89½–120¼
Sensitivity of EK October 110s is .333
Bias of hedge is neutral (long 100, short 99.9)

Forty-five days later, EK is at $95, and the 110 options are selling for ½ with a sensitivity of .15. The bias of this hedge is now bullish (long 100 less short 300 × .15, or 45 shares, so net long 55 shares). You should get this hedge back to neutral.

One choice would be: the October 100 options are selling for $3, with a sensitivity of .30. If you were to sell two of these, you would be almost neutral (long 100, short .15 × .3 or 45 shares + .30 × 2, or 60 shares, for a total short of 105). These are the effects on your profit ranges:

Sell two 100 options at $3 = $600
Downside breakeven is now $83½
Upside breakeven is now $111⅝

Downside is 100 less total premiums received of 16½, or 83½.

Upside is total premiums received—16½—less $100 per point loss up to 110, and $400 (four uncovered options) per point loss over 110.

A second choice would be: repurchase the 110 options at ½ for a realized profit of $900 less the 5-point ($500) unrealized loss in the stock, for a net profit of 4 points ($400) and sell three October 100s at $3 per option.

Now recalculate the breakeven point as if the stock were being purchased at $95. The breakeven range on this position is $86–107.

What are the collateral requirement differences between these two choices?

In the first case it would be:

Situation—Sell 2 EK 100s at $3 each

30% of 9500:	$2850
Less amount out of the money (100–95):	500
	$2350
Number of uncovered options:	× 1
	$2350
plus	
Requirement on 3 EK 110s (1350 × 3):	4,050
Collateral required:	6400
Less value of stock (50% of 100 EK at 95):	4750
Additional requirement:	$1650
Less premiums received on 2 EK 100s at 3:	600
Additional collateral required:	$1050

In the second case it would be:

Situation—Sell 3 EK 100s at $3	
30% of 9500:	$2850
Less amount out of the money (100–95):	500
	$2350
Number of uncovered options:	× 2
Collateral requirement:	$4700
Loan value of stock:	4750
Excess collateral:	$ 50

Premiums received on sale		
of 3 EK 100s at $3:	$900	
½ less cost of repur-		
chase of EK 110s (3 × ½)	−150	
Net cash inflow		750
Excess collateral:		$800

Clearly, the stock's loan value covers the requirements in the second case, while additional collateral is required in the first. Furthermore, should the price of EK rise, the requirements in the first case would increase by $470 per point for the first 5 points (130 × 4 - $50 increase in loan value of stock)—and by $520 per point after the stock would have reached the striking price ($100). In the second case, collateral requirements would rise by $210 per point (2 × 130 - $50 increase) to the striking price ($100), and then to $260 thereafter. This potential increase in collateral requirements must be weighed against the likelihood of the 110 options expiring, which would mean an additional $150 profit (from the expiration of the 110s) versus the likelihood of the extra EK 100 option expiring.

A situation of similar choices often occurs. You must frequently decide whether or not to repurchase an option that is selling for a fraction of a dollar, when a new option is sold to adjust the hedge. There is the commission cost, as well as the repurchase price, to consider. And, even though it is likely that the option will expire worthless, the collateral committed to that position can increase dramatically if the stock rallies. This collateral hit would greatly reduce your flexibility. If a rally were to occur, the neutrality would be affected significantly, because those 100 options would be picking up sensitivity which might call for another adjustment.

The decision, of course, is intertwined with the whole portfolio's picture. How much excess collateral is there? What is the sensitivity of the options? Will you still be able to repurchase for a fraction if the stock rallies sharply?

This problem comes up often near an expiration. Many times the risk is worth taking on a probability basis when expiration is near. However, when it does not work, it can be very costly. If the option has more than 45 days to run, the probabilities of maintaining this position successfully will tend to fall rapidly. With that kind of time remaining, there is too much risk of a sharp rally. In general, it is better to take the course that reduces the number of uncovered options outstanding.

Another common adjustment problem is deciding which new options to sell as the stock declines. Very far out-of-the money options will have such a low sensitivity that you will have to be uncovered on a substantial number of them to lower your breakeven range sufficiently. It is often a better idea to sell much fewer in-the-money options (but with a high sensitivity).

Let us say that you have 300 shares of XRX at $55 and are short 9 XRX 60s with a sensitivity of .333. If the stock declines, you might consider selling more 60s, but with this out-of-the-money option's lowered sensitivity, you might have to sell as many as five to give yourself adequate downside protection. This means a high collateral requirement. Instead, why not consider selling one option with a striking price of $50, which will give you more protection and neutralize the long stock without significantly increasing the collateral requirement?

If XRX declines even further, sell a 45 or another 50 and repurchase the now insensitive and fractionally priced 60s. If XRX rallies, you can consider repurchasing the 50, which will not have increased in price as much as that of the stock, since its sensitivity is less than 1.00.

The objective is to keep the options with striking prices nearest the stock's market price intact, and to adjust, through very out-of-the-money and very in-the-money options. This gives you maximum flexibility without having to make many ''massive retaliation'' decisions as the stock moves around its current price. Working on both ends of the options spectrum, you can gradually change the hedge's bias by, in effect, rolling with the trend.

(And do not worry if you have to buy back an option for more than you had sold it, because the underlying stock—your asset—has increased in value.)

One final adjusting problem concerns your decision as to when you must sell more options to adjust your hedge, when all options on that stock are undervalued. As an alternative to selling undervalued options, you should consider simply selling your stock and closing out the option positions—and be satisfied with earning interest while you wait for opportunities. You will have to determine the degree of undervaluation versus the costs of selling out your inventory and perhaps having to buy it back later.

Remember, you are not in the business of buying stocks; rather, you are selling volatility. If a situation arises whereby you cannot make a profit by selling volatility, you should be on the sidelines, earning interest on your capital with little risk. It is not written anywhere that you must be invested in stocks all the time.

Step 10: Consider the Effects of Commission Costs

The examples used thus far have excluded commissions. Since the costs of a variable hedging program are the commissions, it would be worthwhile to see what effect they have on results. Using the same situation as before—$50 stock, 3 $60 options at $2 per option—what happens to the rate of return under different circumstances? Table 9-5 makes these comparisons.

Step 11: Keep Your Tax Consequences in Mind

Since the passage of the Tax Reform Act of 1976, tax treatment for options sold has been simplified. All transactions in options sold and repurchased result in short-term capital gains or losses. Long-term gains come from holding the underlying stock more than a year.

If your stock is called away on exercise, the premium on that option is added to the selling price (strike price) and the long-term gain is increased by the amount of the premium. Dividends on stock held are kept by the owner and are taxable. Short-term gains are applicable against tax loss carryforwards. These carryforwards tend to act as shelters for an option writing program. Since the holding period for long-term gains is now one year, a variable hedging program becomes even more attractive, since the option selling activity is "financing the holding period." Compare this to merely purchasing a stock and holding it for one year, hoping it will rise in value. Without options, if it does not rise, the year will be fruitless. However, if short-term gains via options are being generated through ownership of the stock, it is a more worthwhile holding, and a decision can be made to continue using that stock as an investment, now that it has the additional value of having achieved long-term tax status against the short-term gains generated.

TABLE 9-5 Rates of Return Including Commissions Costs* for Various Adjustment Strategies

Market Price	Pr. Shares	Gross Investment	Assumption	Options Sold	Premium	Net Investment	Maximum $ Return	Maximum % Return
50	100	5,000	no commissions	3	2 each	4,400.00	1,600.00	36.3**
50	100	5,077	keep stk; opt. expires	3	2	4,514.82	1,485.18	32.89
50	100	5,077	keep stk; buy opt. @ ½	3	2	4,514.82	1,387.18	30.7
50	100	5,077	keep stk; buy opt. @ ¼	3	2	4,514.82	1,462.18	32.3
50	100	5,077	sell stk; buy opt. @ ½	3	2	4,514.82	1,222.73	27.08
50	100	5,077	sell stk; buy opt. @ ¼	3	2	4,514.82	1,297.73	28.74
50	100	5,077	sell stk; opt. expires	3	2	4,514.82	1,397.73	30.9
50	500	25,325	keep stk; opt. expires	15	2	22,454.10	7,545,90	33.6
50	500	25,325	keep stk; buy opt. @ ½	15	2	22,454.10	6,420.90	28.6
50	500	25,325	keep stk; buy opt. @ ¼	15	2	22,454.10	7,133.40	31.7
50	500	25,325	sell stk; buy opt. @ ½	15	2	22,454.10	6,323.65	28.2
50	500	25,325	sell stk; buy opt. @ ¼	15	2	22,454.10	6,736.15	29.9
50	500	25,325	sell stk; opt. expires	15	2	22,454.10	7,148.65	31.8
50	1000	50,520	keep stk; opt. expires	30	2	44,736.20	15,539.80	34.1
50	1000	50,520	keep stk; buy opt. @ ½	30	2	44,736.20	13,613.80	30.4
50	1000	50,520	keep stk; buy opt. @ ¼	30	2	44,736.20	14,438.80	32.3
50	1000	50,520	sell stk; buy opt. @ ½	30	2	44,736.20	12,999.30	29.1
50	1000	50,520	sell stk; buy opt. @ ¼	30	2	44,736.20	13,824.30	30.9
50	1000	50,520	sell stk; opt. expires	30	2	44,736.20	14,649.30	32.7
50	2000	100,800	keep stk; opt. expires	60	2	89,190.40	30,809.60	34.5
50	2000	100,800	keep stk; buy opt. @ ½	60	2	89,190.40	27,509.60	30.8
50	2000	100,800	keep stk; buy opt. @ ¼	60	2	89,190.40	29,159.60	32.7
50	2000	100,800	sell stk; buy opt. @ ½	60	2	89,190.40	26,480.60	29.7
50	2000	100,800	sell stk; buy opt. @ ¼	60	2	89,190.40	28,130.60	31.5
50	2000	100,800	sell stk; opt. expires	60	2	89,190.40	29,780.60	33.4

*CBOE Schedule **Same for all quantities, i.e. 100, 500, 1000 and 2000

A frequently asked question is, "What if the stock rises above the striking price, and I am called?" It should be understood that the fact that a stock is selling above the striking price does not mean that there is a threat of exercise. As long as the option sells for a price in excess of "intrinsic value," there is little likelihood of being called (even the day before going ex-dividend). For example, if you were to sell a call at $50 on a stock that is now selling for $55, there is about zero probability of being called as long as the option sells for more than $5. The reason is simply that it would be irrational for the holder to exercise the option at $50, since he will realize more money from selling the option, and he does not have to put up the $5000 to exercise.

There is another factor to be considered. If there is an irrational exercise which could create a tax liability, stock can be purchased in the open market and delivered against the exercise. If the combination of the exercise price, the premium, and the open market purchase results in a loss, then stock can be delivered in such a proportion as to cause the low cost stock's gain and the newly purchased stock's loss to net out so as to create no tax liability. In this event, the residual holdings will have a higher cost basis. For example,

Client owns 800 shares of Stock A @ $10 per share

Cost basis:	$8000.00
Proceeds from exercise of 100 shares @ $50 per share:	5000.00
Add: Premium received on option sale:	350.00
Total selling price:	$5350.00
Cost of purchase of 100 shares @ $60 per share:	6000.00
Net loss	$ (650.00)
Deliver 13 shares of low cost stock @ $43.50 gain per share:	$ 565.50
Deliver 87 shares of newly purchased shares @ $6.50 loss per share:	(565.50)
Net tax gain	$ -0-
Cost basis of remaining shares:	
787 shares @ $10 per share:	$7870.00
13 shares @ $60 per share:	780.00
Total new cost basis of 800 shares	$8650.00

Recordkeeping for taxes and rate of return should be kept current. Options accounts are difficult to reconstruct. Recordkeeping can and should be done by your broker, who frequently has it computerized so that his reports can be used in helping you prepare your tax return.

CHAPTER TEN

Variations on a Theme: Using Other Securities and Options in Variable Hedging

Are there proxies for stocks and substitutes for call writing in a variable hedging program? In some circumstances puts fit well into a variable hedging strategy—but more on this later. In a much broader range of circumstances, one can use a "stock proxy" that provides an interesting contrast (and some distinct advantages) to the conventional variable hedging procedures previously described.

The "stand-in" is a procedure involving the use of dual fund capital shares in place of the common stocks underlying the written calls. Why? For greater portfolio diversification, for handsome upside leverage plus a downside cushion, and for greatly decreased necessity and costs of making adjustments.

But let us back up first and go through a primer on dual fund capital shares. The original concept behind dual funds (which are closed end investment companies with diversified portfolios) was to give investors one pool of capital to serve a dual investment objective—providing income for investors who wished it, *or* providing capital appreciation for those who preferred that alternative.

Thus these funds have two classes of stock—income shares, which receive all the dividends earned, and capital shares, which receive all the market value above the obligation to redeem the income shareholders at a fixed termination date. Income shareholders have the advantage of obtaining higher than normal rates of return, because they receive dividends on substantially more than the number of shares their investment dollars would normally buy (a privilege they have "earned" by foregoing capital appreciation entirely). Capital shareholders, in contrast, give up their share of the income generated by the underlying diversified fund portfolio in order to obtain substantially more capital appreciation (or conversely, depreciation) than they could normally buy with their dollars invested. In essence, dual funds allow each type of shareholder to leverage his objective by trading off his interest in the companion objective—income for capital or capital for income.

The other salient feature of the six dual funds that we recommend for use in variable hedging programs (see Table 10-1) is that they all have a date of termination, ranging from 1979 to 1985. The capital shares of these dual funds sell in the marketplace at substantial discounts from their net asset values, but these discounts can be expected to gradually disappear as the termination dates approach—since upon liquidation the shareholders will receive net asset value. This narrowing of the discount in the relatively near future provides a protection for the capital shareholders, since the discount *must* be earned between now and termination date. As of December 30, 1977 the discount on the various dual funds ranged from approximately 4.6% to 9.6% per year.

This brief description touches upon some of dual fund capital shares' attractions for the variable hedger. This book emphasizes often the importance of diversification; since dual fund capital shares are themselves shares of a diversified portfolio, they provide the variable hedger with a great deal more diversification (and hence less risk) than the conventional variable hedging procedure of buying stocks in order to sell their attractively overvalued options. One thus gets "more diversification per dollar invested" and can concentrate on selling more diversified combinations of overvalued options.

The leverage feature plus the discounted market prices of these capital shares offer additional attractions. The combination of these two features results in extraordinary upside leverage without equivalent downside risk for the capital share investor. Let us look at a specific example:

The capital shareholder, to reiterate, gets, for each $1 invested, not only assets at a discount, but "twice the bang for his buck," since he elects to take capital appreciation (depreciation) and forego income. The income shareholders, on the other hand, will get a fixed dollar amount upon termination of the fund, with the balance promised to capital shareholders. Suppose there is a liquidation requirement of $20 million for income shareholders in a dual fund of $40 million in assets. If the fund's value increases by 25 per cent, to $50 million, the capital

TABLE 10-1   Dual Fund Comparisons As of December 30, 1977

	Market Price	Discount from Net Asset Value %	Net Asset Value $	Capital Shares Out- standing (000)	Total Fund Assets $MM	Income Share Require- ment at Termina- tion $MM
American Dualvest	7¼	14.4	8.47	1565	36.25	23.0
Leverage Fund of Boston	11⅞	28.2	16.53	2003	60.11	27.0
Income & Capital Shares	6	32.0	8.82	1510	28.32	15.0
Scudder Duo Vest	6⅞	26.1	9.30	5423	100.03	49.6
Putnam Duo Fund	6⅜	33.5	9.59	1505	29.23	14.8
Gemini	19	26.9	26.00	1656	61.06	18.0

[a] Capital gains taxes are paid by the fund. Tax exempt shareholders may apply for a refund.

shareholder's equity increases by 50 per cent. (The $50 million fund upon termination would pay $20 million to income shareholders and $30 million to capital shareholders.) If additionally (and this is almost always the case) the capital shareholder has been able to purchase his shares at a discount from net asset value, his leverage increases substantially. Suppose he were to buy them at a 30% discount from net asset value (i.e., at $14 million) and were able to cash them in at $30 million; he would enjoy a 114% appreciation.

Suppose instead that the value of the fund were to decline by 10% by termination. Then the $40 million fund would be worth $36 million. In that case, $20 million would be paid to the income shareholders, with $16 million left for capital shareholders. On an investment in the fund discounted to $14 million, he would still gain $2 million, or 14%. Table 10-1 illustrates the upside and downside parameters of the capital shares of these six dual funds as of December 30, 1977.

Of course, if the value of the fund were to decline precipitously before termination, the capital shraeholder would have to sustain large losses; but the probabilities of this are low in contrast to the potential for a reasonable return if the fund's assets stay flat—and an extraordinary return if they increase.

In the last chapter the point is made that a variable hedger's profitability is a function of the differential between an increase in one's assets (stocks) and a decrease in one's liabilities (written options). Using dual

TABLE 10-1   Dual Fund Comparisons As of December 30, 1977
(continued)

Coverage of Income Share Require- ment	Date of Termina- tion	% Discount Earned per Month on Initial Investment to Termina- tion	Tax Loss Carry Forward $MM[a]	% Total Assets May Decline and Capital Shareholders Still Break even at Termination	% Appreciation If Total Assets of Fund Have Increased at Termination By			
					0%	25%	50%	100%
1.58	6/29/79	.93	15.0	5.2	17	97	176	336
2.23	1/1/82	.65	6.7	15.5	39	102	166	292
1.89	3/31/82	.75	3.8	15.0	47	125	203	360
2.02	4/1/82	.56	8.4	13.1	35	102	169	304
1.98	1/3/83	.70	3.9	16.5	50	126	203	355
3.39	12/31/84	.44	0	19.0	37	84	132	228

fund capital shares instead of the stocks underlying the written options gives the investor assets which will increase with the market in general, but will decrease less than the market in general—due to both the fact that the dual funds are purchased at a discount and the fact that upcoming termination dates tend to narrow that discount. So they increase the odds of the investor's assets rising faster than they will decline. On the liability side of the ledger, the fact that one is selling overvalued options means that they will increase less as the market advances and decrease more as the market declines.

What are the mechanics of using dual funds in place of underlying shares? There are two major adjustments from the mechanics discussed in the previous chapter:

- *Calculating Sensitivity*

Let us say that there is an attractive overvalued option in Eastman Kodak (EK) that would dictate by its sensitivity a 3:1 write. Further calculation shows that one would buy $10,000 worth of EK stock to establish this variable hedge. To substitute dual fund capital shares, one would start with that dollar amount and adjust for the standard deviation (volatility) of that dual fund compared with the underlying shares. (Your broker's computer model can tell you the standard deviation.)

In general it is wise to diversify amoung the various dual funds within a variable hedging program. Keep in mind that the volatility of the dual funds (since they are diversified portfolios of typically large-capitalization "market-type" stocks) tends to be in line with such "market-type" stocks. Therefore, when selecting attractively overvalued options, it is wise to stay away from selling those special-situation and extremely volatile options whose underlying stocks' volatility varies greatly from the "market-type" stocks.

Using dual fund shares in place of the options' underlying shares does not remove the necessity of making adjustments as the sensitivity of the options changes with market conditions.

- *Calculating Collateral Requirements*

In a conventional variable hedging program, for example, a 3:1 write in EK involves calculating collateral requirements that assume one EK option is covered by the underlying EK shares, while two are uncovered. When we use dual fund capital shares as a substitute in this example, however, we have three uncovered options, and collateral requirements will be greater. Therefore it is more prudent to select closer-to-the-money options, since if one sells too many uncovered options, the collateral costs are too high relative to the extent of downside protection.

In weighing the advantages and disadvantages of using dual fund substitutes for common stocks, remember these points:

- A "pure" dual fund variable hedging program (that is, one that contains no shares relating to the written options) will tend to be more aggressive and more volatile in both directions, since the dual funds themselves are low priced stocks, and a small move has a leveraged effect.

- You will receive no dividends.

- If the market were to decline drastically the dual fund leverage can begin to work against you in spite of the discount.

On the other hand:

- You have more potential for long-term capital gains (since you will not be trading in and out of your dual fund shares).

- You will have fewer transaction costs, since you will be keeping the same underlying shares.
in EK stock when the EK options are no longer attractive.

You will avoid some of the difficult choices that sometimes confront the conventional variable hedger, when, for instance, there are suddenly no more overvalued EK options to sell and one has to make some kind of a compromise· in "rolling down" in EK; or, alternately, one may have to close out the whole position and start over with options and stock purchases and sales in other securities.

Remember, too, that the technique of using dual fund capital shares is not an either/or decision. You can use both these shares and options' underlying stocks within a variable hedging program, and you can adjust the "mix" of this "hybrid," depending upon how aggressive (using only dual funds) or conservative (using only underlying stocks) you wish to be.

How Do Puts Fit into the Variable Hedging Program?

The opposite strategy to conventional variable hedging (buying stocks and selling combinations of calls) is, of course, selling stocks short and selling puts in various proportions. This strategy is not particularly profitable or workable, but puts *can* be used successfully in variable hedging as a substitute for stocks.

First, let us examine why selling short and selling puts has many disadvantages:

- Puts have smaller premiums than calls.

- Short sellers pay dividends rather than receive them, causing a swing in the potential rate of return.

- Execution is more difficult because of short sales' uptick rule.

- There is no chance of a long-term capital gain from short sales of stocks.

- Put valuation methods use the economics of the professional—who earns interest on short sales—while the investor does not. Therefore, puts that appear "overvalued" on a computer model may not be overvalued in the context of the ordinary investor's economic constraints.

How, then, can puts be used profitably? If puts are attractively overvalued, then the sale of uncovered puts should be considered a substitute for long stock (so that a variable hedger would be short puts and short calls rather than long stock and short calls). One real advantage of this stance is one's ability to use "outside collateral," that is, any stocks or bonds one already owns, without having to borrow to finance a conventional variable hedging program that buys stock long. (See "Collateral Requirements" below for more detail.)

When considering the short puts/short calls alternative, you must keep several factors in mind. It is easy enough to find neutral substitutes for the conventional variable hedge's components, but one has to evaluate each in terms of volatility, rate of return, collateral requirements (initial and maintenance), profit ranges, gradient (the rate at which neutrality changes), and transaction costs.

For example, consider various combinations with these EK components:

Stock—$50
July 50 calls at $5   sensitivity = .60
July 60 calls at $1 ½   sensitivity = .20
July 50 puts at $3   sensitivity = −.40*

*Note that the put has a negative sensitivity. This is because the put's sensitivity increases as the underlying stock declines and decreases as it rises. Also the equivalent of long stock is a long call and a short put, that is, a sensitivity of +.60 and −(−.40), or +1.00

A study of the various positions in Table 10-2 shows the differing effects on your portfolio of various combinations producing neutrality. You should make these calculations when choosing strategies, but it is not productive to go through the exercise unless puts are overvalued. If they are not, you are better off using the conventional long stock/short calls procedure.

[It is possible that it could be attractive to own calls instead of stock, but you must first carefully weigh all the factors and make comparisons like those above. More often than not, transaction costs due to the volatility of such a position will eat into profit potential too much to make this strategy worthwhile. Using calls as a stock substitute is usually too risky for anyone but a professional (who has a different cost structure and different margin rules than the ordinary investor) because of the small margins involved and rapid adjustments required.]

When contemplating puts in a variable hedging program, there are two other factors to remember:

■ *Taxation*. Calls cannot go long term now, since the holding period for tax purposes is one year, and calls are only created for 9 month periods. Puts are deemed to cause the holding period of the underlying stock to be negated (unless purchased simultaneously and designated as a hedge). However, buying a put *after* the stock is long term does not affect the holding period.

Buying a put can be very advantageous to an investor with low-cost-basis stocks. The loss, if the stock rises, is short term and the gain is long term. If the stock declines, either the put can be exercised and the long term gain realized, (net of the cost of the put), or the put can be sold for a short term gain—whichever approach is more advantageous.

■ *Collateral Requirements.* The collateral requirements on uncovered puts are the same as those on uncovered calls—that is, 30% of the market value of the underlying stock plus any in-the-money amount, or minus any out-of-the-money amount. Keep in mind the distinction between puts' and calls' in-the-money and out-of-the-money status. With calls, when the underlying stock goes up, the call becomes more in-the-money. But with puts, when the underlying stock goes up, the put becomes more out-of-the-money, and vice versa. Remember, too, that exchange rules require a $250 minimum requirement for each short put (as with short calls). Here is an example of collateral calculation for a short put:

Sell 1 XRX 50 put at $5	
XRX common is at $48	
30% of $4800	$1440
Plus the in-the-money amount	200
Collateral requirement	$1640*

*The premium received may be used as part of the collateral.

If you are *short puts and short calls,* the collateral requirements call for a comparison calculation. You will be required to deposit either the collateral requirement on the put side or the collateral requirement on the call side—whichever is greater—increased by the amount, if any, that the other side is in-the-money. (However, the requirement is not reduced by the amount, if any, that the side having the lesser requirement is out-of-the-money.) For example, suppose you sell:

1 XRX 50 put at $3 and sell
1 XRX 50 call at $7
When XRX common is $52

You must do two computations to see whether the put or call side has the greater requirement:

Call computation	OR	Put Computation	
30% of $5200	$1560	30% of $5200	$1560
Plus the in-the-money amount	200	Less out-of-the money amount	200
Collateral requirement	$1760	Collateral requirement	$1360

TABLE 10-2 Various Equivalent Neutral Hedges

	Long 100 EK @ 50 / Short 5 EK (sens.=.2) July 60 calls @ 1½	Long 300 EK @ 50 / Short 5 EK (sens.=.6) July 50 calls @ 5	Short 1 EK (sens.= - 4) July 50 put @ 3 / Short 2 EK (sens.=.2) July 60 calls @ 1½	Short 3 EK (sens.= - .4) July 50 puts @ 3 / Short 2 EK (sens.=.6) July 50 calls @ 5
Profit range ($):	42½–64%	41.67–62½	44–63	43.67–59½
Maximum dollar profitability occurs at:	$60 per share	$50 per share	between $50 and $60 per share	$50 per share
Initial investment ($):	4250	12,500	1400	2600
Maximum $ profit:	1750	2500	600	1900
Maximum % return:	41	20	43	73
Effect on profitability per point *advance* in EK from point of maximum profitability, in dollars, and as a % of initial investment:	−400	−200	−200	−500
	9.4	2.56	14.3	19.23

Effect on profitability per point *decline* in EK from point of maximum profitability, in dollars, and as a % of initial investment:	−100 2.35	−300 2.4	−100 7.15	−300 11.53
Additional collateral required per point *advance* in EK ($):	470 over 51 per share	260 over 67.30 per share	60 up to 55 per sh. 260 thereafter	190
Additional collateral ($) required per point *decline* in EK:	None	None	−60 to 48.03 +70 below 48.03	210
Change in neutrality (%) per point *advance* in EK:	−25	−6.7	−35	−17
Change in neutrality (%) per point *decline* in EK:	+12.5	+6.7	+22.5	+17

Since the call position has a higher requirement, that is the amount that must be deposited. There is no requirement on the put.

One advantage of using the short puts/short calls strategy rather than the long stock/short calls approach is that you can employ other collateral to support the variable hedging "business" without borrowing. Any profits are therefore incremental.

To emphasize this point; consider these alternatives. Suppose an investor already has a portfolio of stocks and/or bonds and he wants to construct a variable hedging program. If he were to use the conventional long stocks/short calls approach, he would have to borrow against his collateral to come up with the capital needed. His overall variable hedging return then will be reduced by his interest costs. On the other hand the short puts/short calls approach allows him to use his own portfolio as collateral without incurring interest costs, thereby permitting any return to be incrementally profitable (that is, he does not have to earn a return in excess of interest costs).

The disadvantage to taking the short puts/short calls approach is lack of flexibility, since there are presently only a limited number of stocks on which puts are traded, and some of those put series are not very liquid. Also, their combined sensitivity changes much more rapidly, and more frequent adjustments are necessary.

CHAPTER ELEVEN

Summing Up: The Risks and Rewards of Variable Hedging

Making money in the market today is more difficult than ever before. Keeping your capital in the face of the arithmetic of losing is an even tougher challenge.

The survival strategy we recommend is not a gimmicky technique, but it is a whole new approach to the market. It involves subjective attitudinal changes, as well as the use of an objective, disciplined technique that employs the new options markets to position oneself to make money—no matter what the market does.

The attitudes you need to survive the new stock market are in direct contradiction to conventional thinking that holds "winning" in the stock market to be a pie-in-the-sky, hit-or-miss proposition involving making the right guesses about future market moves, or that says that "conservative investing" means buying and holding the big, recognizable stocks. Instead, these attitudes involve learning to manage a stock "inventory" as a businessman manages his product inventory, with a neutral stance toward the market, flexibility, and an ability to capitalize on probabilities. Our survival strategy means that the investor must learn to act as a kind of insurance company—to identify relatively low risk situations in which he will be paid money to assume that future reality will conform to historical probabilities.

The method of variable hedging relies on computer models, plus your own good judgment. The computer models help you to create hedged positions that, by historical standards, are "neutral"—that is, not biased—so that you can profit from market moves in any direction. Judgment comes into play when reality requires that you adjust.

The risks of variable hedging lie not in your new attitudes. These will hold you in good stead, regardless of the mistakes you may make in implementing the method. The risks revolve around the method.

The major risk, though possible, is in fact highly improbable. It involves the chance that two improbable occurrences will happen simultaneously. One is that *all* of the stocks in your portfolio will rise or fall *together* at a *rapid rate* for an *uninterrupted time period*. The other is that, simultaneously with this rapid and continuing rise or fall, *you fail to adjust* your positions. Both these elements must be present in order to suffer real capital loss. You *can* survive a dramatic portfolio advance or decline by skillful adjustment.

This possible but improbable risk is of an entirely different magnitude from the real risk of simply owning stocks in a declining market.

The secondary risk entails a higher-than-desirable capital exposure, but not a real danger of capital loss. It is occasioned by one of the technical quirks of collateral requirements.

Usually a call for additional collateral in an investor's conventional account is a sign that he is losing money, and that he is being called because his equity is declining and the broker must protect himself. If the call is not met, the customer will be sold out in order to pay off his loan (debit), while the assets still cover the liability. However, in a variable hedging account a call for more collateral can occur when the position is very profitable. Since there is no differentiation made for collateral purposes between an option that has 6 months to run and one that has one day to run, a margin call can be made against a very profitable position. For example, suppose you buy 100 shares of XRX at 50 and sell 3 XRX October 60s at 3. Maximum profitability is at 60 at expiration. Your collateral requirement at 50 is covered by the long side; that is:

30% of $5000:	$1500
Less amount out of the money (60–50):	1000
	$500
Number of uncovered options:	× 2
Collateral requirement:	$1000
Collateral value of stock:	2500
Excess collateral.	$1500

Now suppose the stock rises to 59 the day before expiration and the options are selling for ¼ each. Your collateral requirement is now:

30% of $5900:	$1770
less amount out of the money (60–59):	100
	$1670
Number of uncovered options:	× 2
Collateral requirement:	$3340
Collateral value of stock:	2950
Collateral defiency.	$ 390

Yet, as you can see, this call is occurring in a situation when you, the investor, have a profit of $900 in the stock and $825 in the option. Therefore, if you are in the business of variable hedging, you must keep track of the collateral requirements in your entire account in order to avoid possible collateral calls. Sometimes it is wise, and/or necessary, to repurchase options previously sold in order to free up collateral. This is part of the "business" aspect of managing your variable hedges.

The magnitude of either of these risks pales considerably compared to the rewards of variable hedging.

Variable hedging is a survival strategy suitable for bull markets, bear markets, flat markets—all markets. By its very structure the variable hedging survival tool protects the investor from the ravages of the new stock market's volatility, while at the same time producing a good return—regardless of whether the market goes up, down, or nowhere.

Just how good a return can the investor expect? That depends on external factors, as well as his own self-discipline. Generally a conservatively managed variable hedging account should produce an annualized return in the area of 12 to 15% over a period of time that encompasses a full market cycle (that is, peak to peak or trough to trough of a cycle).

The external variable that comes into play is the degree to which option premiums are overvalued during any particular period. During periods of low premiums an investor might be making only, say, a 5% annualized return, but he can expect to make that up in periods of higher premiums, resulting in a 12 to 15% average return over time.

Meanwhile, even though there may be periods when the variable hedger is only earning a 5% return, it is important to remember that he is *not losing.* Thus he is avoiding the quicksand of the arithmetic of losses—so that it will *not* be so difficult for him to later make compensating higher returns in better times.

Self-discipline figures into the variable hedger's potential return this way: The discipline of variable hedging requires that one's positions must always be kept as neutral as possible in terms of a bullish or bearish bias. But the temptation to create a bias to reflect your own judgments on your particular stocks or on the stock market's future direction is always there. If you yield to this temptation *and you are correct,* you can increase your return. If the portfolio, for example, has a negative bias, and the market declines, then the rate of return will be higher than if the market did not decline. But introducing a bias greatly increases your risk. Every time you depart from the discipline of variable hedging you are returning to the old, self-defeating game—trying to second-guess the market. Sticking to that discipline will not produce spectacular "hits," but it will keep you from losing, while receiving a respectable 12 to 15% annual return, over a market cycle.

How do we know that such returns are possible over the long run? Admittedly, variable hedging is a new business. It could never have existed before the creation of national standardized options exchanges. These exchanges have been in operation only a few years, so that we do not have historical perspective for judging variable hedging's long-term performance. Yet since the business, by definition, is based on selling options which are overvalued, you should logically be able to achieve an incremental return over the long-term return on common stocks (which has historically been 9%) of another 3 to 6%.

Meanwhile, variable variable hedging is not just another fad like "formula plans" and "one decision stocks," which in hindsight proved to be pure folly. Each of these fads on closer inspection were really reactions to investors' most recent experiences, so that when reality changed they no longer applied. Variable hedging is really a very old technique—built upon the tried-and-true investment vehicle of options—made facile by the new options exchanges. It is no more faddish than insurance companies' actuarial tables and premium rates.

Variable hedging is a disciplined technique for surviving and succeeding in the new stock market by collecting enough premiums to offset the risks of losing. As long as there are investors who think that they can outguess the market, and who have love affairs with their stocks, there will be profit opportunities in overvalued options for variable hedgers.

INDEX

235